THI

To Dave
Best of everything

Willie Gaard

AKA

Bill Ramey

THE ANCESTOR CHAIN

THE ANCESTOR CHAIN

WILLIE GAARD

THE ANCESTOR CHAIN 4

THE ANCESTOR CHAIN

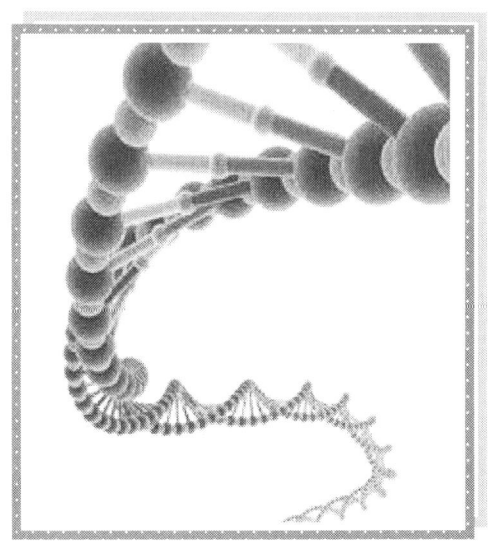

WILLIE GAARD

**ISBN-13: 978-1479258505
ISBN-10: 1479258504
All rights reserved.
This book or parts thereof
may not be produced without permission**

Cover design by W.C. Dragsmar

Dedicated to
Narby Krimsnatch
"Best of 56"

THE ANCESTOR CHAIN 8

INTRODUCTION

You and I have had, without question, direct line relatives living many thousands of years ago…else we could not be here today. Genealogical studies can sometimes trace your family roots, but only for a few generations.

This narrative is about our common ancestors of long ago. Each of these tales is accurate to the living conditions in its calendar time. Locations, historical events and maps are genuine. Names of notable people are true to historical records. Myths of each period correspond to the thinking of that point in time. Archeology represented is based on current studies.

Follow these ten accounts then as they describe possible activities of your ancestors, striving to survive in their personal segment of history. Your forbearers actually lived such tumultuous times.

Their survival brought you to life.

Willie Gaard
Baldwinsville, NY
2013

TABLE OF CONTENTS

RU 50,000 B.C.
The First Marker * Haplogroup R-1B (M168)

The Genographic Project

POV 7400 B.C.
Jericho

Catal Hoyuk

RIPHATH 5600 B.C.
Geography and Archeology

Deluge

OTZI 3300 B.C.
Remembrance

Iceman Otzi

GEAAD 1600 B.C.
Sculpture

Danube River Delta

Minotaur

Egypt

REIJO 400 B.C.
The Amber Road

Shape Shifters

BAETAN 133 B.C.
Celtiberians

Spain

RUGA 413 A.D.
Britannia

Flight into Darkness

HAAGAN 1020 A.D.
The Unicorn's Horn

The Saga of Haagan * Haplogroup M173

ROGAARD 1200 A.D.
Epigenetics

Egeskov Slot

The Northern Crusade * Haplogroup M343

Love and Deception

EPILOGUE

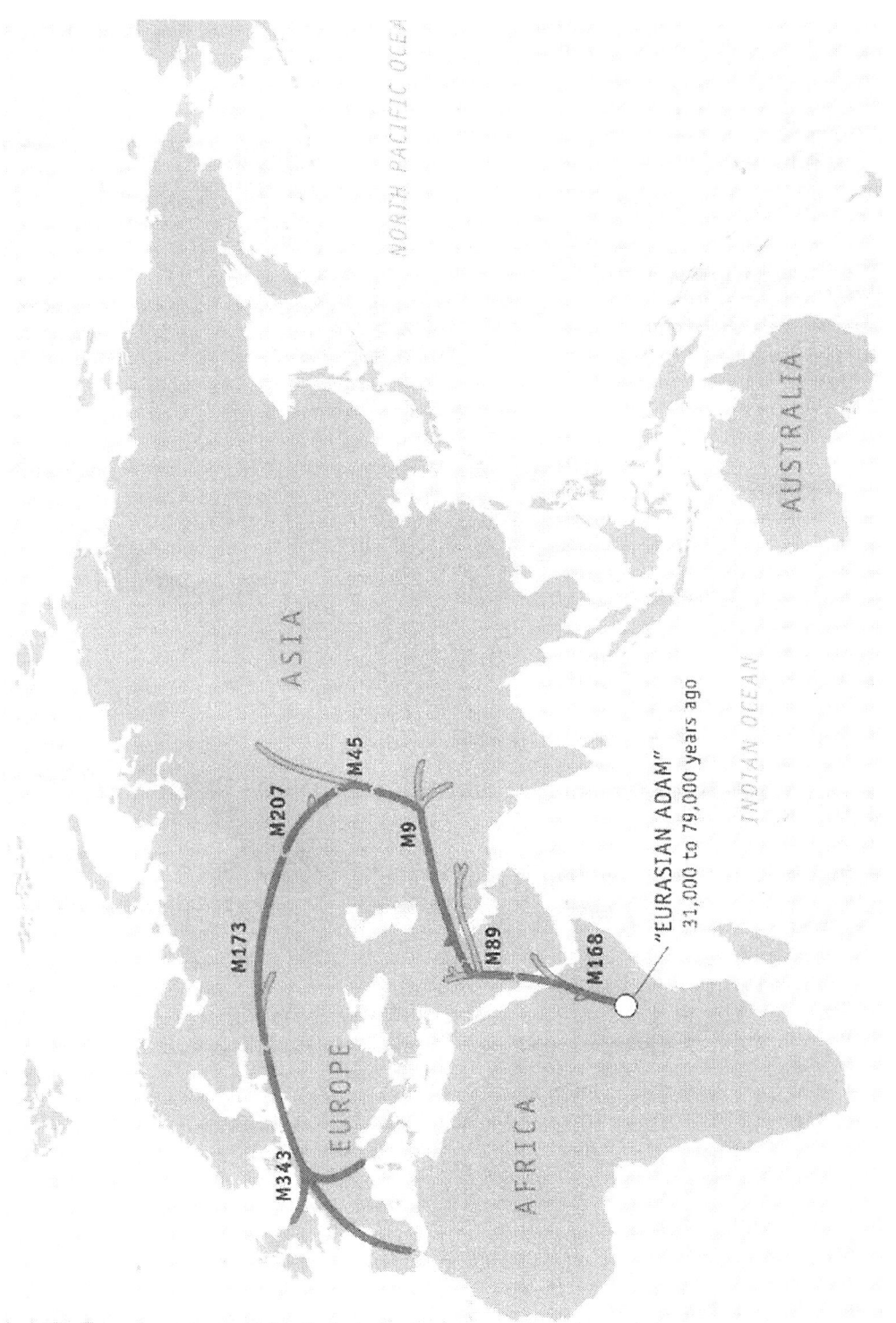

THE ANCESTOR CHAIN

One

Ru
The First Marker
50,000 B.C.

Muk slept fitfully. He was lying on his left side in the tiny shallow depression of the limestone plateau. It was his bed. His torso was pasted by his own drying blood to the grass bedding beneath his body.

A light flashed onto his face. Suddenly he was wide awake. He blinked repeatedly. The round hot orb of the day was casting brilliant sunlight directly into his eyes. This blazing orange globe was sitting between the rim of the earth and the dark endless cloud blanket overhead.

Muk tried to turn away from this blinding source of light. His sudden movement forced a hoarse scream from his badly chapped lips. His bellowing shriek channeled a throbbing pain throughout his being. Violent distress immediately flashed through every nerve ending in his body. He fainted.

As the physical agony subsided, Muk slowly drifted back to consciousness. Now he was cautious not to move. His breath came in tiny snorts. Still, as the pain receded, he could only marvel at the light in his eyes! It was so strong it penetrated his closed eyelids. There had been only one other time in his life that he remembered seeing, for just a moment, the hot burning fire that warmed the day. He knew that the round fire slowly passed overhead every day. It somehow created the day.

He remembered that once, many uncountable moons ago, an old muk using sign language, had told the tribe about this hot bright orb from an earlier time. The old tribesman motioned that one day thick gray clouds had come to hide the hot orb. The clouds would not go away. It had been the work of some strange evil god.

For every day of this muk's life that gray blanket had filled the air above his head. Even a rare ash filled rain did not diminish the dreary high barrier between sun and earth. Just now the orb no longer pressed his eyes shut. It had climbed over the gray clouds and into the upper sky.

Dimly Muk recalled the source of the agony caused by his movement. His leg and foot were crushed. A bone with sharp edges was sticking through his skin just above his knee. A great animal that they were hunting had suddenly turned and trampled him. Old Muk and Young Muk must have carried him to his dream spot on the limestone rock. Muk could not remember. He woke there one sun time ago…or was it longer?

Once, Young Muk had come by with some pulled fresh grass to soften the place where he lay. An ooola had laid part of a roasted snake near his hand. It was his only food but he dared not make the stretch movement to reach for it. The pain of stirring any part of his body was too great.

The tribe knew Muk would soon die. Early on, he had tried to pull the jagged bone out of his body. The violent stabbing pain from his pull immediately drove Muk into a death sleep. Since that one attempt to cure himself, he was only sometimes awake. Now he breathed quietly, afraid to move at all… even while insects feasted on his festering open wound. Muk dared not lift his head to see them. It didn't matter, except that, if he could catch any of them, then he would have something more to eat, maybe even a little liquid for his swollen tongue.

Daily survival was more than difficult for the Muk tribe. It was a constant challenge to stay alive. Game was always scarce. Many seasons of overcast had reduced vegetation to almost nothing. Animals had little to eat. The ooolas could not find edible roots or fruits. Clan Muk was on the edge of extinction almost every day. The oasis, which was their home, was rapidly failing from years of drought. The last date palm tree no longer bore fruit. Their bubbling water source, a spring, was almost dry.

"Move," Old Muk shouted in a guttural grunt with arms waving and a shoulder shrug.

"What?" Hork, the tracker of animals responded. He was surprised. Old Muk seldom spoke any words. The tribe mostly communicated with head and hand movements and occasional grunts. This little group of humans, living in the dawn of mankind, had no more than an eighty word vocabulary.

"Move," Old Muk repeated the command. He pointed downstream of the trickle of water running from the spring. His order meant traveling in the direction where the dim light of the day started. Some long dead male muks had indicated that this journey would take them to a bigger water flow. That water course moved north. There were legends of a very big water flow in that direction.

Yet all knew that some of the tribe would die on such a journey. It was recognized that there was no food to be had along this rocky defile. These primitive people had no way to preserve food. Each day was a test to find enough nourishment to survive until the next day. Even the bravest living muk had never gone more than a half day's journey down the stream flow. And the ooolas almost never strayed out of sight of the encampment. Their little oasis, with a spring to create the stream, was the entire world of Clan Muk. It had been so for generations. Moving away was unthinkable. Change was always to be feared.

Old Muk stood. He picked up a small rock and smashed it into one that was bigger. This time the sound got the attention of all the ooolas and their offspring. "Move!" There was anger in his shout. He started out. No one dared oppose him. The ooolas gathered their skinning tools, the fire-starter and the few offspring too young to walk. There were no blankets or other possessions to bring. They had no clothes.

The Muk Clan followed Old Muk. In the countless ages of this clan's existence they had migrated many times. Still, this was the first move for every currently living clan member. The oasis had been a good home. To move away from it seemed almost impossible.

The Muk Clan of early man was typical of the time. Short, stocky, very hairy and dark skinned. Life at the most, rarely exceeded forty years. Few males, muks, and none of the females, ooolas, had names. Only Hork, the best hunter in the clan, was the exception in this tribe. He had a name. The ooolas, among themselves, identified each other and their children by sounds unrecognized by the males. In only a hundred or so generations this would all change. Everyone would have a name.

The trip became three days of exhaustive climbing over large rocks and down steep defiles. Along the way there was nothing that they could find to eat. One of the youngest offspring died ... his ooola had no milk. Another ooola gave birth on the second day of the trip. No one stopped to help her with the birth. It was not the way of the Muk Clan to do so. Alone, she caught up to the group the next afternoon.

Finally, the group arrived at a large river. On its muddy banks they immediately found an abundance of food in the form of clams. Greedily, all but the youngest ate with vigor. Eventually the clams filled their bellies. Most could not remember a time when they could simply eat no more. Two of the clan, though full, just kept on eating, but then returned the chewed clams from their stomachs back to the mud. With full stomachs, the other clan members sat and laughed at the gluttons. Laughter was a rare sensation. At the dawn of mankind humans seldom had any occasion to enjoy life.

Those ooola mothers with weaned, yet tiny offspring began chewing clams into mush for their small children. Old Muk, who had almost no teeth left in his mouth, could not bite the clams. He found small clams and swallowed them whole. His first ooola, from his youth, chewed the larger, meatier shellfish for him and transferred the gruel to his mouth. For many days Clan Muk feasted on clams.

On a new day, Hork entered the muddy river water with a spear. He snagged a large fish. The ooolas roasted it over hot coals. Again, the clan feasted. Only Hork was able to catch fish. His quickness with his spear could not be matched. All the young muks tried to imitate Hork, but without success.

Another day, as Hork fished in almost waste deep water, the children watched squatting and playing in ankle deep mud. Suddenly one of the older boys pointed to Hork and screamed, "Snake!" The large crocodile caught Hork before he could even turn to look. Most of Clan Muk saw the fight in the water and heard Hork's screams. Now there was only a bloody pool in the river. None had ever seen an animal like that. They turned to Old Muk for guidance.

He said, "Stay away water."

Two nights later there was a horrible tumult in the camp. Everyone woke. From the dim light of the night fire they watched as a croc carried a screaming half grown muk into the water. The rocks they threw at the beast did nothing at all. A flint pointed spear just bounced off the animal's tough hide.

All huddled close to the firelight to await the dawn. Every night sound terrified them. In the morning Old Muk again banged two rocks together for attention. He said, "Bad place! Move," and he pointed downstream. Clams would no longer be collected from this mud bank.

The little group of kinfolk began walking together in fear, almost clinging to one another in a compact circle. They watched everywhere for the monster that had taken Hork and the young muk to their doom. Only the ooola who had birthed the lost muk looked back. Then she too moved on. He was forgotten. She had other little muks and ooolas.

Their journey became terrifying. Now, they recognized there were many of the monsters watching them, with only eyes above the water. Death was floating silently in the river.

Around a small bend the mud turned to sand, here rested more crocodiles than any muk or ooola had fingers. The band of humans shrunk back at the sight. Their leader, Old Muk, held his ground. He had fought many beasts, some even bigger than these strange animals. A few of the crocs sensed that Old Muk was there, but they did not move.

Suddenly Old Muk yelled at the top of his lungs and took small steps towards the crocs. He alarmed everyone, both human and crocodile. The nearest of the beasts turned and fled towards the water. Seeing that the crocs could be frightened, the tribe began screaming with Old Muk and moved slowly forward as a group. Every crocodile turned, waddled away and finally splashed into the water. A hunter's cheer of triumph rose from the clan. Fear was now replaced with caution.

As the Muk Clan moved forward, they found a plethora of clams. Then a real treasure…eggs! Old Muk watched as the ooolas gathered the rich bounty. This was good. Most important, he had learned that the crocs could move very fast on land. Their short legs also told him that they could not climb. The tribe would be safe on higher ground. When the egg gathering was completed, Old Muk again crashed two stones together. With his back to the river he pointed up the hilly bank and said, "Move."

Reaching the crest of the high embankment was as difficult as the descent to the river a few days earlier. These early humans were of very limited stature. The biggest of the clan, strangely an ooola, was barely over five feet tall. The way was steep and the vegetation thick with thorn bushes. At the top the land was a barren plain. It was all rock and light brown sand away from the river as far as anyone could see. The water gave life, but only close to its banks.

The group followed the ridge and the flow of the river northward, walking further away from their old oasis. The river, and often the adjoining sandbanks filled with crocs, was almost always in sight. Finally they came to a bluff covered with trees. The ooolas immediately recognized some living date palms. A wide stream was flowing sharply down to the river. Here there were no clams to be found … but also no crocs. There would probably be birds and game for the muks to hunt in this small forest. The stream to the river flowed swiftly and was a barrier too deep to cross. But the tribe, led by Old Muk, had found a new home.

Life suddenly became as gentle as the tribe had ever experienced. Existence had always been a daily fight for food. Now food was plentiful. The crocodiles could not reach them. No spoor of dangerous large animals was found, not even the deadly lion.

One morning two young muks were at the stream bank. A loud squawk from across the water made the young boys look up. There they saw a terrifying site. It was someone like them, a human, but not of the Clan Muk. In this primitive world of early man, the true Homo sapiens groups rarely, if ever, encountered another human tribe. The land was very big and the humanoid branch numbered less than ten thousand beings. They roamed widely, always in small groups. Each little clan exhausted the plant and animal food supply that lay before them. Then they moved forward. Meetings with other humans were rare. Still, this extraordinary event did occasionally happen.

The small muks ran back to their ooolas screaming, "New muk, new muk!" They waved their arms toward the stream. The boys had seen babies born and heard the ooolas call them 'new muks.' Now they used these same words. It was as close as their limited language allowed them to describe the sight they had just seen.

All the ooolas, followed by their children ran to the stream. All expected to see a newborn. There was nothing to see! The bank, opposite of where the boys had been playing, showed only the normal trees, some green knotty reeds and the rocky outcrops of the oasis. Several of the ooolas mouthed angry sounds at the two small muks. One of the adult ooolas cuffed them both. Three little ooolas, of the same age as the muks, giggled at the boys' misery.

Days later, an almost full grown ooola, also saw what the boys had observed. She too ran back to the group screaming, "New Muk!" She also made motions to indicate that this was a full grown human.

This time the entire clan came to the impassable stream. They saw indeed, another muk, but not a member of Clan Muk. The grown ooolas noticed a difference, slight certainly, but yet a difference. The stranger had a somewhat lighter skin color and much less hair on his body. The three adult muks were busy waving their flint tipped spears and shouting at the intruder. The ooolas had none of this. They were more interested in the appearance of the male. Now, almost daily, this incident was repeated. Then, one day the newcomer did not appear. Each new sun time Clan Muk returned to the stream bank. But now, the opposite bank was always empty.

Drought, a concept not understood by the clan, continued to suffer the land. It was severe. The gray cloud covering the sky produced almost no moisture. Plant life continued to wither. Day after day the remaining three adult muks of the clan, returned from the hunt empty handed, Clan Muk would need to move again soon, Old Muk knew that. His plan was cancelled the very next morning.

The stranger had appeared again. Fear rippled through the group. This time he was on their side of the stream! The muk men howled and waved their spears as they had done before but did not advance towards the outsider. He too kept to a safe distance beyond spear and rock throwing range. He yelled sounds that none understood. No one moved. Finally, he reached down into the tall grass at his feet and held up game he had killed, many rabbits and two large rats. Next, he walked away leaving his gift. There was sufficient sustenance now for the entire tribe. They would live another day.

More game was left in that same spot almost every day. At times the stranger was there, other days they did not see him. Clan Muk no longer had great fear of him or screamed at him. Yet, all stayed safely beyond the range of a thrown spear.

Old Muk and his two grown muk men could not locate the source of the animals that the stranger brought to them each morning. Where was the game coming from? Old Muk realized he had to bring this person closer to his tribe to hunt with him. How? Originality was not part of the early human thought process. The only exception was trapping and hunting. Old Muk needed to trap the stranger.

Early the next morning, with barely enough light to see the pathways, Old Muk grabbed a young ooola who had only recently freshened. She thought that Old Muk wished to take her so she stretched out on her bed of reeds. The clan leader shook his head to say 'No' and pulled her to her feet. She was confused. He made her walk, in the breaking dawn to the spot where the stranger left his daily presents. She knew the place. All the ooolas knew it. They went there every day to collect his donations of food. Among themselves they admired the skills of this strangely different provider.

At the location of the food drop Old Muk pushed the ooola down. He signed strongly for her to stay in this place. She began to tremble and wail. She understood! She was to be given to the stranger. Her primitive fear was that the hunter might eat her.

Old Muk could not describe what he had done or why he had done it. The clan did not have enough language for that. When, at last, there was sufficient light, the tribe could see the food gifts were in their usual spot. The stranger was not to be seen. Also one of the younger ooolas was missing.

The stranger failed to appear for the next two days. On the third day the tribe heard his cry from afar. As he came into sight, they could see the missing ooola following behind. She carried a heavy burden across her back. The three hunters in the clan immediately recognized what she carried. It was a fat gazelle. This was a rare catch.

At the trading point she was allowed to drop the animal. It was fresh. All could see blood from the animal smeared across on her back. With the heavy weight gone, she could raise her head. She saw her tribe the short distance away and immediately started to run towards them. In two steps the stranger caught her by her trailing long black hair, pulled her back, and then slammed her forward into the ground. With one foot on her back he raised his spear and howled, warning the tribe to stay back. No one moved.

The stranger brought the ooola roughly to her feet. Her face was bruised from the fall. Blood trickled from her nose. He violently turned her around onto the path they had come, prodding her to move with his spear. She was not to return to the clan. Old Muk knew inwardly that he had made a good trade. The ooola did not matter. The tribe would eat well for many days. The stranger might return again.

Days passed. The stranger, the ooola and more gifts did not appear. It had never occurred, in the dim minds of the muk hunters, to try to follow the stranger's trail. Then, the same two boys, who had first seen the stranger, saw him again. They alerted the tribe as before. This time both the stranger and the ooola were on the opposite side of the stream. Old Muk, for the first time, realized that there had to be a way to cross over to the other side. His clan had yet to find it. Perhaps that side contained abundant game. The ooola and the stranger finally turned and walked into the trees.

Once again, many gray days followed by dark moonless starless nights passed. The stranger and the ooola were all but forgotten. One morning a yell came from the field near the food drop. It was the sound of the stranger. Clan Muk was starving again and ran out to greet him...yet keeping a spear throw distance from the man.

Both the stranger and the ooola bore large game on their backs, unloading them in the usual spot. This time the ooola did not run. She held up a clutch of rabbits and waved them at the clan. With her other hand she took the stranger's arm. Then both of them took a step forward. Immediately Clan Muk, moving in unison, took a step back. Again she waved the rabbits before moving another step forward. Old Muk held his ground this time. The two came closer. Finally the ooola reached Old Muk and handed him the rabbits. She pointed to the clan leader and said to the stranger, "Muk." In turn she pointed to the stranger and said, "Ru." Lastly she waved at the females crouched behind the three muk men, and said, "Ooola." The tribe had no way to yet describe more than one of anything. All the females were simply 'Ooola.'

Old Muk raised his fist to strike this impertinent ooola. She had spoken directly to him...without permission. She had looked openly at him. Her eyes had not been downcast in the customary subservient position. Old Muk did not strike. He saw the newcomer tense and slightly raise his spear. *Best not to fight*, he thought. The clan needed this man Ru to ward off starvation. Old Muk, the still growing Young Muk and the third muk all needed help to hunt. Ru would help. Tribal custom was not that important.

Ru had no language skills at all. He could make sounds, but did not understand any words of the muks or the ooolas. Ru and the three muks communicated with body movements and hand signals. Since he had made growling noises towards the very frightened ooola given him by the Muk Clan, she in turn had taken the sound and made it his name, Ru. He was intelligent and quickly understood that she was 'Ooola.' Still, he could not manipulate his tongue to make the sound of her name. His temper was always short. He guided her to his needs with sign language or beatings.

Clan Muk and Ru learned much from each other. Ru taught them to make snares. He showed them how to bait a trap with some part of a decomposing animal they had previously caught. There was now excess food to do this. Clan Muk began to put on weight. The ooolas, secretly to themselves, said Old Muk's swelling belly meant he would soon bear a new muk.

Ru, without language, could not explain how he grew up or where his tribe wandered. Never-the-less, the muks and ooolas marveled at his hunting skills. Ru, in turn, also learned new things. The muks could make better spears than those which he had. They painted their bodies with juice from certain plants to ward off insects. He found he could mate with any ooola. Whenever he felt the urge, one of the ooolas would eagerly comply.

The ooolas noticed that Ru often made a sign that seemed meaningless. He would take the thumb and first finger of his left hand and squeeze his nose shut for just an instant. It was a sweeping motion that happened at random. It did not appear to convey any meaning they understood. The ooolas mirrored the squeeze of nostrils to Ru. He ignored it. The muks did not notice it. It was senseless to all but the newcomer.

Ru settled into clan life with surprising ease. He had missed the companionship of other humans. Sign language served all of them well. The long missing clan of his origin never had developed words for objects or actions. That did not matter to the muks. His hunting skill made him wanted by the tribe. Perhaps the ooolas appreciated something more.

One morning Ru was roasting a small pigeon. It was the last food item in camp. He and the muks would need to hunt for game this day. As he held the bird over the fire two very young ooolas raced passed him. The second girl stumbled and fell into the squatting man. He was thrown off balance and fell into the hot coals, searing his mating tool. His temper flared. He quickly caught the little ooola. Kneeling over her, he began pummeling her with his fists.

The little ooola's mother was only a short distance away scraping a gazelle pelt with her flint knife. She saw that her child was being savagely attacked. Without thought she stood, stepped to the hunched over man and stabbed him in the neck. The sharp flint severed his carotid artery. Ru's life bled away in just a few minutes. The child also died.

The tribe was not shocked, nor did it mourn. Occasionally someone in the tribe died or was killed. Usually it was an ooola or a child. It just happened. It was just part of their existence. There was no punishment or remorse for a killing.

Clan Muk was no longer short of meat. They feasted for several days.

The three muk hunters left the clan in search of new game. The wildlife in the area was again near exhaustion. They could roam only a half day's journey before turning around. If night separated them from the rest of the clan there was great fear they might never find their way back. Such was the primitive tribe's thinking.

The search for food was almost useless without Ru. Somehow he had been able to see game where they found only dried grass and sand. Still, on the second day of a new hunt, Young Muk did find the droppings of a large animal. Tracks pointed to a box canyon that they knew. They ran to it. Muk and Old Muk guarded the narrow entrance. Young Muk was sent through a narrow defile at the back to force the animal out to the two stronger hunters. Ru had taught them this trick.

Muk and Old Muk heard the other hunter yell to startle the animal. Suddenly, the flushed beast came roaring out of the narrow canyon opening. It had horns. It was the largest beast they had ever seen. The brown juggernaut swerved towards Old Muk. He threw his spear into the animal's flank just as Muk closed from the opposite side. The pain from the spear caused the animal to turn. Muk was too close. He tripped backwards and was trampled.

Old Muk and Young Muk carried the unconscious man back to camp and placed him in his shallow sleeping place in the sandstone rock. He would be left there to die. Burial was not yet a clan custom. So too, using the flesh of a tribe member for food was taboo. They would simply leave Muk where he lay.

The next daylight, Old Muk banged two rocks together for attention. "Move," he shouted. With sign language he indicated that they would cross the stream where Ru first appeared. He pointed to the ooola, that he had traded to Ru. She was now obviously with child. She was to lead them to the crossing point. Old Muk was sure that much game and plant food existed on the other side. If he was wrong, if it was barren, his group was doomed.

As the tribe was leaving, Muk awoke or perhaps regained consciousness. He understood what they were doing. It was the way of Clan Muk.

As they departed, one of the little ooolas wistfully looked back at Muk. She turned and ran to him as he lay, almost immobile, on his death bed. This confused Muk. She was the small ooola that he most disliked. He had often cuffed her, just to move her out of his path. Sometimes he had enjoyed hitting her for no reason at all. Now she approached him, but stayed out of arms reach.

For just a moment she looked at him, her eyes sparkling. Then she reached down, picked up the snake portion that her mother had left as food for Muk. She hurled it away, far beyond his grasp.

Done, she ran to catch up with the departing tribe.

A BIT OF HISTORY

The first marker, Haplogroup R-1B (M168), was present in some of the signature groups working their way north out of Africa fifty to seventy thousand years ago.

THE ANCESTOR CHAIN

THE ANCESTOR CHAIN

Two

The Genographic Project

Christopher puzzled as he watched his father. Michael was sitting at his desk in the family room swabbing his mouth with something like a tiny toothbrush.

"Dad, what are you doing?"

Michael held up his index finger to Chris, as a signal to wait. He looked at his watch, swabbed his cheek a few more turns, then he took the little brush out of his mouth and put it into a tiny canister.

"What is that?" Chris again inquired.

Michael smiled. Teenagers didn't often talk to their parents. "I'm sending a sample of my DNA off to a lab to be analyzed."

Chris was suddenly worried. "You mean they are checking you for some sort of disease?"

"No, Chris. This is part of something called the Genographic Project. It is a research scheme. It will give us an idea about where our ancestors came from."

"We already know that dad. They came from Denmark and Germany and Ireland and maybe a few more places. Every kid does a family tree in school. I think I made one years ago in the third grade."

"Chris, this is not about our relatives that came from Europe a few generations ago. This is a deep, deep ancestry study. I expect we will find out the origins of our relatives hundreds or maybe thousands of years ago."

"But Dad, we didn't have any relatives back then!"

Teenagers, Michael thought. "Okay Chris, then how did we all get here?

"Oh, I see ... I guess"

It was always a joy to see understanding develop; especially in one of his own children. It reminded him of his years as a teacher. As Chris pondered this information, Michael, squeezing his left index finger and thumb, pulled the two digits down over his nose and lightly pinched his nostrils. He sometimes remembered that his father had done the same thing. *Must be something in the family genes*, he briefly mused.

Chris finally said "I guess I get it. Our grandparents had grandparents who had grandparents and so on. So this DNA test will tell us if we are related to someone famous way back, maybe George Washington."

"No."

"Well then..."

"Chris, this will only give us an idea of the physical paths our ancestors followed. All humanity's roots are in Africa. At some point we, I mean our first true human ancestors, came away from the African savanna and colonized the world. As far as we know today, human development began on the African continent."

"So that little swab will tell us if we came from cavemen?"

"I don't think so Chris, but maybe. We'll get results in about a month."

"But Dad how does that work?"

"It's a bit complex. Here, read this little paper. It came with my test kit. It might help explain how this works."

As human DNA is passed from parents to offspring, most of it is re-combined, and mutated giving rise to all of those characteristics that make each person unique. Some components of our genetic inheritance, however, remain relatively stable over the course of generations. Occasional mutations in these components are easily identified and accumulate in a particular order and at a particular rate so that, compared across a broad spectrum band of DNA samples, they act as kind of a time line. These 'genetic markers' never disappear but are passed on to each generation. Over eons, different populations accumulate their own set of markers.

Christopher shook his head. "Wow! So we'll find out if we are related to a hairy caveman whacking dinosaurs?"

"Not really." Michael was now just a little annoyed that his son was losing the concept. "I'm pretty sure Chris that way, way back we are all related to what you think of as a caveman. Somehow we had to have a beginning. But then I really don't know how much we will learn about cavemen. I think the results will give us some sort of generalizations about where we, as humans, got started. The test is especially designed to tell us the paths that our particular line of ancestors followed across

Africa and Europe, That's long before any of our relatives ever came to this country."

The young man thought this all over. "Will this swab of DNA tell us if we are related to somebody famous?"

"I don't think so Chris… I really don't think so. I'll share the results with you and the rest of the family when I get them."

Three months later

The week that the Genographic Project results arrived in the mail, was just a few days before Chris arrived home from college for the summer. The first thing the young man did when he came in the door was to raid the refrigerator and eat everything in sight.

"Didn't they feed you in college?" His mother asked. "You look so thin."

"I didn't have much time to eat, mom. I was studying for all those exams." He lied. He had really run out of money, but why worry his mother.

Later, after eating and talking with the family, Chris and his younger brother Matt had time to share together. They were only a year apart in age. Matt was especially interested in the Ancient History course that his older brother had just completed. Their father's DNA test for their ancestry had particularly sparked Matt's curiosity.

"You got an A in Ancient History?" Matt challenged. "You don't get 'A's' in anything as I remember."

"Yup, I got an A. It was the easiest course I've taken so far. In fact, it was so much fun, I may change my major."

Matt grinned. "Did you know that dad is tracing our ancestry with something called the Genographic Project?"

"Yes. Mom told me about that on Facebook. Besides I was home the day dad did the cheek swabbing."

"Well, his results came in the mail a while back. Dad was excited about it. It really doesn't look like that much to me. I made a copy for you with the computer. Here, take a look."

Matt prattled on while Chris scanned the documents.

"Well?" said Matt.

"Well what, little brother."

"I don't know. I guess I just expected more. It's a map, but it is mostly just a flow line. Were our ancestors only nomads? Didn't they ever stop and plant roots some place?"

"Probably did Matt. According to that ancient history course I took, one of the earliest towns that has been ever identified is what we now call Jericho. We got that name from the Bible. I doubt the first settlers ever called it by that name.

"Where the walls came tumbling down..." Matt grinned as he half-sang the words.

"No and yes and maybe."

"Huh?" Matt screwed up his face. "I don't know what you mean."

"This Genographic Project starts us back fifty, maybe seventy thousand years ago in Africa. Back then our ancestors might have lived in caves or were nomads. Archeologists so far found that the oldest known settlement, a place where humans first stayed permanently, was Jericho. That was a long time ago Matt, about 8,000 B.C. One of the genetic markers I see on this report for dad is M89. That means you and I also have that marker because we would have inherited it from dad. Look at it on the map. Jericho is located in what was called The Fertile Crescent. This map just gives us a rough idea about how people wandered. I guess eventually they got tired of moving and found a place to settle where their needs could be met. There was water; food and maybe an economic basis to stop wandering and start a permanent home…create a town. A permanent location made life easier. Jericho, it seems could have been, perhaps, that first town."

"What was the reason to settle there and then start a town?" Matt was now interested.

"Salt probably. Jericho is in a valley where the River Jordan flows from the Sea of Galilee to the Dead Sea. People and animals need salt. It also preserves food. Jericho provided that salt. The nomads who became settlers in this new town could trade salt for other necessities. A town meant something brand new… commerce."

"Wow, maybe we had relatives in Jericho."

"Maybe. But also, think Matt…you are the one who is good at numbers. At that time, in 8,000 B.C. there were an estimated 5 million humans alive. They had spread all over the world….even into China and Australia and some had managed to get into North America. But our ancestors, labeled with a new gene called M89 were in the Fertile Crescent."

"How did we get that M89 thing?"

"I have no idea Matt. That was a long time ago."

"How many generations would that be back to then, Chris?"

"Well, at a rate of four generations every 100 years, and ten thousand years, that would be about 400 great grandfathers. So, that means, we could draw a direct connection back through 400 men and you and I might find a male relative in Jericho."

"And women too."

"No Matt. The Y-chromosome markers in the Genographic Project trace only males. We can only trace through males...fathers and grandfathers."

THE ANCESTOR CHAIN

Three

Pov

Jericho 7400 B.C.

The small settlement of Jericho had been in place for hundreds of years. Its name meant something like 'smell' or 'odor'. Indeed the area did have a very strange aroma. It came, not from the salt collected from the Dead Sea, but from the bitumen dug from the dark merky shallows of that nearby body of the water. Those two valuable products, salt and bitumen, changed the way of existence for some nomads who had wandered the Fertile Crescent for millennia. For the very first time in the history of mankind there was a permanent settlement. Jericho was not just a temporary encampment, it had developed into a community. It was a town. The number of inhabitants had grown to more than 600.

In Jericho, the townspeople built a wall for protection. Yet the wall often failed to shield the small population from wandering bands of raiders. Violent hunter bands sought the riches of Jericho. A second inner wall had been built for additional protection. This first town of mankind, consisting of small round houses, each made of dried clay, had a double ring of defense.

Those clansmen without strong family ties, a few bonded servants and even fewer slaves, lived between the outer and inner wall. The privileged and their families shared space inside the second fortification. Jericho was often attacked. Sometimes the warring party became exhausted and was driven away before breaching the first wall. At other times raiders broke through the outer wall and were satisfied to pillage the poorer part of Jericho. Occasionally the double walled defense was completely overwhelmed and the entire town was temporarily brought to ruin.

Tog a merchant, was the semi-official leader of Jericho. He was as physically strong as his size indicated. His coal black hair hung half way down to his waist. His skin was an olive brown. A dirty loin cloth somewhat covered him. There was a deep scar on his left cheek which reminded everyone of the terrible fight that, many years ago, had won him his position of authority. His enemies and their kin had also paid a price that day…their lives! He was widely known as a man to be feared.

Tog had many sons. All of them lived inside the second wall. His extended family was the largest in Jericho. That alone made Tog the arbiter of a town of just a few hundred humans. Tog liked his position. He was not a fool…power was good. He conducted his daily life using power.

Tog's women had produced many sons. Daughters were discarded at birth. But, as Tog's sons grew towards manhood, his women produced fewer children. Then, after a time, there came no children at all. A crone, who made spells and hexes, was consulted by the man. She told Tog he needed a younger female to produce more sons. The very next day a trader appeared. He came from the land of the great river far to the south. He wanted to barter for salt. He offered Tog leopard skins and one of his two slaves. In turn he would take all the salt his burros could carry away. Tog had no need for the black male slave, but the young female, perhaps fourteen, caught his eye. It was an omen.

"I will take the animal skins and the female slave for the salt," Tog told the man from the south.

The trader smiled. "You have made yourself a poor bargain Tog. The male is strong. The girl is nothing but a problem. She is insolent and lazy. I am glad to be rid of her."

Tog inquired, "Have you had her a long time?"

"All her life," the trader replied wearily. "She is one of my many daughters. Her name is Lahg."

Tog quickly found that Lahg had been trained by the women of her clan in the special arts of pleasing men. She knew things that Tog's women did not know, and Tog for the very first time, was overjoyed to learn them himself. Just thinking about her brought a smile to his face. In a matter of only two moons young Lahg was installed as First Woman. The other females jealously hated her. Tog commanded that none of his sons could use her. This was a violation of the family custom. But since everyone feared Tog, none of them dared to disobey.

In just a short time, Lahg was obviously with child. Tog was delighted but his women understood something different. In only five moons a full term girl was born. Tog ordered the issue destroyed. His women mocked him behind his back. He had been taken for a fool. After beating Lahg, he questioned her about being with child.

"It was not my fault," she cried. "It was the man who sold me to you. He told me he would kill me if I said anything. Now that I am free of his burden I can give you a son. Let me show you."

Lahg's offering was perhaps no longer possible. Tog's youngest son was now ten seasons old. He wondered drearily if he could sire any more sons. Yet, true to her word, Lahg produced a boy barely a year later. She named him Pov. Tog was overjoyed and rewarded Lahg with soft robes and sparkling gold rings. The other women of his clan raged in jealousy. Not once had Tog gifted any of them for bearing children. They could only think of revenge.

The oldest of Tog's women visited the crone of the hexes and bought poison from her. It worked quickly. The women explained to Tog that the strain of childbirth, on such a young girl, had killed Lahg. Pov, her baby, had been the cause of her death. Tog mourned. He could not forgive his new son for the loss of his beloved Lahg. He directed the woman of the hexes to take his new son and raise him away from his family in the lower part of Jericho. He could not bear to look at the tiny boy.

With the death of Lahg, everyone noticed a gradual change in the man. He drove his many sons relentlessly at the work of panning salt. He organized the Jericho population into forced work parties to raise the town walls another four feet. He became a bitumen tradesman, buying slaves to collect the black sticky gobs of tar. He no longer visited his women. Tog's temper was to be feared. He was a man alone.

Pov grew in the loving care of Kella, the hag, the maker of potions and the giver of hexes. She had been childless and Pov now filled a deep void in her heart. In such a small village it was not easy, but Tog did not see his son again.

Pov was an inquisitive and intelligent child. As he grew, she allowed him to assist her mixing some of the simpler healing potions. She explained what problems they were meant to cure and how they worked. She had him taste and smell the substances in the unmarked containers on the shelf above her pallet. The concept of writing was still many generations into the future. There were no markings to identify the material. She relied on the different shapes of the many jars and unique texture or smell of its contents for identification.

One morning, while Kella was baking a bit of dough for breakfast, the young boy pulled a container from the back of the shelf. He did not recognize the contents. It had a delicate odor that he could not distinguish. As he was about to taste it he called to Kella, "What is this?"

Kella turned, saw what he was holding and screamed at the top of her lungs, "Stop!"

Pov was terrified by the angry screech. He dropped the container and started to wail. Kella had never before yelled at him like that. In turn, Kella was both horrified and relieved. She scooped the crying five year old onto her lap and comforted him.

"Pov," she said, "what you had in your hand was poison. I sell that to the people of Jericho. They use it to kill rats in the food bins. Did you smell it?"

"Yes," came a weak whimpering reply.

"Pov, never forget the smell from that jar. Just a small taste of that powder will kill anything, human or animal. If you had put just a few grains in your mouth you would be dead now."

Pov scuttled more deeply into her arms and cried even more.

Kella had lied to him. It was poison, but not for rats. She sold some of it only once since coming to Jericho…to the woman who had poisoned Lahg.

As Pov grew a little older, he wanted more freedom from Kella. He wished to explore beyond her tiny house situated between the two walls. One cloudless morning he woke early. Kella was snoring. He went outside into the bright dawn sunlight. Urinating at the ditch where townspeople emptied their nightly honey pots, he noticed that the gate through the inner wall was open. He had never been in that part of Jericho. Kella told him he was too young to enter there. She indicated that the upper town was sacred and he was not cleansed. At age seven he already knew not to believe all that adults told him. Pov would find out for himself.

Kella woke suddenly, as if from a nightmare. But she had not been dreaming. Something was wrong...terribly wrong. She saw immediately that Pov was missing. Someone had taken him? No!

At the doorway she saw the town's upper gate was open. Had he disobeyed and gone to the upper part of Jericho? She had warned him that he could not go there, but he was a headstrong boy. Moving as fast as her short legs could carry her, she ran up the hill to the open gate. It was much too late...Tog was there holding Pov's arm tightly clamped in his enormous hairy fist. He saw Kella.

"Is this little runt my son," he asked.

"Yes Tog. I am so sorry. He got away from me. I know I promised that you would never see..."

"Quiet woman! I see Lahg in his face and in his movements. How old is he now and why is he so small?"

"He is in his seventh year Tog. Remember that Lahg was also tiny."

Tog thought for a moment about Lahg and a rare smile came to his face. "The boy pleases me. I will take him back. I am reminded of his mother. Your duty is done women. I will send a gift to you. You have served me well. What do you call him?"

Kella, with breaking heart replied, "I use the name Lahg gave him. I call him Pov."

"He is little, I will call him Runt."

"My name is Pov," the boy cried in a childish scream as he tried to escape Tog's grasp.

Kella was horrified by the boy's reaction. Tog had severely punished others for much less.

Instead, Tog laughed. "Just like your mother, are you boy? She would fight me all the time. It will be a joy to battle with you."

Initially, Pov sorely missed Kella. Yet, life was much sweeter in Tog's house. He was given a fine new pair of sandals. Now that he was no longer barefoot he could run faster. Pov could also eat until he was full. That happened rarely when he had lived with Kella.

Tog enjoyed calling Pov by his new name, Runt. When his women or older sons were present Tog would freely call the boy, 'Runt'.

"My name is Pov," the seven year old would shout with some anger in his voice.

"See, he is spirited, as was his mother." Then Tog would hold his big belly and laugh.

Pov found that his older brothers did not share their father's joy. Out of Tog's hearing they all called him Runt. If he tried to correct them, they would hurt him in ways that would not leave marks on his body. The women equally disliked this issue of the hated Lahg woman.

Pov had a mental quickness that none of his brothers possessed. He was allowed the honor to sit at Tog's foot. Sometimes he would even question some of the reports given Tog by his brothers. As he grew Pov dared to make suggestions and occasionally, but privately, challenge some of his father's directives. His brothers and the women could see the danger. If young Pov became too powerful, he might be made the heir to

Tog's property. Siv, the eldest son, would be disinherited. The structure of the clan would change for all the other sons and all of the women.

"We must do something about Pov," Siv told his brothers.

"Kill him!" one suggested.

"How?" Siv asked. "Father will blame us if we do that. Then he will have us killed." At those words the sons all turned and looked at their largest brother. He was called Ox. Only Ox had the physical proportions of his father. Yet he was the slowest of the somewhat dull-witted group of siblings. Ox was Tog's tool of control. If his father ordered it done, Ox would break a man's arm. If a captured raider, now a slave, disobeyed a directive, Ox might be sent to strangle the man. He did everything as Tog commanded, and without passion. His brothers had reason to fear him.

One of the women, Cam by name, serving food to the group of brothers answered Siv's question of 'how to kill Pov?' She whispered quietly in Siv's ear. At first he was going to bat her away. Then Siv's eyes lit up and he listened carefully. He replied noiselessly with a nod and sent her away.

"Brothers," Siv said, "we have a way to rid ourselves of that Runt. Tomorrow we will join our father in the feast of the North Goddess. I will send a special dish to Runt. It will be poisoned. He will die and we will be rid of that open sore the bitch Lahg made for us." The brothers all cheered except Ox. He did not understand.

The next afternoon the feast was held in the small open plaza near the upper gate. None of the small round houses in this early village of mankind was large enough to hold more than a few people.

Siv was careful not to be directly connected to the poisoning process. He had the woman, Cam, instruct a new serving girl to present a special lamb dish directly to Pov. She was told to say to Pov that it was seasoned with a new spice. He would be the first to try it.

The servant girl was very young. She trembled as she approached Tog and Pov. The young boy was sitting in his customary position at the feet of his father. As she offered the lamb, it was Tog who reached out for the meat. Siv was horrified. As Tog brought the meat to his mouth, Pov jumped up and knocked it out of his hand. The feasting group was stunned. Pov had actually hit his father! This was an offense punishable by death!

A sound started to come out of Tog's throat, but Pov's scream overpowered it. "Father that was poison!." The lamb piece had fallen to the ground. It was instantly consumed by one of the many dogs in the courtyard. In moments the dog's eyes bulged, her tongue flopped out of her mouth and she fell dead on the ground. All were stunned into silence.

"Pov, how did you know?" A shaking Tog asked.

Pov smiled. His father did not call him Runt. "I...I learned that smell when I was with Kella. She taught me."

Siv was shaking too. Without thinking he blurted, "Father, it was not meant for you. It was for the Runt." Too late, Siv realized he had confessed to the crime.

Overwrought, perspiring from his close brush with death, Tog said in a weak voice, "Ox, take Siv to the gate in the wall and hold him there. I must think on this. Everyone else leave, but Pov, you stay with me."

Tog took Pov by the arm and forced the boy to sit beside him. "Pov, your brother tried to kill you. It is your choice to decide how to punish him. It is not right to have Ox strangle him on the feast of the North Goddess. Yet, if that is what you want, I will command Ox to do it. Better still we can wait until tomorrow to punish him."

"Father, I would never want to kill my brother," Pov knew about the abhorrence his brothers and the women had for him. He knew he had replaced some of them as his father's favorite. That came at a price. The young boy was conflicted. He was too young to order a man to his death…especially a brother. "I don't want him killed father" he begged.

Tog rejected Pov's plea. "He must be punished Pov. I just don't understand why he would ever want to harm you. Our law is an eye for an eye. It is our way. It is simple. It is just."

"Father, you are the most powerful man in Jericho. You make the rules and you can change them. Siv is your blood and also mine. Trade him to that caravan leaving tomorrow. He will become their slave. That is a fair punishment for what he has done. Slavery is far worse than death."

Tog thought about that for a moment and then nodded in agreement. He was inwardly pleased at Pov's good judgment. He ordered Siv to go to his house and wait there. After that, he had the wailing servant girl brought to him. Between hysterical sobs she told Tog that his first woman, Cam, had sprinkled some powder on the lamb. Then she was ordered to take the dish only to Pov.

Tog ordered the girl sent to a brothel in the outer town where she would now pleasure the caravan drivers. It was a mild and fitting punishment.

Ox was sent to fetch Cam. She was dead. She had taken the remainder of the poison knowing the servant girl would seal her fate. Before the next dawn Siv slipped out of the gates of Jericho. He had assumed his punishment would be death. He had decided not to wait for it.

During the next few years Tog found that the bitumen that his sons and slaves pulled from the muck at the Dead Sea for their own use was equally a much sought after trading commodity. Bitumen was a good adhesive with many possibilities. Wooden boats were caulked with it, reed containers were water-proofed by it and ceramics repaired using the mastic properties of the material.

As Jericho became a more important trading center for salt and now bitumen, Tog became aware of the profit from a new product called obsidian. This sharp glass-like stone was not new to him, but tradable quantities of the material had never before arrived at Jericho. Today a trader had come over a great sea and followed the narrow track to Jericho to get Tog's bitumen. In trade he offered obsidian. Tog discovered from the trader, his name was Dagg, that obsidian was mined far to the north, almost in another part of the world. The place was called Catal Hoyuk.

Tog was amazed as the trader showed him how a slight blow to the obsidian created a seashell like piece of mineral with the sharpest edges he had ever experienced. He could cut hair with it. He could even shave his beard with the glass-like material. While this stone-glass was far too fragile to be used as a weapon, it would cut flesh and bone if handled with diligence. It could become a wonderful tool in the preparation of animal products.

The trader explained that his obsidian was mined at the base of sacred mountain named Hasan Dag. This mountain occasionally spit fire from its top and had two cones shaped like a woman's breasts. Hasan Dag was a difficult four day journey north of his home village of Catal Hoyuk. Collecting the obsidian was dangerous work. Dagg said that the fire goddess of Hasan Dag did not like her treasure stolen. She often sent puffy hot clouds of smoke down the sides of the mountain. Everyone who breathed the strange smoke died. At other times this angry goddess sent rivers of boiling hot melted stone flowing over the cliffs. Obsidian collectors were often trapped by the flowing liquid fire and died. The mountain goddess was powerful and all Catal Hoyuk worshiped her fury. Currently no one dared to tempt her by collecting more of her precious glass-stone. Too many collectors were dead.

Later, after the trader retired to use the brothel in the lower town, Tog called Pov to his side. "Pov, I made a bargain with that trader Dagg, who brought me this obsidian. He will take you and your brother Ox with him when he returns to Catal Hoyuk."

Pov was upset by his father's words. "Why father? Why are you sending Ox and I away with such a strange man? I think he is not truthful with us."

Tog laughed. "I have been dealing with traders all my life Pov. They are all liars. This man, Dagg, is a very big liar. I am glad you can see that. Can you imagine a mountain that shoots out fire?

Pov shook his head with a 'no.'

"Or melted rock?"

"That cannot be father."

Tog smiled. "Exactly! Dagg is trying to frighten us. He knows how valuable this glass-stone will be in trade. I have made a deal with him. I will give him freely, without trade, as much bitumen as he can carry. In turn he will take you to the place where he mines obsidian. Then, when he returns here with you, I promised him another free load of bitumen. It will be worthwhile for him and for me."

"How is that father? Oh, wait. I see. Then I can tell you how to find the obsidian and we can get it ourselves. We can collect it from the mountain without trade."

"You are a smart boy, Pov. None of your brothers are as quick as you. But I will send Ox along with you."

"Why Ox?"

"Because Ox is so big, everyone fears him. I will tell him to do whatever you say. He will keep you from harm. Robbers and pirates are everywhere. You need to be protected. This trip will take two moons each way, according to Dagg."

"I can take care of myself father! I don't need Ox."

"Don't argue with me, Pov. You are still just a boy. I would send one of your older brothers, but none of them have your sense. You can learn the route to this treasure. Dagg says he has a boat waiting that you must take. It sails on a sea that has no end. I don't believe that tale either. Dagg says there are monsters in its water and creatures called sirens, which are part woman and part bird. They lure sailors to their deaths with magic songs. Again, I don't trust these wild stories. You are to go with him and find what the truth is."

"Father, if Dagg knows we are going with him to find the glass-stone, he will try to fool us, or maybe never bring us back. He might even kill us."

"Don't worry Pov. Remember that I am a trader and I know how one thinks. I have told Dagg that our witch, Kella, said I must have younger women in order to have more sons. I heard that the women of the north are very fertile. Dagg thinks you are going to select new women for me. He is a fool. He believed me."

Pov sat quietly with his father and contemplated his new adventure. As he thought about it, he took the thumb and forefinger of his left hand, squeezed his nostrils and pulled downward. Tog did the same thing. Neither noticed the common family gesture of the other.

The trip was grueling, and yet amazing at every turn. At first, when they reached the sea, Pov could not believe his eyes. His keen sense of smell anticipated the water long before they walked over the last ridge. Even from a great distance he saw that the waves were enormous and the sea, just as Dagg had said, was endless.

Arriving at the sandy shore Pov took his brother by the hand and led him into the water. The waves knocked Pov down but Ox laughed at his little brother and easily returned him to his feet. Pov came out of the sea spitting a mouthful of the water. It was far less salty then the Dead Sea.

As the waves washed over them, and the sand brushed them, Pov noticed a change. The soot of the cooking fires, the dust of travel and the heavy grease patina of sweat and oil was washed from their bodies. Pov saw that Ox's body was fairer than any he had ever noticed in Jericho. Ox also had brown hair...not black. To his surprise, as he looked down, he found his skin was also lighter.

Finally, he realized that the odor of his body and that of his brother was gone! How could that be? Did this huge sea change smell? When they rejoined Dagg, Pov found he could immediately smell the ship captain. All the odors of food, animals and the dusty tract they had followed to get to the coast were with Dagg. He turned to Ox. No smell at all. He and Ox no longer held that mixture of strong aromas.

Dagg's little boat was waiting. It smelled of fish, rotting wood and something he could not identify, but that odor was near or in the single sail. If he stayed at the front of the boat, sailing into the wind, there was only the fresh salt air in his nostrils. He thought now he would take Ox into the water and sand at every opportunity. Cleanliness was a new experience. Pov delighted in it.

They sailed north and west, but only by day. The sea was miserable for Ox and almost as bad for Pov. The constant motion of the tiny boat made both of them sick. Dagg and the two sailors who made up his crew mocked them constantly. Tog's sons lost all they had eaten over the side of the boat. It happened every morning. After just a few days they both refused food at the start of the day's sailing.

The little boat always sailed within the sight of land. Dagg did not know how to navigate on the open sea. Each night the boat was beached, a fire built and a guard posted. Sometimes small groups approached their fire at night. All of the intruders scattered when Ox was called to stand upright and told to howl. His size terrified the raiders.

After many days at sea, high winds of a storm struck from the north. The little boat was beached and the sail made into a tent to protect the group from the driving rain. Dagg sent his two men in search of fresh game, berries or even dry firewood while they waited for the storm to abate.

Sitting under the tarp like structure, Dagg began to muse about his trip to Jericho. "Pov, you know that I came to Jericho to get bitumen. I expected that your father, Tog, would take my obsidian in trade. It would have been a fair bargain. Yet he gave me the bitumen freely and additionally, gold for my obsidian and still more gold to take you and the Ox to Catal Hoyuk."

"Yes, I know all that."

"So you can find Tog a young woman for your father to have more sons?"

Pov was not sure that he could respond. He had not yet learned to lie like a trader. He remained silent.

"I have to tell you Pov, I think your father is crazy. No mere woman is worth what your father has given me."

"But don't forget Dagg," Pov sputtered, "part of his trade is also to bring Ox, me and a woman back to Jericho for my father."

"I won't do that Pov. You and Ox...fine. But I will not have a woman on my boat. They are bad luck."

"You never told that to my father," Pov replied angrily.

"True. The trade was too good for me. I had to take it."

Pov breathed heavily in frustration. "Then how will Ox and I get back to Jericho?" He was suddenly worried.

The ship captain smiled. He rose and walked to the edge of the tarp and urinated onto the sand. "Pov you are intelligent. If you watch me, you will see how I use the sail to turn the ship. Look back as we travel...see where we came from and remember landmarks. Tog told me he gave you gold to trade for a woman. You can use some of it to get a boat...women are very cheap in Catal Hoyuk. You can buy any woman you find acceptable and then sail your own boat back to your father."

Pov was stunned. The gold was not for a woman. It was to pay for guides to lead him and his brother to the obsidian. Still, he thought, perhaps this was best. Dagg might learn the true reason for their trip if he failed to bring back a woman. That could be dangerous. As they sat by the small fire, Pov seriously told Dagg, "I will watch you and learn."

That night as the group slept on the beach, Ox left his watch position and gently woke his brother. He signaled Pov to follow him a short distance down the beach where they could sit on driftwood tree trunk.

"Pov, Ox must tell you..."

These few words from Ox were more than the young man had ever heard from Ox at one time. It sent a chill down his spine. He gripped Ox's arm interrupting, "Yes Ox, please tell me."

"Everybody think Ox stupid. Ox not stupid. Ox understand things. Two men say they will kill Dagg, then us, for the boat and your gold. Said they would be much rich."

"Who Ox? Dagg's two crewmen?"

"Yes."

"When, Ox?"

"That all I hear little brother. Don't want those men to hurt you."

The next day the storm was gone but the seas remained too high to safely travel. Dagg again sent his two crewmen to forage. While they were gone, Pov explained the plot that Ox had overheard.

Dagg's face turned red with rage. "I will kill them both with my bare hands. Better yet, I will have Ox do it and watch them die slowly."

Pov disagreed in a commanding voice, "No! He obeys only me and I will not have him do it. Let us leave this place without them. I want no blood on my brother's hands." Pov began to value that he had some measure of power, even at his young age.

Ox nodded in appreciation. The three of them pushed the small boat into the water and although the waves were dangerously high, they set sail to continue north. The two deserted crewmen screamed at them from the shoreline as they departed. They ran along the beach until they became exhausted and were left far behind in the dunes.

It was another ten days before the boat reached the mouth of a small river. They sailed the stream for another three days until they came to a small group of huts. Dagg was known here. He hired men and burros to carry his cargo of bitumen over a mountainous trail.

"Dagg, you told my father that Catal Hoyuk was on a river. Why are we now climbing these hills?"

"I also said that it was a two moon journey. Have we traveled two moons?"

"No." Pov replied sullenly.

"Well, little man, we have to cross a mountain range to another river in order to get you where you can pick a bride for your father."

Dagg smiled to himself. He knew the bride story was a lie.

Four

Pov

Catal Hoyuk

It took MANY days to cross a seemingly endless range of mountains. Pov had never seen peaks so high. Some appeared to almost touch the clouds. To his young eyes the valleys were even more incredible. Each was lush with green plant life. Many places held gigantic trees. This land was nothing like the bone-dry valley of the River Jordan. Finally, after days of trekking they came to the Carsamba River. It showed itself to be a broad shallow stream of crystal clear water.

"It flows down to Catal Hoyuk," Dagg said.

A day was spent at the riverbank constructing a log raft for the cargo of salt and bitumen. Pov had noted that the newly hired porters knew Dagg but obviously disliked him. He wondered why? They were surly to him but they followed his directions.

Ox helped the porters carry the heavy timbers to build the raft. He needed to be busy doing physical things. In the meantime Pov once again cleaned himself. This time he bathed in the clear cold river. Each time he did this, his sense of smell improved. Now at the end of the day, he made the sweat covered Ox also wash himself in the water.

Dagg gave all the orders but still managed to spend most of his day fishing. Supper was a feast of roasted carp sprinkled with some delicious spice brought by the porters. They called it 'savory'. It provided a tang to the fish that Pov had never experienced. It made the meal delicious. The aroma of that spice would not be forgotten.

Two days later, rounding a bend in the river, Pov saw Catal Hoyuk for the first time, its brick walls were gleaming in the sunlight. The town was the largest cluster of structures Pov had ever seen. They all appeared to be connected? *It was...it was...perhaps ten Jericho's all in one...*Pov thought. He searched his mind for a descriptive word...to explain to himself the odd aggregation of buildings. Perhaps something like *'clump'* or *'beehive'* might do. *No, neither was right.* This was all just too unexpected and so different from Jericho.

As they drew near, Pov could not see any protective town wall. He asked Dagg, "Where is the wall to keep out bandits, robbers?"

"There is no wall," Dagg replied. "Catal Hoyuk is far from any regular path. The mountains shield us from bands of raiders. Then too, the goddess of the mountain Hasan Dag also watches over us. Those who know of us, they fear our goddess. She spits fire."

"What name do you give the goddess? Is she also Hasan Dag?" Pov asked.

Looking a bit confused, Dagg replied sharply, "The goddess has no name. Only the mountain has a name."

Pov's amazement continued as they got off the raft and walked towards this immense structure... the town that was called Catal Hoyuk. It was all, seemingly, one mass of brick with no doors or windows or any place to walk. There were no paths or lanes of any size. In Jericho spaces separated the dwellings from one another. He saw very small doors at ground level, probably for household animals. There were also ladders against the outer walls for town people to reach the roofs.

"Dagg, how do we....?"

"I know your question. I will explain. In your town of Jericho each dwelling is separated by some space from the next house. In fact, everywhere I have traveled there is space all around for people to walk between structures."

"Yes, except those houses attached to the town wall."

"Well none of that is true in Catal Hoyuk. Here a new building starts at or close to the outer wall of an older building. We climb ladders at the outer-most buildings and walk over roofs until we arrive at the place where we live. Then there is another ladder going down into the living space. The opening in the roof lets out smoke from our cooking fires and admits light and air to breath. You have such roof openings in Jericho but here in Catal Hoyuk it is also our door. The door you see is in the ceiling of each home. Most of our time, however, is spent on the roof. We go into our houses only to cook and sleep or worship"

"And when you sleep you take down your ladder to keep enemies out of your house."

"Good thinking Pov, but I have no enemies in this town. We are a place of brothers."

Another lie, Pov thought to himself. While he was still young, he was not a fool. It had not taken long during the voyage with Dagg to learn that this man often invented the truth. It was also noticeable that as soon as the townspeople recognized Dagg they turned their backs or scrambled downs their ladders to avoid him. A few dared to send looks of disgust, in his direction...or was it hate? *What had this sea-captain-trader done to earn this enmity of so many?*

With Ox guarding the cargo, Dagg hired new porters to carry the heavy bundles of goods from the raft to his house. It would be a slow process to move all of that material. Dagg took the young man from Jericho by the arm and the two of them went on ahead. His house could only be reached by crossing the roofs of many other dwellings. The roofs were of uneven height which made passage somewhat difficult. Cooking smells rose from some of the ventilation holes. Occasionally Pov heard a snatch of conversation or the play-voices of children. Like everything else on this trip, it was all very extraordinary.

Dagg stopped at a vent hole, motioned Pov to follow and quickly descended the ladder. Women below began to joyfully shriek and call out Dagg's name as he went down the ladder. There were five women in the house. Three women were close to Dagg's age and two were much younger. The younger of the two girls had not yet blossomed. Both shyly batted their eyes at Pov. After some initial fussing over Dagg, all the females left to prepare food and drink. Waiting, Dagg and Pov reclined on thick wool rugs of a unique beautiful design.

"You must be very rich Dagg to have a house like this? And it is not round as are the houses in Jericho. This room and the others we crossed seem to have straight walls with square corners. And the walls are...."

"Dried mud bricks first and then the walls are plastered, Pov."

"Plaster?"

"Yes," Dagg replied with a very wide grin. "Pov, you have much to learn. I will show you how we make plaster, maybe tomorrow. The world is large and much of it is not at all like your Jericho."

"I am learning that every day. May I ask you about some things?"

"Of course you may Pov. What do you want to know?"

"Well who makes these wonderful mats? My father would trade much bitumen for some of these."

"My women make them. They weave these rugs from the wool of sheep. Many of the women in Catal Hoyuk do the same thing, but my women make some of the best. I trade salt and bitumen for wool for the weaving and for food from those men who choose to gather grain and hunt animals.

"Our rugs have two uses Pov. First is trade, we barter them for many things. My best arrangement is for gold. Many people in Catal Hoyuk make jewelry from the gold. We are a town of traders and craftsmen. The second use for these rugs is to bury our dead. We wrap our departed kin in one of these rugs. The more important is the person, the richer is the rug. We bury the dead person beneath our fire hearth here in his house. Then, after a time, we have to build the house a bit higher because the floor is not even in all of our rooms."

Pov shuddered. "Is that why the roofs we crossed are of different heights?"

"Yes."

"And are some of your kin buried in this house?"

"Of course! All of our ancestors. We honor them by keeping them near."

"But what of the odor of the dead? That must be awful. No one has been buried here for a long time because I don't smell anything."

Dagg grinned. "You do not understand our customs young man. Here in Catal Hoyuk, when a person dies we place the body outside. After the vultures clean the bones for us we respectfully paint the skull and bury it with the skeleton wrapped in one of our rugs."

As the women appeared with steaming trays of food and drink, Pov wondered if he was sitting on the grave of someone in Dagg's family. Dagg followed the young man's eye movements and laughed.

"Do not worry Pov; we bury our dead under the hearth. You are not sitting on anyone." The women all laughed. Pov thought it not at all proper to have women laugh at him. In Jericho a female would never dare laugh at a man.

The meal provided another surprise for Pov. But it was not the food. The women and even the two girls sat and ate with them. They even dipped into the common dishes of food. Another strange custom. In Jericho, women served men and never ate with them. These women were very different. They directly engaged Dagg in conversation and talked about the weaving and the rug trade as if they owned the process.

"Pov, you are surprised that my women act this way?"

Putting his head down so as to not make eye contact with any of the women, Pov mumbled a quiet "Yes."

Dagg firmly declared, "Your way is not our way."

The women began to question Pov about the customs and the women of Jericho. He was offended to be directly questioned by women, yet he did his best to maintain his status as a guest. As they talked he failed to notice that the oldest woman, Shala, had called Dagg aside and the two were engaged in a quiet but lively conversation.

Dagg suddenly became animated. To Pov he said, "Go to the roof and wait for your brother. He should be along very soon. Have the salt and bitumen brought into the house." To the women Dagg said,

"Feed the giant man who comes here. He is Pov's brother. His name is Ox. He will not harm you. Now I must leave immediately. All of you be careful!" The words were spoken with authority. No one refused to comply.

It was not until evening that Dagg returned to his house. After another whispered conversation with Shala, he called for Pov to sit with him as he ate and drank for a second time. He had a worn-down look on his face.

"Pov, my situation here in Catal Hoyuk is far worse than I imagined. There is an old grudge held against me. Four brothers and their father must kill me in order to preserve their family honor. I choose not to let them do so"

"What did you do?" Pov asked.

A look of rage flashed across Dagg's face.

Pov immediately saw he had made a grave social error with his question. "I mean...I mean," he stuttered, "why do they want to harm you?" Pov knew that his words were still wrong, but at the same time Dagg seemed to calm himself. He continued with eating his meal and ignored the unwanted questions. The long silence spoke to the young man's blunder.

As Dagg noisily chewed his food, Pov detected a new unpleasant odor coming from the opening in the roof. "Dagg, I think...."

"Yes Pov, I have hired men to guard our door for the night. I am surprised that you heard them."

"Well, I...I..." Pov did not want to tell Dagg that he had smelled them. Best not to tell this man too much. *Change the subject,* he thought. He said, "What happens now Dagg?"

"I don't know. We will wait for tomorrow."

The next day, and the next after that, brought no trouble at all. Dagg relaxed. While he stayed out of sight in the house, he let Pov and Ox wander about Catal Hoyuk, on their own. The two soon discovered that a large area on the side of the town away from the volcano was a daily market place. Here were traders offering goods Pov had never imagined existed. There were live birds and bleating goats and cut meat of hunted animals, all available for trade. He found baskets of different grains and fruits unknown in Jericho. It was all very confusing, very colorful, very exciting.

On their next daily trip to the market Pov found the two young girls who belonged to Dagg. They were trading. Females certainly held a much more respected position in Catal Hoyuk than Jericho. The oldest girl, about Pov's age, was named Lira and her younger sister was called Pata. Lira carried a small satchel with obsidian. Apparently it was quite valuable since many of the traders in the market place knew of the contents of her pouch and hailed her by name to come see their offerings. One man covered with grime and blood was persistent, shooing the flies off of his recently killed meat. He was extremely ugly. His face appeared to have been chewed by some animal.

Pov and Ox joined the girls and found that Lira was a hard bargainer. Then too, it was obvious that the vendors wanted her obsidian. Pov asked, "Why is your obsidian so valuable? I thought that it was much available at the mountain called Hasan Dag?"

Lira went limp. The meat vendor groaned loudly. Lira quietly snarled to Pov, "It is not permitted to say the name of the sacred mountain of the goddess, except in a house shrine. It is great offense to say her name outside. Never do that again!"

"I did not know, Pov muttered. "I am sorry. I never meant to offend your customs."

Lira was still angry. "It is terrible bad luck to do what you just did Pov. That caused my father to ..." her voice trailed off. Her little sister Pata stared at the ground. The vendor was trembling. There would be no trade.

Lira took Pov by the hand...a gesture never done by any female in Jericho. In the hot sunny trading plaza, with all to hear, she said, "Come with me, I must teach you about the goddess."

Pov quickly learned much about life in Catal Hoyuk. They visited several houses. Inside each house he found a room devoted as a shrine to the fiery goddess of the Hasan Dag, the volcano mountain.

"What is the name of your goddess? Is it the same as the mountain?" Pov asked for a second time. He wondered if Dagg had told the truth about a goddess with no name.

Lira replied, "She has no name. She *IS* the fiery mountain. We honor her in every house so that she will not send poison clouds and melting rock down upon us. We only say the name of her mountain inside the shrine of each house. Never Pov, *never* say the name outside of her shrine room, not even anywhere else in the house. Many people have died on her mountain."

"Do they go there to worship the goddess?"

"No Pov, most go there to steal her obsidian. She sometimes punishes the thieves with fiery death."

"But..."

"I know what you are thinking, Pov. I have obsidian. I did not go to the mountain. I have never been there. Dagg gives the obsidian to me and has me take it to the market to trade for food. I also trade for wool to make our rugs. Only Dagg trades for gold.

"Know too Pov, *death*...often...comes to those who go to the mountain to steal the sharp green glass of the goddess. While we have her obsidian here in Catal Hoyuk there is not a problem. The goddess seems to forget about the obsidian once it is gone. But it is bad luck, sometimes very bad luck, to steal the obsidian. Also you dishonor the goddess by saying the name of her mountain outside the room of a house shrine. Is it not that way in Jericho?"

"We know nothing of your goddess in Jericho," Pov told her. Both quietly absorbed this information from the other.

They continued the tour of several of the nearby houses. Each contained a shrine room. Every room was neat, clean and the plaster walls coated with some white material which Lira called 'whitewash.' At first Pov thought that the women in these houses were relatives. They certainly treated Lira and Pata with a noticeable level of deference. After returning to Dagg's house, he inquired about it.

"The women in the houses we visited all work for my mother, Shala. We give them some food and many of their other needs and the wool to make rugs. Their men are hunters or traders. You saw some of their men in the market place. Very few of them are as brave as Dagg to go gather their own obsidian. So Dagg gathers obsidian for hunters and other trades people. In turn their women make rugs for him to trade in far places."

"Dagg brought no rugs to Jericho?"

Lira shrugged with a motion of puzzlement.

Pov said, "I wonder why he brought only obsidian. I will have to ask him."

Lara nodded a second time. "He is often very mysterious. None of us dares to disobey him, even Shala. But she has a way. He listens to her. I think she is the true master of the house. She is very powerful."

"And who is the master of Catal Hoyuk? In Jericho it is my father who makes the rules and punishes those who break his commands."

Lira smiled broadly. She almost laughed. "Oh Pov, that is awful. Here we have no one person telling the others what to do. I have seen your surprise at how we women act with men. Here we must be very different, I think, from your Jericho women."

Pov certainly had to agree with that. "Does your mother Shala…"

Lira interrupted. "Shala is not my mother. I just call her that and Dagg is not my real father. They bought me and Pita from a traveler when we were very small. You need young girls with small fingers to tie the knots in our rugs!"

That evening Pov thought about all he had learned that day. He was taken aback by the power of the women of Catal Hoyuk. Then too he was especially pleased talking with Lira. It somehow gave him a feeling that he had not experienced before. His reverie was disturbed by Ox, who was bedded beside him.

"Pov, you still awake?"

"Yes." This was a bit unnerving. Ox rarely spoke.

Ox whispered in a quiet but demanding voice, "Tog sent us away with Dagg to bring back young women. It is time you pick some so we can return to our father."

"Tomorrow, Ox. We will look tomorrow." It was a false promise. Perhaps he should tell Ox the truth that they were really sent to find the source of obsidian. Maybe, tomorrow. For now Pov wanted to fall asleep with Lira in his dreams.

Something was wrong! Pov shuddered awake. In the deep gloom of the entrance room, lit only by a small wax light, he could barely make out the shape of Ox snoring lightly beside him. What had caused him to be startled? *The smell!* He could not detect the smell of the men set on the roof to guard Dagg, They were gone!

Quickly he rose and he went to the next room where Dagg slept with his women. He gently shook the man. Almost instantly he felt a knife at his throat. "Dagg, it is me. It is Pov."

"By the goddess, Pov, you frightened me. I almost slit your throat."

"I know."

"Why did you shake me? Dagg asked.

"I had to. I think something is wrong. The guards you hired are all gone."

"What! How do you know?" Dagg said quietly, but at the same time was holding Pov's arm with extreme pressure.

"Something woke me Dagg. Then I realized the smell of those men was no longer in the air. I was worried…"

"Pov, be quiet. Go wake your brother and tell him to guard the entrance. I'll wake the women."

It all happened in a blur. Dagg explained that men were coming to kill him and he must flee. There was a secret door to escape from the house and he had to use it now. The men, he explained quickly, would abide by the customs of Catal Hoyuk. They would never harm the women. Pov and Ox were also safe because they are strangers from afar.

"If they ask where I am…I know they will, Shala you are to tell them I have gone to Hasan Dag to get more of the green glass obsidian. I will leave a trail so they will follow me. Perhaps the goddess will protect me there."

Shala snorted, "You don't believe in the goddess you old fool."

Dagg dismissed her remark. He turned to the young men from Jericho. "Ox, you are so large that the men will not cause trouble. Let one man come in to search the house for me. No more than one man. Tell him you will break both of his legs if more men come down the ladder."

"He will do as you say," Pov quietly agreed.

Just then they heard many footsteps near the ladder. As one they turned and focused for just a moment on the ladder. When they looked back, Dagg was gone. The events of that night proceeded as Dagg had predicted. Now they all waited for his return.

Two moons passed without a word. Pov became, first an assistant, then a leader to Lira trading for goods in the market place. He discovered that the group of women weaving rugs for Shala was much larger then he had first imagined. In turn a very large number of the men supplied hunted game for the weavers. They were paid with obsidian and sometimes gold. Lira was the go-between.

Time passed quickly for Pov, yet each night Ox would ask Pov about young women and returning to Jericho. Each night Pov wondered if Ox would understand that they had been sent with Dagg, not for women, but rather to find obsidian. Could Ox be told the truth and not inform anyone else?

As the days went by, Pov and Lira spent more time together. She was so different from the women of his home. She spoke up to him, she disagreed with him and occasionally she took his hand or arm. He tingled at her touch but failed to understand why. Each day Ox would ask about returning to Jericho, Each day Pov would think about Lira. He did not want to leave Catal Hoyuk.

In the third moon after Dagg's departure, the earth shook. It was early morning. Pov and Ox were at the trading plaza with both girls. Without warning the ground under their feet moved. Pov had never experienced the frightening power of an earthquake. He nearly lost his balance as the earth seemed to shift sideways. Ox stumbled to his knees…terrified! Stalls of food and other goods were toppled as if by a giant invisible hand. The earth itself cracked open, directly in front of Lira's feet. The fissure was accompanied by an ear shattering roar that filled the air. One house near the market suddenly crumbled, immediately another followed suit. Then many others collapsed. People, petrified by the sudden quake prostrated themselves towards the mountain. Pov turned in that direction. Through the clouds of dust, churned in the market place, he could see huge ash plumes and flames belching from both cones. Liquid fire was starting to flow down the slopes of Hasan Dag.

"It is the goddess," Lira whimpered. "Come, we must get to Shala.'

The damage to Catal Hoyuk was extensive. Many houses were destroyed. Two of Shala's weavers were dead, buried in the rubble. Many others were hurt. All talk centered on the goddess. Why was she angry? Who had violated her? What could they do to please her?

The volcanic eruptions and occasional shaking earth continued for many days. Winds blew the smoke and ash away from the village. Eventually, normal life resumed. Ox especially had been deeply impressed by the eruption. Finding paints, he decorated one wall in Dagg's house that he dedicated to the goddess. It showed the volcano and the houses of Catal Hoyuk. It was a talent that impressed everyone. Pov particularly was astounded. He never realized that his big brother possessed such a gift.

Meanwhile Pov was also enjoying some delightful experiences with Lira's help. She, almost daily showed him some different ways of Catal Hoyuk. But alone, his almost unnatural robust sense of smell, often drove him from the odors of the town to the Carsamba River. He would immerse himself in the cold water. Then he diligently rubbed sand over his body to remove the grimy soot and odors that clung to his skin.

"What are you doing Pov?" Lira along with her sister Pata had followed him one day. She was inquisitive by nature. She had to know what he did on these lone excursions.

Pov was startled; He tried to cover himself as the girls made silly giggling noises. He blushed. Finally he found his tongue. "I need to get rid of the stink of Catal Hoyuk from my body. I wash it away with sand and water."

Lira pouted a little. "Do you think that I stink?"

Time in the market place had taught Pov to meet difficult questions with subtlety. He was enamored by Lira so he responded with what he considered a great deal of tact. "Lira, you don't smell as bad as most of the others in town."

There was no reply. Instead Lira stamped her foot, then with a menacing look she picked up a fist sized smooth gray stone and threw it at the naked young man.

The action was so fast that Pov could not scramble out of the way. As he tried to turn, the stone hit him directly in his testicles. With a small sound escaping from his lips, he sank below the cool clear knee deep water.

A gasp of horror escaped from Lira's lips. Pata put both of her hands to her mouth. Lira shouted, "Pata help me get him out of the river. He might drown." Together they dragged his limp body to the rocky beach. Pov was breathing but immobile from the pain. Gradually the sting wore off as the girls, not knowing what else to do, carried handfuls of cold river water to him and poured them on his groin.

Lira was crying, "I'm so sorry Pov. I never meant to hurt you. Please forgive me, please!" Turning to Pata she said, "Run and tell Shala what I did. Find how to make him better."

The pain was severe and Pov groaned loudly as Pata turned and ran. Slowly he sat up. "Lira, help me to move back into the water. The cold will ease my pain." Slowly but surely they both rose from the rocky shoreline. By hanging on to Lira he managed to walk the few steps to the water and sit. The jolt of putting his bottom into the river caused him to nearly pass out a second time. Lira sat beside him helping him to stay upright.

The pain gradually subsided but Lira was still tearful. "Do you hate me, Pov? I never meant to hurt you like that. You made me so mad, saying that I smelled bad. Do you still think that I do?"

Now Pov was now especially cautious. The sensation of violent hurt was gone, yet he was still very sore. He was not sure what to say. He certainly did not wish to be hit again…not like that. He just shook his head.

Lira understood. "You do think that I smell bad, don't you. Well, if you can wash the odor away, so can I."

By the time Pata brought a running Shala to the river, the older woman saw that both Lira and Pov were standing naked in almost waist deep water. They were laughing and rubbing each other with handfuls of sand. "Come Pata," a smiling Shala exclaimed, "I think Pov is better now."

It was almost six moons before Dagg returned to Catal Hoyuk. Lira was not yet showing any outward signs, but both she and Shala new she was carrying Pov's child. Pov did not know. Yet he did learn, guided by Shala and aided by Lira, the methods of being a successful trader.

Ox, in turn, was angry that they were not yet bringing a young girl to Tog. He even suggested that Pata would do. Ox told Pov that he would obey him for only one more moon...then he would find a woman and return to Jericho with or without his brother.

A few days later, Shala, hurriedly returning from the morning market, took Pov aside and whispered to him, "Dagg has returned. He wants to meet with us and he fears that his enemies know he is nearby. We have to join him outside of the town."

"How do you know...how did he...?" Pov stuttered.

"No time for questions. Get your brother. He wants Ox to be with us when we meet him."

Ox was not to be found. There was no time to search for him. Shala's urgency demanded they go to the meeting place as quickly as possible. It was at a grove of trees far out of town. Nearing the site, they noticed three men, in the near distance, all running very hard, away from them and away from Catal Hoyuk.

Shala took it as an omen of very bad luck. She uttered an oath to the goddess, even using the name of the mountain. But it was too late. They found Dagg. He was sprawled on his stomach with a spear in his back. He was dead.

With some difficulty Pov turned the man over. He had been pinned to the ground where the spear had completely pierced his body and the point entered the earth as he fell forward. There was a small pool of dark blood on the ground.

Shala knelt over his body and shook him. She could not return him to life so she began to wail while pulling her hair. As she sobbed uncontrollably Pov sensed movement in the dense undergrowth behind them. A bearded unkempt man appeared. Pov stared. He recognized the specter. It was Framm; one of his many half-brothers bore by one of Tog's women. Pov pulled an obsidian dagger from his belt. "Framm, did you do this? Did you kill Dagg?"

"Brother," he cried, "I would never do that. Dagg saved my life. He brought me here from our home in Jericho. Three men found us only a short time back. Dagg knew them. He knew they wanted to kill him. He told me to hide while he found a place to fight all three of them. The tallest man had a spear. He threw it at Dagg. It would have missed except Dagg could not see it coming towards him and he swerved into its path. When the three saw you coming towards this place, they ran away." Framm was now sobbing and his words came in short spurts. He staggered, then collapsed at his brother's feet.

Pov didn't know what to do. He could see blood on Shala's clothing where she had tried to raise the dead man. Now it appeared that she had fainted. The three killers were no longer in sight, having disappeared over a ridge towards Hasan Dag. He needed to learn how all this came about so he pulled Framm to a sitting position and said, "Tell me about this. How did you get here? Why are you and Dagg together?"

Framm gradually quieted his shattered emotions. He spoke slowly, glancing occasionally at the body covered partially by the woman. He said "Runt…"

"Don't call me that ever again! My name is Pov." There was power and authority in Pov's voice that brought Framm's head up. He stared directly into Pov's hazel eyes. This was no longer the young boy who had left Jericho.

Pov had to know what happened. He repeated his question. "Framm, how did you come to be with Dagg?"

This time the older brother was more respectful. "Dagg came to Jericho again just a few moons ago. He brought another load of obsidian for our father Tog. He also explained that he would try to bring you back to Jericho on his next trip. He told Tog that you liked the women of this place so much that it would be hard to get you to return.'

"Dagg lied to our father. He must have had other reasons…" Pov did not continue. His voice trailed off. "Tell me more, Framm."

"Perhaps Dagg did have reasons. But the very next day a very large band of raiders attacked Jericho. The walls would have held except the leader of the brigands was Siv, our oldest brother. Remember he ran away after he had tried to kill you with that poison."

"Of course I remember."

"Siv knew about a secret escape tunnel from the upper town that existed in case we were ever overrun. None of us knew it existed. Siv used the tunnel to get into Tog's house. He killed Tog."

"He killed our father?" Pov lamented.

"Yes. Next he and his men slaughtered all of our family. I had been away at the salt beds so I was spared. I met Dagg on the road running away and he warned me not to return to Jericho for surely Siv would kill me like the rest of the family. He told me to accompany him and find you here at Catal Hoyuk."

Pov was startled by Shala's voice. She was no longer sobbing, "Did Dagg tell you where he had been for these many months?"

Framm shook his head negatively. "I only met him in Jericho."

"Did he tell you where he hides the obsidian?" she pleaded.

"No."

"Maybe he told you why anyone wanted to kill him."

Again from Framm, a negative nod of the head. "He never spoke or told me much. I knew that Runt, I mean Pov, was here in your town. I also knew I would be killed if I returned to Jericho, so I just followed Dagg. I didn't know what else to do. I didn't want to die."

Pov was surprised to learn that even Shala knew nothing of the reasons for Dagg's death. He had been a trader and a manipulator and certainly a liar. But here was also a man who had many deep secrets he shared with no one.

Now, without delay Shala returned to her home to prepare everyone for the news of Dagg's death. In the meantime Pov and Framm struggled to carry the heavy body to the town. They were almost there when Shala came screaming to meet them.

"Pov," she cried, "your brother is gone and forced Lira and Pata to leave with him."

"Where…?"

"I don't know," Shala replied. "The other women in our house believe that he is taking them to Jericho for your father."

"But Tog is dead!" Pov said with the sound of fear in his voice.

"Ox doesn't know that. Pov you have to bring the girls back. Lira is carrying your child."

Pov turned ashen with that news. "Framm stay here with Shala. I must bring them back. If I know Lira, she will fight Ox every step of the way and I can catch up to them before they leave the river and start to cross the mountains."

It did not go well. The girls and Ox had already crossed the Carsamba River. Pov raced up the trail crossing the mountains, running as hard as he could manage during the daylight. At dusk on the second day he realized that Ox could not possibly get the girls to move this far so quickly. They must have taken a different route.

Slowly he returned down the mountainous path. It was now four days since they had disappeared. He didn't quite know what to do.

Nearing the Carsamba he heard voices, then laughter. It was Lira. She and Pata had Ox in the water. They were washing him! He had a look of rapture on his face as Pata rubbed him with sand. It made Pov smirk.

The girls were facing the shore line and saw Pov at the same time. They both shouted his name. "It took you long enough to find us," Lira said with smiling indignation. "Pata and I walked as slowly as we could. We took a circular trail that I know. It brought us right back to the river. Finally we told Ox he smelled so bad that we must stop and wash him to get the stink off. He is big!" she said with a gleam in her eye.

Pov was angry. He ignored her and went directly to his brother. "Ox, what are you doing? You can't steal Dagg's women. I told you we would find some girls and return soon. You don't even know how to get to Jericho"

Ox hung his head.

"Come out of the water and sit by me Ox. I have some bad news. Our brother Framm is here. He told me that our father is dead. Siv returned with a band of men and killed Tog and the rest of our family. Framm ran away with Dagg, who was trading again in Jericho. They just returned here."

"Father Tog dead?" Ox asked.

"You saw Dagg?" Lira screamed. "Tell us how he is, is he home with Shala?"

Pov's shoulders slumped. Now he had to give Lira and Pata bad news. "Dagg is also dead. He was killed by three men who ran away when Shala and I approached. Our brother Framm was hiding nearby and came to meet us. We carried Dagg's body back to Catal Hoyuk and it was there Shala told us you were gone."

"Father Tog dead!" Ox repeated mournfully.

That day was one Pov would never forget. He returned three wailing morose people back to Catal Hoyuk. Still, it was the start of a new life. With the subtle guidance of Shala and Lira he became a prosperous trader of rugs and spices. Lira, and later Pata, each gave him several sons and daughters. Ox and Framm decided to return to Jericho to avenge their father. They were never heard from again.

Pov lived to the ripe old age of forty-three.

A BIT OF HISTORY

In approximately 5,600 B.C. the town of Catal Hoyuk was abandoned. At that time Pov and his family had been interred under the hearth of their house for over 1,700 years.

THE ANCESTOR CHAIN

Five

Geography and Archeology

"What are you working on Chris?"

"I have to do a lot of research and write a paper on the environment. It's going to be about the impact of global warming on the human race. I've decided to make a special emphasis on the shrinking of that enormous, mile thick ice cap in Greenland. If that thing keeps melting and the oceans continue to rise, the high water will wipe out a lot of our most expensive real estate. For example, did you know Matt, that Key West Florida is only about three feet above sea level? Maybe the whole town and the Keys could go underwater."

"Chris, I think some of that college stuff you are learning is going to turn you into a tree-hugger. The arctic ice could never melt to the point of causing a disaster. That's crazy talk."

A big smirk came across Chris' face. "Sit down brother and learn a little. I've got a story to tell you about our climate.

"Do you remember when dad sent away for that kit on the Genographic Project?"

"Sure."

"Well Matt, early humans came out of Africa maybe fifty to seventy thousand years ago. They moved north because the climate was warming. The glaciers had been receding for tens of thousands of years. In those early days there was a big fresh water lake in a major depression of the earth between Europe and Asia. That very low area is what we now call the Black Sea. There were, and still are, three big rivers that pour fresh water into that low lying ground...the Don, the Danube, and...and, right now I forget the other one."

"So...." Matt hated his older brother's long drawn out explanations.

"Well In a series of expeditions just a few years ago, a team of marine archaeologists led by a man named Robert Ballard identified what appeared to be ancient shorelines. He found freshwater snail shells, drowned river valleys, tool-worked timbers, and man-made structures in as much as 300 feet of water. The freshwater finds were under a deep blanket of salty sea water. That all helped preserve what was below the salty water.

"His discoveries were made off the Black Sea coast of modern Turkey. He used sophisticated underwater cameras to locate stuff. Radiocarbon dating of the freshwater mollusks that he found told us that the age of Ballard's discoveries. He made everything there to be about seven thousand years old."

"Again Chris I have to say, so what? What does that have to do with glaciers melting, sea water rising and global warming? How are you putting this together as climate change?"

"It may be related to that ancestor project that dad is doing. Remember we talked about the very first town...Jericho? The town was there about 8,000 B.C. That was, if you count four grandfathers every 100 years, maybe 400 lined up grandfathers...400 males in our family line...to way back to then. Now let's move forward 2,400 years to 5,600 B.C. We now have about 300 direct line ancestors lined up behind us from that time. And the earth continues to go through a warming cycle. According to my environment professor, this global warming had been going on and off...more on than off...for maybe 50,000 years... The glaciers that fed the Don and the Danube and that other river that I can't remember were shrinking and less fresh water was going into this low lying Black Sea Lake. The lake was receding, evaporating, but ever so very slowly.

"With all the ice melting all over the world, the oceans and the Mediterranean Sea were rising. The Black Sea or Black Lake was 350 to 400 feet lower than the ocean water. This higher ocean water, in the Mediterranean Sea probably started as a stream overflowing the narrow land bridge we now call the Bosporus. This stream flowed into the Black Lake. Eventually about 5,600 B.C. the land gave way. It was much like an enormous dam suddenly breaking. The scientists estimate that ten cubic miles of water poured through the opening each day. That's two hundred times what flows over Niagara Falls. The Bosporus flume roared and surged at full spate for at least three hundred days. Some 60,000 square miles of land were inundated. The Black Sea shoreline expanded significantly in all directions. The lake's water level was raised many hundreds of feet. It changed from a fresh-water landlocked lake into a salt water lake-sea connected to the world's oceans."

"Wow!"

"That's right, Matt – *Wow!* A lot of people believe that this flood was the source of the story of Noah in the Bible. A great flood was described in writing in the Babylonian Epic of Gilgamesh. In that ancient book, the heroic warrior Gilgamesh makes a dangerous journey to meet the survivor of a great world flood. He wanted to learn from the survivor the secret of everlasting youth. If a memory of the Black Sea flood influenced the Gilgamesh story, then it could also be a source of the Noah's Ark story in the Book of Genesis. Bible scholars have long noted that there are striking similarities between the Gilgamesh and Genesis flood accounts. They have suspected that the Israelites got their version from the Gilgamesh epic. This flood happened thousands of years before humans learned to write. There must have been a common oral history, told and retold from the real catastrophe. Eventually it was put into writing…when writing was invented long after the flood."

"So global warming" Matt said, "caused all of this?" As he talked he took his left hand and pulled it down over his nostrils.

"Yeah, I us think so. Our earth has been warming and cooling in cycles for just about…well, forever. That's why my paper is so important. If all the ice melts in this cycle, coasts and cities will gradually be flooded. It won't be anything like the Black Sea deluge, but still it will be very bad for much of the world population that lives near the edges of the oceans.

The two young men sat silently for a few moments. Finally Matt said, "I wonder Chris, if we had any ancestors in Noah's Flood?"

Six

Riphath

Deluge 5600 B.C.

Noah thought of himself as a generous and friendly man. How could he not be that? He was patriarch of this entire small river valley. His large family and many retainers all shared in his enormous wealth. Bounded by a river to the west and a low lying ridge to the east, and with distant mountains to the south, this idyllic green valley was home to all he held dear: his wives and sons, but especially his ever growing flock of sheep.

Noah had the largest flock of sheep that anyone had ever seen. It was not possible to know just how many sheep were in his flocks. Knowledge of how to count beyond fingers and toes would still have to wait some thousand years into mankind's future. For now, sheep were simply uncountable in numbers. It was a mystery … but a happy one.

In order to remedy the counting problem, Noah placed around his narrow waist a cord-like belt with a small gray pouch attached to it. Inside this pouch was one small pebble for each sheep. At the time following each full moon his retainers gingerly passed all of Noah's flocks through a crude chute. As each animal passed, Noah would remove a pebble from the pouch. Rarely was there a pebble left in the pouch. Usually, laughing with fevered excitement, he was forced to add new pebbles as his ownership grew larger with every counting.

The land was good to Noah. The huge mountains kept bands of nomad raiders and chill winds away. In the other direction it was a three day journey, walking over a flat grassy plain, to reach the endless expanse of fresh water. Everyone called the water 'The Ubykh Sea' because of its dark color of the wavy vastness.

When he was a young man Noah had walked, with his brothers, to this great body of water. They simply followed the slow moving streams flowing from the mountains of the south through their pastures, past seemingly endless green prairie, until they came to the broad sandy shore of the calm blue-black Ubykh. It was a beautiful sight he would never forget.

Shortly after they turned, starting their return journey home, Noah and his two brothers heard terrified screams in the near distance. Running over a small sandy rise they caught sight of eight or ten filthy wanderers stealing sheep from two small boys. The boys shrieked to no avail. One vagrant grabbed the smallest boy and threw him to the ground. The man howled with contempt as he stood on the young lad's back.

Without thinking, Noah and his brothers charged into the band of brigands. Because of his very broad stature and heavy body Noah overpowered two of the men and easily broke their arms. He broke another man's neck while his brothers scattered the rest. The attackers ran away...leaving the dead man. Noah chased them, caught one and broke still another neck. He had become infuriated, screaming and wildly beating the body of the dead man. No one stole sheep! It was the greatest of crimes in his mind. Noah's brothers were astounded at the depth of his rage.

The boys were unhurt and led the three brothers to their master. He thanked the three with food and a place to rest for the night. Noah learned a great deal from this experience. Many people were not as safe as his isolated family in their secluded valley. Those living along the coastal plain were often attacked by groups of raiders from the direction of the sunrise. Noah had also gained knowledge of his core value from this experience: protect yourself at all times with physical force especially while saving sheep.

As he aged Noah became the natural leader of his family. Everyone feared his enormous strength and rare bouts of violent temper. He was basically a good-natured man but never shy. He often used his muscles to lift objects beyond the ability of any other man in the valley. He moved boulders and other large objects to build pens for his sheep. Legends grew around the man maintaining that he had killed thieves by crushing them to death. He never denied it. The stories allowed Noah to keep order in his clan.

Noah had one single obsession in life...his sheep. Everyone disliked the time of the full moon and the demanding parade of sheep. If Noah had any pebbles left in his bag at the end of the count, then the pain-staking process of driving the animals through the chute, one-by-neE had to be repeated. If the count still failed, all the lands of his valley had to be meticulously searched. Finally, neighbors might be accused of thievery. If there was no way to find any of the missing sheep, Noah turned into a recluse until the next full moon counting. He would remain agitated and angry in all that time. Nothing could soften his mania except a larger count of sheep the following moon. Noah might even become so angry during the wait that he would banish some of his retainers, occasionally one of his own grandchildren, from their comfortable life in the valley. His anger, his fixation with his sheep, was to be feared.

Eventually a grandson named Riphath, the eldest son of Japaeth, found a solution for Noah's terrible spells. After another dreadful month caused by a short count, Riphath took action. During the spring period, when many lambs were born, Riphath with his brothers culled a few sheep from the flocks. They took these animals to a shepherd outside of their valley. This man was told to secretly tend this flock for Riphath. After each full moon he was to bring the flock immediately to an isolated pasture in Noah's valley. If the count was short then Riphath would 'find' these sheep, thus forcing Noah to add pebbles to his bag. Noah's fixation now always ended with delight because of a positive count every single moon. The valley people could retain their idyllic life without disruption.

It would not last forever.

On a very hot summer afternoon one of the Noah's many shepherds came running into the main farm area. The man was covered with sweat and grime. Exhausted, choking for air, the man fell at Noah's feet desperately trying to deliver a message.

Startled, Noah asked, "What is it…wolves? Has something happened with my sheep?"

The shepherd was so out of breath that he could not answer. He could only shake his head negatively while pointing to the north, the direction of the valley opening facing towards the Ubykh Sea. These were the great waters that Noah had visited in his youth.

"Give him something to drink," Noah commanded.

Finally the man rose to his knees. "Stra....strangers," he gasped.

"Strangers! So, are they thieves?" The sound of his own voice made Noah more apprehensive. His first thoughts went to his precious sheep. He would stop them from taking his property. He....

The retainer was again shaking his head but also this time saying "no" in a clear, but trembling voice. He did not want any part of Noah's wrath on his head.

"Well what is it then?" Noah demanded.

"It is…it is an entire tribe. Many, many people are coming up from the shores of the Ubykh. They have their own sheep, a few pigs, and all their belongings."

"Why are they coming into my land? Why don't they stay where they belong?" Noah's voice was raised and his hand reached out to grasp the terrified shepherd.

The man wisely shrank back. With almost a scream he cried, "I don't know, I don't know!"

Noah understood that this was a time for action. *Who were these people*, he wondered. He called urgently for his sons and grandsons. He ordered them to arm themselves with clubs. Next he told the exhausted shepherd to lead him and his little army back to the trespassers. He would put a stop to this intrusion.

Noah was surprised as he met the group. He knew the leader. He had traded for many years with Obed. This was no stranger. Obed was a fair and honorable man.

"Why are you here Obed on my land with your tribe?" Noah, now calmed, asked gently.

"Our land is gone, Noah. I beg you to allow my family and animals to travel through your fields. We must find a new home far from the dreadful Ubykh. We go towards the mountains"

The plaintive tone in Obed's voice worried Noah. He knew his friend to be a man of strength. "Tell me Obed, are you being driven away from your land by raiders? Are there many of them? Will they come here?"

"No, no, NO! There are no raiders." Obed almost shouted the words. "It is the water. The Ubykh Sea has suddenly started to rise. It has flooded all of our land. Our fields and houses are all gone. There is nothing left. The water now covers even the tree tops where we pastured our animals."

Noah visualized Obed's land. A chill ran down the powerful man's spine. "That just cannot be Obed. Your pastures are high above the black water."

"I do not lie, Noah. Ask my sons." Obed's voice was tinged with frustrated rage.

Noah sought to calm his disturbed friend. He said quietly, "I know you to be a truthful man, Obed. I do not need to question your sons. But still, this is the dry season. These past moons have given us almost no rain at all."

"I know that," Obed spat back at him.

"And the waters that flow from the mountains snows are barely filling the streams."

"I know that too Noah, I am not a dolt. Yet the black water lake is rising more every day, increasing almost half way to my knee by each and every sunrise. It has devoured our land. It has buried our houses. We have nothing left. We must find new land or die."

"So how can the waters of the Ubykh be increasing so very quickly?"

"I have no idea, and there is something else. It frightens me a great deal."

"Yes, tell me Obed," Noah growled. This was becoming too much to absorb.

"The rising water is now salty. All the fish that we used to catch are dying. It is so strange. We had a witch in our clan bawling at us that this is the end of the world. She was terrifying everyone. When we left, I made her stay behind in her house at the edge of the water. I tied her to a post. That house is now completely covered with water. I think the witch must be dead. I had to do it. She was upsetting everyone."

"I would have done the same," Noah said without the slightest bit of pity for the woman.

The two leaders lapsed into a silence. Neither quite sure of what to do or say next. Then as the two men were lost in thought, more groups became visible on the far horizon of the nearly flat plain.

Japaeth, Noah's eldest son, quietly came to his father and asked what they might do about the new groups walking towards their valley. Noah suddenly recognized an opportunity and motioned all his sons to join the meeting with Obed. "I have a proposition for you Obed. Stay here with your clan. Live on my land in this part of the valley with my gratitude. Even here at the low end of the valley we are high above the level of the Ubykh. The water will never reach us. In turn, however, I will ask you to stop all others from entering my valley."

Obed motioned for his elders and his sons to join the discussion. He explained Noah's offer. There was much discussion and head shaking. Noah's three sons were surprised that a clan leader would consult others…even if they were elders and sons. That was certainly not their father's way. Finally an agreement appeared to be reached.

"I myself would honor your request. It would be good for both you Noah and also for my clan. But many of my people are terribly frightened. Some in my clan are in a state of panic. Several of the women and two of my men cannot stop crying. One man hung himself last night. I suspect they all have a desperate desire to get to the high mountains. We do not have the will to be able to stop all of those people that you and I can see fleeing towards us. Then too, some of my people are afraid to stay here. They fear the rising water will come here to your land. Some, no many, are repeating what the witch said. She claimed that it is the end of the world and the gods are punishing us."

"Bah!" Noah cursed. "There are no gods. That is foolish witch talk. Cross my land with your tribe. I wish you good luck in finding pasture towards the mountains. My son Cush will lead you."

Noah had quickly determined a plan. He called Cush aside and charged him to lead Obed, his people and his animals, by the most direct route, across his land towards the mountains. Next he instructed Cush's sons to follow and plant stakes, each with lamb's tails attached. This would mark path for all the others to follow. Then Noah ordered his retainers to send all additional newcomers, fleeing the water, to travel up the marked trail. With his problems solved and his sheep safe, Noah started his long walk home. He was a happy man.

Although he was the leader of his clan, Noah was certainly never an introspective person. Yet he wondered about the water. What was happening? The summer heat was burning the land. The pastures were turning brown and the valley streams were almost dry. Could Obed be right? Were there some mysterious gods punishing humans? He took his left thumb and forefinger and squeezed his nose in a downward motion. Then the thought was gone as his stomach told him it was time to eat.

Three days later a new adversity struck Noah. A runner came, this time from the mountain direction of Noah's valley, away from the troublesome sea. The man said, "Tribes are passing through your lands going to the mountains. Some are stealing your sheep Noah. They are too many. We can't stop them all."

The news was greeted with a roar from Noah. His face turned as red as a sunset, then the upper part of his almost naked body followed with the same flush color. "Steal my sheep! No!" Noah screamed. He lurched forward smashing a wooden post with his fist. "No one steals sheep from me. I will follow them. I will kill them. I will…"

Noah fell to his knees and pounded the ground with his fists. Foam came out of his mouth. His people had never seen anything like this from their leader. He was a hard man given to violent rages, but this was exceptional. They were horrified at the sight. His sons did not know what to do. Finally, with slow steady movements, Noah rose to his feet. His eyes were glazed. In a guttural voice he slowly began to organize his men into a party to follow and capture the thieves.

At this moment of crisis, a second runner appeared. This man came from the direction of the flooding Ubykh. "Noah," the man cried from a distance, "the black waters have reached the end of the valley. We can see bodies of many dead people and animals in the water. It is…"

He never finished his message. He had reached Noah and was standing in front of his clan leader. With senseless rage Noah lashed out with his powerful fist striking a blow to the man's head. The messenger slumped to the ground at Noah's feet. He was not dead but he would never again be a whole man.

Noah stormed. He stepped over the hapless messenger lying face down on the ground. The man was oozing blood from both ears. Noah paced and ranted strange words. He seemed to dance in a small frantic circle. Finally quieting, he ordered his men to follow on the quest to punish the thieves and recover the livestock. "Take clubs and knives," he ordered in a strange rasping voice. "Japheth, you and your sons are to stay here and guard the rest of the flocks. If any sheep are missing when I return it will be on your head." His eyes drilled holes into Japheth's trembling being as he voiced this veiled threat.

Japheth was stunned. He was the oldest of Noah's sons but yet, the most timid. None of Noah's three sons had ever been allowed to think for themselves, or make decisions or take actions without their father's permission. Suddenly he was left in charge. His lips trembled as he tried to ask Noah what he should do. Seeing that Japheth was too stunned to act, his son Riphath ran after Noah for instructions.

"Grandfather," Riphath pleaded, "what shall we do if the water reaches us here?"

Noah responded with a slap that flattened the teenager. He shrieked "Just take care of it. I must get my sheep back." Then, this suddenly unstable patriarch was gone with most of the men of the tribe.

Two days later, the flood began creeping up the valley floor. Some of the water could now be seen from the high point of the settlement. Riphath went to his father, "We have to do something father or we will all soon be covered with water."

Japheth sat with his head in his hands and moaned. "Noah told us the water would not reach here. I must believe my father."

"Noah was wrong father. We must follow the other tribes up into the mountains or we will all die. You can see the water rising. Do you want us all to die? We must go to the mountains."

Japheth moaned again. "I don't know what to do. If we lose any of the sheep my father will banish us or even kill us. He is a violent man. Look at what he did to the messenger. If we leave the valley and go to the mountains some animals might be lost. We must stay here and wait for Noah to return."

Riphath could see that his father was paralyzed with fear of retribution. But something had to be done quickly. "Father," Riphath said, "tell the people that we have to move to the higher ground on the hill across the stream. It is as high as ten men. When Noah returns he will see us and know you acted wisely to protect his sheep. He will reward you."

A small light suddenly gleamed in Japheth's eyes. *Yes, that would do,* he thought. He called the people together and told them to follow Riphath's orders. Now, if something went wrong, it would not be on his head. His son would take the blame.

Riphath could almost see the water rising towards them. Strangely, he also thought he could hear it. He organized work groups and ordered the shepherds to move all the flocks to the hilltop across the almost dry stream. The rest of the clan was told that the flood would soon drown their encampment. "Move everything you can carry. Follow the sheep to the crest of the hill," he said. By sundown most everything had been moved. Still Noah had not returned. Japheth could not stop pacing frantically.

At the next dawn Riphath discovered the water to be within a strong stone's throw of the old settlement. Looking over the placid advancing flood he saw an unbelievable sight. A man, woman and two children were floating on a small raft of logs far out in the middle of the flooded lower valley. He could see that there was a post in the middle of the flimsy wooden structure and two sheep and a goat were tethered to it.

The adults were using their hands as paddles to attempt to reach dry land. Riphath looked at the hill where all of Noah's people and possessions were gathered. Then he turned to view the rising water. He would have to act again.

Riphath ran quickly to seek out his sleeping father. He realized that the hill might soon be an island and after that the ominous inundation from the gods might consume even this highland. Then it would kill them all. They would drown. The tribe needed to move to the mountains.

Japheth refused! Worry had torn at his mind to even move to the hilltop without Noah's direction. His father's word was law, never wrong, and Noah had said, as he repeated to Riphath, 'The water will never reach where we stand.' "We will wait for Noah." His father's inaction was stunning to Riphath. It was cowardly and stupid. Something more had to be done quickly before all was lost.

In one more day the water of the flood had risen to ankle depth at the tribe's old homestead just below the bottom of the high hill. Today also, there were fewer hilltops to be seen between their hill crest and the direction of the Ubykh Sea. Some hills he noted, in fact even most hill tops, were completely under water while others were islands. If those hills could disappear, so might this refuge.

Again Riphath looked over the waters filling the valley. The raft he had seen earlier was drifting towards a very low hill on the far side of the water. The animals were there but Riphath could not make out any of the people. *Had they fallen off and drowned?* He wondered silently.

Increasingly Riphath realized the extent of the danger. If the flood continued none of them might survive. Noah was gone. His father, Japheth, would not take any more actions and none of the tribe dared to carry out any plan on their own without orders. At last he had an idea.

Calling everyone together he ordered the children to tend the sheep. The adults were to return, down the hill, to their old encampment and retrieve all the large logs they had used to build their simple lean-to shelters. Next they were to cut the few trees up on the hill for more logs. All would be lashed together to make rafts for the people and sheep.

Four days later three large rafts were being assembled. Pens were also being constructed on each raft to retain some sheep. It was obvious to Riphath that most of the sheep would be lost. There was too little wood for enough rafts. Water was now a third of the way up their hillside. Noah had still not returned.

As the men worked, Riphath decided to walk along the ridge towards the mountains. He wanted to see if the water might inundate their only escape route. He was shocked. The Ubykh flood waters had almost filled their only possible exit from the hill crest. There was now only a strip of earth barely wide enough for a flock of sheep to pass. By the next dawn they all might be trapped by water on every side. As he stood there musing, Riphath heard his name shouted from the direction of the mountains. Startled, he looked up to see, at last, the clan men returning from chasing the thieves. A few of them were completely naked. They had stripped off their cloaks making a litter to carry someone. Four men in the group struggled across the narrow land bridge with their heavy burden. The litter contained Noah.

Shem, Noah's second oldest son was in the lead. Both Shem and Riphath spoke at the same time, "what happened?" Then both tried to reply to the other. Riphath stopped talking first and nodded to his uncle to speak.

"We don't know what happened, Riphath. Your grandfather was like a wild animal, He kept screaming about his sheep and thieves. Noah is the strongest man I know and he forced us to run and run. No one has his endurance. The men began to drop from exhaustion and Noah got farther and farther ahead. No one could keep up. Ham and I finally stopped and waited for the others to catch up. When we had most of the group we started out again. Almost immediately we came upon Noah. He was lying in some mud. He could not stand or talk. He could not move his left arm and leg. He made strange sounds we could not understand."

Riphath asked, "Was he wounded? Had he been attacked or fought the thieves?"

"We did not see anyone or even animals. He had no wounds" Shem replied. "We made a litter and have been carrying Noah for the past three days. From a distance we saw everyone on the hilltop and turned this way. Why has everyone moved from our camp?"

Riphath thought his uncle was dim-witted to ask such a question. The flooded old encampment was visible to them from the top of the ridge. Still, you never made light of your elder's errors in the clan. He replied evenly, "The water forced us to move."

By this time the litter bearers had struggled to the point where Shem and Riphath were standing. Riphath noticed that Noah was clinching his left fist and muttered words that might have been 'sheep' or 'thieves.' He could not be sure.

Noah's third son Ham was following the litter. He said, "Father is beginning to regain his tongue. He is also moving his hand. He could not do that yesterday." The procession then slowly made its way to the new encampment.

Noah's women ministered to him while the three brothers and Riphath gathered together for a counsel. They sat by a smoky fire as the sun set. Women brought them food. Shem and Ham praised their older brother Japaeth for moving the tribe to the hilltop. Japaeth failed to admit that it was Riphath's doing. Instead, wiping gruel from his lips he asked, "When will the water stop rising?"

The other brothers shrugged and said nothing. Finally Ham spoke, "We must wait until Noah recovers and can tell us what we must do."

Riphath, while inferior to the counsel of brothers, could hold back no longer. He violated tribal custom and spoke directly to his father and uncles without being asked. "We can't wait for Noah to get better. The water is rising every day. This past sunrise I planted a stake at the water's edge. The top is as tall as I am. Tomorrow at sunrise I will show it to you and you will all see the flood is still coming to us. The black water will cover us and kill all of our clan and all of our sheep in just a few more days. We must flee to the mountains."

The strength of Riphath's plea shocked the brothers. They again sat in silence. There was no history of decision making among them. Only Noah could decide. They would wait.

The next morning the brothers found that the stake was now knee deep into the water. Noah was also better. They could understand the word 'sheep', but he was still paralyzed. Since all the brothers were now in camp the men would no longer take orders from Riphath. Raft building stopped. They waited.

In three more days it was obvious that the waters were still rising to a point of overcoming the hilltop. Meeting with his brothers Ham said, "I have given orders to my people to gather their sheep and belongings. We are going to cross that strip of land that we traveled to get here. I want us to be on the mountain side of this horrible water."

"But that strip is now under the waters, and father has not given us any direction," Shem worriedly told him.

Ham replied, "I understand that, but the water will soon drown us. I went to the crossing earlier. I waded through it this morning. It is quite deep, but we will carry our sheep on our shoulders, one-by-one. We will do the same with the children and make more trips with our goods and even bring our sick."

"You will desert us and our father and the clan,"

"No! I will wait for you on the upland side of the flood. We must save all we can."

"Father did not tell us we could…."

"Shem, stop being such a baby," Ham replied. "If he doesn't get better we will all die anyway. I will save my people."

Riphath smiled. At last someone was taking action.

The very next morning with the water still higher, Shem said, "I and my people will follow Ham."

Japheth shook his head. "You can't do that Shem. The water has risen again. Ham's tallest people were wading almost up to their necks. Some of the shorter women had to be carried. And remember when Asok slipped. He and his sheep both drowned."

Shem angrily replied, "I understand all of that Japheth. Do you think I am stupid? We will use one of the rafts that you were building. That was a smart move on your part to make them. I must honor you. We will take one of them and ferry my clan and sheep and goods over to Ham's side of the water. He, by the way, has gone. I don't know where. You can stay here and drown Japheth. I think you are too cowardly to do anything else."

With Ham and Shem and their portions of the family gone, there were too few men to build additional rafts even if wood could be found. Riphath estimated the rafts might hold, in addition to the people, just a few sheep. Again he approached his father. "We must follow Ham and

Shem before the water gets too deep and we lose sight of the land to the mountains."

"No!" replied Japheth. "Noah said the water would not reach us. I must do as my father says. You, in turn, must obey me. That is our law. Noah put me in charge. We stay here until my father tells me what to do."

The waters continued to rise. Riphath could build no more rafts. He strengthened them and built small shelters for people and pens to hold sheep in the remaining space. Even with Shem and Ham's groups gone the water was beginning to crowd the top of the hill. It was touching the end of one of the rafts. The water between the hill crest and the higher lands towards the mountains was widening. Yet, Japheth stubbornly refused to move.

Riphath now became concerned for Noah. The older man could now sit up but he was unable to move his legs or talk. Japheth allowed Riphath to move him to the largest of the rafts. He would stay dry there if water rose to cover the hilltop. If the flood waters gradually increased, the raft would float. Others in the clan seeing this began to claim spots on each of the rafts. It became apparent that some of the clan might have to be left behind to drown. Taking any sheep was out of the question. Japheth agonized. What might he do to save his father's precious sheep?

That concern was now just a dream. The blue skies and calm winds of the past weeks were giving way to gloomy weather. Heavy dark clouds approached and lightening appeared to the west. The waters, which had been placid for a moon, began suddenly to churn violently, driven by a howling wind.

Heavy waves started to roll towards the hill crest. Abruptly all three rafts were afloat. As the unstable structures shook, a few people fell off the sides of the rafts. Since the water was not yet deep most of them were able to scramble back up onto the rafts. The noise of the howling wind was deafening. There was panic.

Riphath saw that his father and Noah were drifting rapidly towards the mountains to the south. He felt relieved, yet angry. They could have saved so much more if only Japheth had not been so fearful and stubborn. Riphath realized that the people on his raft were now voicing soundless screams and pointing towards the violently churning Ubykh. He turned, barely in time, to see a wind-driven wall of water boiling towards him. It was twice his height. The surging wave washed everyone from the raft and then destroyed it.

By some strange will of the gods, Riphath found himself clinging to a large log that had been part of the smashed raft. There were no other survivors in sight. The monstrous wave had washed away all those people he knew as Clan Noah.

Controlled by new currents, the log and its single passenger drifted far to the west before finally beaching a day later. Riphath searched vainly for his family as he walked farther to the south away from the continuously rising Ubykh.

He would never locate any of his clan.

A BIT OF HISTORY

Writing, using words, was not developed until 2,000 years after the Great Flood. The Epic of Gilgamesh, describing this flood from oral history, was written approximately 500 years after the written form was in common use.

The Bible story of Noah is thought to have been composed still another 1,500 years afterward (approximately 4,000 years after the flood) and was based on the Epic of Gilgamesh.

The Genesis account of the Ark with animals two-by-two is widely considered myth by Bible scholars.

The impact of this immense natural catastrophic event on mankind had been kept alive by oral tradition for thousands of years.

Seven

Remembrance

Chris and Matt were at the cemetery. They were participating in the spring community clean-up. It was a chore they did every year. The cleaning also turned out to be an Eagle Scout project for one of the younger boys in their Boy Scout troop. The two brothers had been to this particular area of the burial grounds quite often since their grandparents and even some great-grandparents were buried here.

As they were clearing the weeds and brush in the area of the family plot, Matt was surprised to see his brother bring out a camera and take a picture of the much worn headstone of their great-grandparents. It was so weather-worn that the engraving was barely legible.

"Chris, what are you doing taking a picture of that gravestone? Is my older brother turning into some kind of ghoul?"

"You are the odd one little brother. You only live in the present. Buried here are relatives we never met. This stone marker is just about all we have in order to make a family connection with them. We don't even know what they looked like. Photography wasn't invented before they died and they were not rich people…so no portraits. Pretty soon even their names will have eroded from these sandstone markers."

Matt nodded. "I guess that makes sense. In a couple of generations no one will know who is buried here. We sure won't be here to tell em."

"That's why I'm taking pictures. But you know what? I also learned in one of my college classes that scientists are working on imagining systems to be able to read these old stones. People like to be identified and remembered. Look at all the taggers who scribble with paint spray on buildings.

"My history professor even brought up a little saying by Benjamin Franklin in Poor Richard's Almanac. It was so funny, I even memorized it. It goes, 'If you would not be forgotten, as soon as you are dead and rotten, either write something worth reading, or do things worth writing about.' "

"That doesn't even rhyme Chris."

"I know. Still, people have been erecting stone monuments for thousands of years. We've got the pyramids in Egypt and those strange Stonehenge sites erected, probably for religious purposes. There are also marker stones all over Europe. Those markers are often thousands of years old. I believe those stones, they are called 'steles.' were…maybe… planted to mark territory boundaries of groups of people.

"A lot of our human recollection is written in stone."

Eight

Otzi the Iceman
3,300 B.C.

Otzi lounged with his back firmly planted against the outside wall of his hut. He was at peace in the warmth of the late summer sun. For a man of his age, there would always be many aches and pains. It was expected. Yet today he felt quite well. Life was good. His right knee did somewhat trouble him. That he normally anticipated. But truthfully, his ankle and back felt sound. He was comfortable on this beautiful cloudless morning gazing at the high peaks above his settlement.

In each of the commonly painful locations on his body, there were a series of round black tattoo-like scars burned into his skin. Many in his clan felt this medicinal treatment often eased the deep bone ache of old age. Perhaps it helped. He wasn't sure. Otzi was almost forty summers old.

There was no cure for the deep wound in his deformed groin. That injury was incurred just as he had attained his manhood. It had nearly killed him.

Hunting with kinfolk in the nearby forest, he accidentally stumbled onto an Alpine brown bear with her two cubs. Before he could retreat, she clawed him. His terror was so great that he did not feel some parts of his manhood had been mauled and torn away by the animal. He lost consciousness, perhaps in fright, perhaps in pain. That wound had changed some of Otzi's views towards life. Still it did not prevent him from siring many children,

On this grassy hillock, like his father and their ancestors, he had raised many sons. High ground was desirable…it was easier to defend. The land was also an ideal place to grow grain. Furthermore, the surrounding forests below the cleared hilltop still held enough game for an occasional rousing hunt. Yet with good reason he still feared the bear.

Watching from his warm seat, Otzi smiled as the women harvested their ripened crop of einkorn wheat. Far beyond his vision, his sheep and goats grazed in the higher mountain pastures. They were driven there each spring as the snow melted. The animals fed on the lush upland grass of the summer meadows. It had been especially ideal this year, a productive year for all of his kin. Their larders would soon be brimming with supplies stocked away for the cold Alpine winter ahead.

Now it was almost time to fetch the flocks back to the lower protected winter fields. In just a few days at the next full moon, his three young grandsons, acting as shepherds, would return with the animals. Those grassy summer fields, above on the high mountains, would then be set on fire. That burning would somehow ensure a plentiful re-growth of the meadow for the next season. Otzi did not understand why this was so, but he knew this burning had to be done.

When the animals arrived home from their high summer pasture he and his sons would harvest wool and meat as additional provisions for the snowy season to come.

Otzi's gaze drifted towards the marker for his band. Long ago, beyond memory, Otzi's fore bearers had placed a carved claiming stone in the clearing. It was surrounded by the huts that made up his clan's settlement. It was a typical stone found in almost every tribal community in Western Europe.

These small flat pillars of stone, half-buried in the ground, declared identity and ownership of the area for the inhabitants living here. No longer were they roving bands of hunter-gatherers. This land was theirs. It was their home. The Stele of Otzi's clan was typical of the times. It had eyes and a nose, but no mouth. It watched over the clan. It was respected but not worshiped.

Otzi suddenly decided it was time for action. Some strange ache, deep in his bones alerted him to an unseen change in the weather. He called together the six adult males of the site. They along with the fifteen or so women and children comprised his village.

"The winter winds will soon be upon us," Otzi told them. "It is time to repair our shelters to withstand the cold. We need also to gather the wood for our winter tasks."

The men grumbled but obeyed. Otzi was their leader. He had also fathered all six of the men. As they walked to the forest to start the annual task of felling trees, the second oldest son remarked, "The chill is reaching the old man earlier every year."

His brothers laughed in agreement.

Brun, the oldest, directed the work party. "It is late in the day so we will gather firewood. In the morning I will stay in the camp and cut the wood to size. The rest of you will go down the mountain to the water pond glade and gather stems of the wayfaring bush and yew logs. In the winter we will fashion arrows and sturdy bows from them."

The brothers nodded but Ludolf complained, "The water pond glade is almost a day's journey. We will have to stay overnight to complete the gathering before we can return."

"Don't be a child, Ludolf. The weather is good now. If you all go we will have enough material for two winters and we won't have to do it again next year."

"But who will protect the stele if we all go on the marrow? There are still roving bands of hunters looking for places to winter." The youngest brother made a challenge to Brun's the directive. He was really hoping to avoid making the long overnight trip.

"Otzi is here. I am here. What more do we need? We haven't seen robber bands in several years." That boastful assessment would soon cost Brun his life.

Early the next morning Otzi decided to join his grandsons at the high meadow pasture. It was another clear warm day. He would supervise their trek bringing the sheep and goats to the village stele. He dressed carefully, aware that the colder upland air might further distress the aches of aging in his bones. He stuffed extra grass in his boots for insulation. He put on his bearskin hat and a knee-length cloak woven of long reeds. He was too warmly dressed for the village but not for the high pasture.

Otzi never left camp without his bow and quiver filled with at least a dozen arrows. Today he decided to bring his precious copper axe on the journey. He failed to notice that Brun was the only adult male left at the encampment. Brun, in turn, never saw Otzi leave.

Otzi was excited to once again climb to the high pastures. Many years had passed since he had been there. It made him feel young again. The path to the upper pasture was a long gentle slope. The animals could not manage the steeper direct route. Otzi decided to follow the moderate path. His legs would ache if he struggled up the more vertical climb. It took the slow moving animals three full days to travel between the high meadow and the stele. Walking at a brisk pace, he would reach the summer pasture by mid-afternoon.

In late morning he neared the first overnight rest spot used for the uphill spring trip with the flocks. Already he could feel the chill of the air flowing down from the snowcapped mountains. He shivered. Such cold had not bothered him in his younger days.

Otzi passed through a copse of cedar into the grassy flat space where the herd would overnight before the final downward push down to the village. He was immediately surprised as he came into the open field! The sheep, goats and his three grandsons could all be seen, not too far above the field. The three boys were already moving the animals towards this overnight resting place. They had abandoned the high meadow days before the full moon.

Ruzid, his oldest grandson spied him, smiled and then shouted, "Otzi!" The young man sprinted forward, but his smile, as he approached the older man, stiffened to dread. He knew he had disobeyed Otzi's instructions by bring the flocks down to the village at the time of the full moon. He stopped in front of Otzi and knelt in expectation of a beating. Nothing happened.

"Ruzid, get up. Why did you leave before the moon was full?"

Surprised at not being struck, Ruzid slowly rose to his feet. He discovered he was now as tall as his grandfather. He could look him directly in the eye. It took him a moment to find his voice. "It was time to leave Otzi. The meadow was filled with icy rain for the past many days. I was afraid we would lose animals to the cold. Some might even fall on the ice and die. The moon was not full but the weather told me winter is arriving early this year."

Otzi grinned. The young man reminded him of himself when he had been a youth. How tall he was now. You could see life rippling through his strong body. "Ruzid, you acted wisely. I did the very same thing when I was your age. The moon can only be a guide. It will take the animals one more full day to reach our stele so let us overnight here. This is a special chance for me to hunt high on the mountain and with luck I might catch us a feast for tonight."

Luck was with Otzi. Not far up from where the flocks were congregating he heard the distinctive sound of a clash between male Ibex. Near the cold season was mating time for these animals. The sound of a conflict was coming from behind an outcropping of boulders. Even before he saw the battling males, a waiting female came into view. Silently he strung and loosed an arrow into her mid-section. She went down but struggled to regain her footing. Otzi quickly ended her thrashing with his copper hatchet. The two fighting males detected his presence and were nowhere to be found. He never saw them.

As daylight was beginning to fade, he and the three boys feasted on the success of his hunt. Otzi divided the prized Ibex heart into four pieces and shared them with his grandsons. Normally only adults ate this cut of the meat. Most often the hunter who made the kill shared none of it. The heart was known to provide energy, bravery and long life. The old man felt exceptionally generous. Besides the Ibex horns he had culled were highly valued as cures for many aliments. He would trade them for copper in the more populated valley encampments near the bottom of the mountain.

With full stomachs they huddled together for warmth. Ruzid asked, "Otzi tell us the story about your fight with the giant wolf."

The boys all smiled as the old man spun his tale of the great fight he had with a giant wolf. They had heard it many times before. The youngest, Ertwin, giggled and pulled his nostrils shut with his left hand as he listened. Each telling made the wolf larger and Otzi's fight much more daring. They laughed hard when Otzi told how he crept up on the huge beast from behind and cut off its tail. It was, they knew, just a story but it pleased them to hear it again. It was always a bit different. Finally they all slept for the night.

At sunrise, they prepared to finish driving the flock down the mountain. Otzi pointed to one of the rams that had wandered back up the trail. The animal was visible near a high outcropping of rock that was called 'the seeing point.' It was the single place on the trail where their clan village, far below, could be seen. Ertwin immediately scrambled up the trail to catch the animal. At the seeing point he turned and screamed to those below, "Fire!" He pointed towards their stele site lower down the mountain.

The others quickly moved to reach him. Otzi, out of breath, was the last to get there. "What is it?" he demanded. His eyesight was not as good as it had been in his youth.

"It is your hut Otzi. It is burning and there are…look…look, I think I can see people lying on the ground."

"Marauders have attacked. They wanted the warmth of our village as a place to winter. Our men, your fathers, must have driven them off."

Young Ertwin was choking, almost sobbing. He had exceptional vision. "No Otzi," he cried "the robbers are still there. One of them just shot an arrow at my little sister. She is down. They killed her!" Ertwin fell to his knees. His little sister was the only young female toddler in the group. It had to be her.

Otzi's face flushed with fury. His body became rigid. Then he spoke, "Ruzid, get your weapons and come with me. We will kill those men. You boys stay here with the flock. Do not make the last day's journey until we come for you. It is too dangerous."

Ruzid and Otzi dashed down the mountain slope. Nearing the settlement Otzi grabbed his grandson by the arm. "Stop, Ruzid! Wait! We can't rush wildly into camp. We must find out what we are fighting. We will crawl to the bushes near where we dump the honey pots. We can see everything from there."

Shaking with fear, but nodding in agreement, Ruzid followed his grandfather. Creeping forward on their bellies the sight shocked them both. There were four filthy brutish men standing around the village stele laughing and urinating on it. Behind them another beast of a man was beating two of the village women. They were tied together with a long rope. Both females were naked and one was bleeding profusely from her smashed nose. Otzi could see his son Brun dead on the ground in a pool of blood. Two children and another woman were also obviously not alive. No others were visible.

Otzi pondered this strange state of affairs. Where were the men, his other five sons? Then he realized that they, so foolishly all of them, must have all gone to the water pond glade. He did not remember that he had sent them. Brun had been alone when the raiders attacked. Otzi was now unruffled. He understood. Ruzid however was frantic. "Grandfather we must attack and kill them all," he hoarsely whispered.

"Calm, Ruzid. Be calm. They are five, we are two and you are not yet experienced in a fight. Now you must do exactly as I tell you." He drew a deep breath saying nothing for a moment, collecting his thoughts.

"We need to find the rest of our kin to help us. I am sure they are at the water pond glade. I want you to creep over to that clump of bushes where the path starts towards the glade. I will fire an arrow and kill the big man with four fingers. I know of him. He is a very bad man. When I shoot my arrow, you must also fire an arrow at those bastards. They will think there may be many of us. When they turn towards you I will kill another and show myself a bit while you run down the trail to fetch our men. Do you understand?"

"But Otzi…"

"Do as you are told boy. We must save what we can. You are too young to be a good fighter. I will get them to chase me away from the stele. I will go up the steep path towards the summer pastures. That will give your uncles time to get here and help me kill all of them. Now start!"

The events failed to go as Otzi had planned. In his nervousness Ruzid stumbled as he attempted to get into place. He reached for a branch to stop his fall. The rotting limb broke with a loud crack that caught the attention of the intruders. The four-fingered leader stooped to pick up his bow just as Otzi let loose his arrow. The projectile missed its target. Instead the missile struck the man directly behind Four-fingers.

This man had opened his mouth in a cry of warning. The arrow entered his open mouth, cut off his tongue and partially exited the rear of his skull. He fell to the ground dead. Unflustered, Otzi let a second arrow fly. It hit Four-fingers in the side. It was a deep wound. The man fell to his knees just as Ruzid sent an ineffective shot into the center of the stele. Four-fingers saw the boy and screamed a name. A very fat bandit ran out of one of the huts pulling his loin cloth over himself. He saw where Four-fingers pointed…towards the boy running down a path. He grabbed his bow to start a pursuit. Now Otzi was forced to stand. He had to shoot an extreme distance to hit the obese man. The arrow pierced the soft flab of the man's thigh forcing him to the ground. It was only a moderate wound but it would immobilize him. He would be unable to chase Ruzid.

The two men left with Four-fingers saw Otzi and pointed at him. Their downed leader screamed a word in an unknown language, but the old man readily understood. The word was "Kill." As Otzi turned to lead them away from the village another thug appeared from nowhere. Otzi had not scouted well enough. At least three, maybe more of this band would be chasing him.

Ruzid scrambled down the path at a breakneck run. In just moments he came upon the group of women and children who had fled the village earlier at the first sign of the attack. They grasped at the boy crying for help. "Let me go! Where are the men? Are they at the water pond glade? I must get them."

As he said this the five brothers, in a long strung out line, came panting up the hill. "What is it?" Ludolf, the first to arrive yelled.

"Marauders," Ruzid gulped, equally out of breath.

"We saw the smoke, dropped our gatherings and started back on the run. How many are there Ruzid?"

"I saw four men, no wait, there was another chasing me so there are five. I don't know what happened to him. Maybe he saw you and turned back. But Otzi killed one and maybe a second one. Brun, your brother, and some others of our kin are dead. They have some of the women as prisoners. We must hurry back and help Otzi. He is fighting them alone"

The brothers did not move. They feared an ambush. After some lengthy discussion and frantic urging by Ruzid they moved cautiously up the trail. They were tightly followed by the women and children. All watched in every direction for the marauder who had followed Ruzid. Finally arriving at the clearing they all were devastated. Otzi's hut was still charring. The heavy support timbers were licked by small flames. They could see a dead thief by the stele and the badly wounded Four-fingers at his side. Blood was gushing from his mortal wound.

Ludolf immediately noticed the fat wounded robber, an arrow protruding from his upper leg. The man was slumped, bleeding and partially conscious, laying in the doorway of the hut. Ludolf could make out the wailing tones of his woman inside. He understood what had happened. He ran forward and quickly dispatched the beast with his hatchet. Meanwhile the other brothers dragged the moaning Four-fingers to the smoldering debris of Otzi's hut and threw him on the burning embers. His screams went unnoticed. They were drowned out by the wailing women and children finding the bodies of Brun, some of their youngsters and friends. The two abused and hurt women were still tied together. Ludolf's woman, naked and badly bruised, came staggering out of her hut. All added to the confused howling din.

As they searched for other intruders, Ruzid rushed up the steep path to aid Otzi. By the time he had reached the overnight resting spot where his brothers were waiting he realized that his grandfather had not come this way. Otzi was not to be found.

Wounding the man who was about to go after Ruzid had forced Otzi to expose his hiding place. But he had intended to let them see him anyway. He wanted the remaining hooligans to chase him. He needed to protect those of his people left in his village by drawing these men away. Hopefully his sons would get there soon. In the meantime he might be able to waylay the pair.

Otzi had thought there were only two others, but suddenly there was another man who was now blocking his way of escape. Where did he come from? Could there be even more of this gang? This one stood between Otzi and the steep trail he expected to take towards the summer meadow. Each man remained frozen for just an instant staring at the other. Then both started to run.

Otzi recognized that the man, while big and powerfully built, did not have a bow. If he managed to catch Otzi it would be close hand-to-hand combat. The old man was not afraid. He had killed other intruders over the years who tried to invade his village. Still, none of this was good. The man chasing him was heavy set but appeared to be much younger with strong legs and arms.

Because he was between Otzi and his chosen escape route, Otzi now would be forced to take an extremely difficult steep path up the mountain. He could not go down the mountain because he would quickly lose any race to his youthful attacker. Even of more concern…where were the other two men? He could not fight three at one time.

Otzi started to run up a steep path. The hard rock surface soon turned to slippery loose shale as he climbed. Suddenly he was sliding backwards, on his belly, down the slope towards his pursuer. The simple weight of his body had started a small rockslide. He slid downward directly towards his aggressor who was being pushed back and partly buried by the same shale flow. The rock surge was carrying Otzi directly into the path of his enemy. The man had a knife poised to strike. Without leverage Otzi could only feebly grasp his axe.

Abruptly his glide downward turned him to the left of the man. He twisted to keep out of the reach of the knife. The move was only partially successful. As he slid swiftly past, the knife wielder managed to reach out and slash at him. Otzi received a severe cut on his right hand.

In just a few more feet his fall stopped and he was able to regain his footing. The man, now above him, was grunting…struggling to free his lower legs buried in the loose gravel. Below, Otzi heard the shouts of the other two raiders who had been at the stele. He had to hurry to somehow get past this big man blocking his way in order to reach the safety of the high ground. He had to eliminate this man.

Gripping his axe in his left hand, Otzi started back up the loose stone. He would chop the man down before he freed himself from the stones. The raider turned, as best he could, roaring menacing oaths into Otzi's face. The older man waited for his chance, and then cut into the trapped man's leg with his axe. The fierceness of his blow caused him to fall forward on the up slope. Somehow it also freed his attacker from the stones. The larger man fell down the slope on top of Otzi. They rolled and grappled until they came to a halt on a flatter part of the slippery stones. The attacker had lost his knife in the scramble. But now he held Otzi from behind in a bear hug. This man was strong! Otzi felt the breath of life being squeezed out of his body. Then he felt a terrible pain as two of his ribs broke.

Acting on pure instinct Otzi found his scabbard with his knife. He pulled the short weapon out with his left hand. Twisting his head to one side he drove the sharp weapon back into his attacker's face. The brute screamed and dropped Otzi. The knife had pierced an eye. The man turned away bent over in pain clutching his face. Otzi, lying on his back, using every ounce of energy, managed to kick at the wounded man with both feet. The attacker slid, and then plummeted farther down the steep slope, finally rolling like a plunging boulder. The thug's head struck a large rock and lay motionless.

Otzi snorted out a sigh in relief, yet every breath he now took became a fresh stab of agony to his broken ribs. The old man managed to find his knife and axe. For the first time he noticed that his right hand was bleeding badly. Using a torn strip of cloth from the top of his boot as a bandage, he tried to stem the flow of blood from his hand. A firm wrap was impossible using only his left hand. The deep knife wound continued to bleed.

With considerable effort he sloshed his way, for a second time, up the loose gravel. Near the top of the loose stone he located his bow, and his quiver, but only two arrows. The bow was broken. It would have to be repaired if he was to have any chance against the other two men, provided they continued to follow him.

Looking down he saw them. Both had stopped. They found the body of his attacker. Their loud keening sounds told Otzi that he had killed an important member of their group…perhaps even a father or a brother. Their need to avenge his death would drive them forward. All his life he had been a hunter…now he understood that he was the quarry.

Looking uphill from the dead man, they saw him. Otzi had foolishly watched from the top of the gravel slide where he was visible. Now he would have to escape higher…perhaps to…to…where? He didn't know. He turned and ran.

As he resumed his climb he recalled that once in his youth he had come up this very trail. Eventually he had arrived at a divide where you could go to the left or right. He had chosen one. It led to a pinnacle with nowhere to go except to retreat back down the almost impossible steep slope. Today, if he took the way that he had followed years ago, it would surely mean his death. He had never gone up the second, almost invisible track that might lead to the next valley and safety. If he could just get over the high mountain pass and set off downhill, they would never get him. He had friends there.

Otzi knew they were still pursuing him. He could hear them screaming. He thought they might be on the loose shale where he had fought the big man. Where were his sons? Now his climb was becoming more difficult. In some spots it was close to a vertical ascend, his wounded right hand was of little use. The weather too was turning against him. The sun had gone behind the clouds. It was rapidly getting colder. He shivered. He had never felt such a violent quick chill taking over his body. It was strange!

Grasping rock handholds Otzi heaved himself slowly upward. Breaths were coming in painful rasping snorts. He tried to protect his broken ribs but that was not possible. Each jolt of the climb was torture. Without warning a new disaster befell the old man. His prized copper axe slipped from his belt. It clattered down the rocky slope, bouncing onto a small ledge. He had to retrieve it. His bow was broken and his knife would not be enough to protect him from the two men following him. *I must get my axe back,* he thought.

Slowly Otzi descended to the shelf near where the axe rested. The narrow rock ledge was split vertically and he would have to stretch over the open space to reach the axe. If he slipped, he would fall to his death. Grimacing, he clutched a protruding rock with his bloody right hand. He stretched to reach the axe but a sudden dizzy spell passed over him and his knees weakened. He nearly fell backwards into what would have been a fatal plunge. Otzi struggled to lean forward against the rock face. Finally the near faint cleared from his head.

Fiercely grasping the rock wall, a second time with his cut hand, he screamed with pain from the pressure of the grip. He swayed back and forth twice, and then lunged. This time he managed to retrieve his precious axe. He heard a sound that, at first he thought, was an echo of his painful yell. It was not. The two men far below were starting up the narrow defile he had just so painfully climbed. They were yelling, telling him he was about to die. They were coming for him. They had found him by the sound of his scream.

Otzi's continued his flight in a daze. Much of the time he had to crawl on hands and knees. Blood flowed faster from his wounded hand. He had made the wound even larger grasping the outcropping. *But I had to have my axe*, he thought. Once he collapsed in bewilderment. He cursed all the raiders, especially the two men below and somehow he cursed this tormenting mountain…wishing them all to depart to the underworld.

Climbing again, Otzi was finally able to stand. The ground was almost level. He had reached his destination…but why? He stood unmoving for a long time pondering why he had come here. Then his mind cleared. This was the place where the track split in two. One path was the dead end he had taken as a youth. The other might carry him to the pass over the ridge and safety. Which path had he trod those many years ago? His mind was too tired to remember. He failed to recognize any landmarks.

Like the wounded animals that he had tracked, he must try and throw his hunters off his scent. Purposely he picked the easier appearing path to the right, marking his way with spots of his own blood. Here and there were small shrubs where he broke branches. Then removing the blood soaked bandage from his hand, he draped it on a high rock ledge above the trail. The two killers would see it and pause, concerned about a trap. Finally he took off his bearskin hat and wrapped it around his dripping hand. It would hold back the seeping blood until he was far up the other path.

The ruse had invigorated the old man and he ascended the left hand trail with newfound energy. Now it might be possible to survive. The climb was very rocky but not as vertical. Still, as he gained more altitude, the thinning air made him gasp agonizingly for every breath he took. Finally he had to stop once more and rest. *I had such a good day yesterday. Why should I be so tired? But of course, I haven't eaten today. Ruzid and I started this morning running down from the meadow to the stele. I have been running ever since I killed one raider and wounded the Four-fingered man.* Mentally reviewing the day brought back one more memory. *I have some meat from the ibex in my pack. Best I eat now for strength.*

The old hunter ate and immediately fell asleep. Then a tremor passed though his body and he was instantaneously awake. *How long did I sleep*, he thought. The sun was very low in the sky. He would have to hurry to get over the pass and down into a warmer climate before dark.

Trying to rise, he fell back in terrible pain. The damage in his chest made him roll onto his stomach. He wondered how he might be able to rise upward without stressing his ribs. He almost fell again finding that his right hand would not support him. His hat bandage was filled with blood.

Finally, finding support from a large boulder, he staggered to his feet. Again he started climbing slowly up the rock strewn slope. Otzi knew he had to keep moving. The cold of his body told him that something was very wrong. Cold rain was pelting him and freezing immediately as it struck the rocky ground around him.

Medicine would not explain how cold affected a human body in Otzi's condition for another 5,000 years. With his body temperature now at 86 degrees, his heart, its electrical impulses hampered by chilled nerve tissues, became arrhythmic. It was now pumping less than two-thirds the normal amount of blood. The lack of oxygen and the slowing metabolism of his brain begin to trigger visual and auditory hallucinations.

"Otzi, come sit by the fire. Eat with us and tell us another story."

"Ruzid, you found me. Help me to your fire. I am so cold and hungry. Did you…did you kill those two men following me?" The vision of his grandson faded as quickly as it had appeared. Slowly Otzi again comprehended where he was. Now with a potency developed by a life of hardship living in the mountains, he moved one step at a time towards the top of the pass. It was just in sight.

A flush of warmth suddenly came over him. He again lost track of where he was going. His vision blurred. He was unbelievably tired. The weight of his weapons became too much to carry. He set down his broken bow and quiver. Next he laid his axe on a nearby rock. He would sit down and rest for just a short while before he moved on.

Otzi froze to death approximately three-hundred vertical feet from the top of the pass.

A BIT OF HISTORY

Ötzi the Iceman is the well-preserved natural mummy of a man from about 3300 BC (53 centuries ago). The mummy was found in September 1991 in the Schnalstal glacier in the Ötztal Alps, near Hauslabjoch on the border between Austria and Italy. The man's name comes from Ötztal (Ötz valley), the region in which he was discovered. He is Europe's oldest natural human mummy, and has offered an unprecedented view of Chalcolithic (Copper Age) Europeans. The body and his belongings are displayed in the South Tyrol Museum of Archaeology in Bolzano, northern Italy.

Nine

Sculpture

It was late in the afternoon but Matt decided to stop by his cousin's house and say hello. Besides there was always something good to eat there. If he was lucky he might get invited to stay for supper. It had happened before.

"Rex, what in the world is that thing you're working on?"

"Oh, Hi, Matt. This is a sculpture I'm making for my art class."

"Really! That doesn't look like anything to me except a funny green shape. Maybe it could be the body of some animal…a dog, maybe?"

Rex frowned. "This is abstract art Matt. I'm making a clay model. It's a bull. Don't they have any art out west in Omaha where you come from?"

"Sure they do Rex, but nothing that looks like that. Why did you paint it green? Where are its horns? Are you sure that thing is really a bull?" Matt's grin was so wide that Rex finally had to smile too.

"Now I understand Rex. Your sculpture represents something which is not exactly real. That's just about like an ancient history story that I had to read in class. It told about a man-bull-god in ancient times. It was a myth. Your sculpture is sort of a plaster myth, I mean a clay myth"

Rex asked, "The story…the myth…it's like a fairy tale…huh?"

"Well, I'm not so sure. This legend happened so long ago that I'll bet people must have believed that it was true. They didn't have TV or reporters or bloggers to investigate anything. They thought whatever they were told was the truth. Back then everything was all by word of mouth. It is called oral history."

"Tell me the story Matt. Maybe I can add something about it to my sculpture."

"I don't think so, Rex. But, I'll tell you anyway…it's kinda funny and scary too.

"The way I remember the story is that in the Mediterranean Sea…you know where that is don't you Rex?...the Mediterranean Sea? Well there is a big island in the middle of it called Crete. Thousands of years ago there was a king living on Crete. His name was Minos. He was rich and powerful. This was a time when people believed in all kinds of weird gods. The king supposedly controlled a monstrous thing called a Minotaur. It was by all accounts a god-like creature that was part man and part bull. It lived at the center of a palace, a great big building called the Labyrinth. Part of it was an elaborate maze-like construction built for King Minos and designed by the famous architect Daedalus. He and his son Icarus were ordered by Minos to build it to hold the Minotaur."

"Wait…Matt…wait! I know about this. My father is an architect too and he told me about the Labyrinth. He's got a book with a picture of the Minotaur. Now I remember. Dad told that story to me one night when mom was out and he put me to bed. He likes architecture stories.

"I was kinda scared after he told me about the Minotaur. I was little. Then dad told me about a big maze called the Labyrinth. He really liked that part of the story a lot, because it was about Daedalus the architect. Dad told me that Daedalus had to run away from the law in Athens, 'cus he was caught getting kick-backs from contractors. He ended up in Crete. He went to work for King Minos. He designed and built the largest and fanciest building ever, called the Labyrinth. Then he did some bad stuff with the Queen, so King Minos shut him up in a tower along with his son. But Daedalus was smart and made some wings for both of them out of bird feathers and wax and they both flew away. But I guess his son Icarus flew too high and the wax holding the feathers was melted by the sun. Icarus fell into the ocean and musta died. His father couldn't help him so he flew away."

Matt shook his head in surprise. "Rex you are a pretty smart kid to remember all that."

"I wonder if any of that could be true" Rex pondered.

"Well Rex, your father is an architect. Do you think he could make wings like that?"

"I'll bet he could. He can make anything. But could a person really fly with just bird feather wings?"

"I don't think so Rex, but that was a long time ago. We'll never know for sure. I think that story might be just as accurate as your sculpture looking like a real bull."

They both laughed.

Ten

Geaad

Danube River Delta 1600 B.C.

The Lipovans were an ancient tribe of humans. They had lived, seemingly since eternity, at the edge of an enormous marshy river delta. They worshiped a goddess named Io. She was the deity of the endless and usually placid nearby waters. The river flowed quietly but forcefully past reed covered flat islands into the Black Sea.

Change for the Lipovans was almost unknown. This rich marshy area of plentiful game fowl, fresh water river fish plus occasional salt water sturgeon from out of the dark water sea, provided abundantly for their needs. These gentle yet cautious people called Lipovans lived well. Otter, wild boar and roe deer provided meat. Mink and ermine gave them luxurious fur garments, first of course for the males of the tribe. Yet pelts were so plentiful that most of the females, in the colder weather, could cover themselves with the same luxurious furs. A wide variety of colorful bird feathers were used to decorate hair, head, and the modest waist wraps worn by the adults.

The reedy marshes also provided security for the Lipovans. Their village was on high ground on the southernmost side of the wide river flow. The dense water-land swamp of the delta, with a maze of confusing channels, separated them from the principal river highway. That water road often carried dangerous manmade activity.

There were only two threats for the tribe. One was flooding. It occasionally filled the marshes. For the sake of safety, the Lipovans had settled their huts on a high forested hill. From this elevated vantage point they would hungrily watch the occasional rising waters. Floods kept them from their main food source of daily caught fish. The river overflows appeared randomly, but had never reached them on their knoll.

The other threat was far worse. Too often, the warmer seasons brought bands of cut-throat brigands paddling and sailing downriver. These were the hard men of the north pursuing riches from the more civilized peoples of the south. These men could easily be identified by their blonde hair and often red beards. Rarely did any of the marauders pause to search out the Lipovans. The marsh was too confusing. The Lipovans had no treasure. Yet, once in the long sing-song oral history of the tribe, a raiding group of starving men had, in desperation, managed to reach their small village. While there were few goods of value to pillage, food was stolen and most of the tribesmen were killed. Captured women and children were carried off to the north as slaves…never to return. The small number of Lipovans, who had managed to escape, re-founded the tribe. Consistently, in the generations that followed, security was foremost in the minds of the elders. They moved the tribal huts deeper into the forest and farther away from the prime food source in the delta marshes

For extra safety, each day, young boys were sent to lookout points up and down river. They were there to provide early warnings of any bands of men on the river. When an alarm was sounded, Lipovan hunters and fishermen withdrew to the village mount. Fires were quickly extinguished to prevent smoke signals as telling signs of human habitation. This effort had worked successfully for ages beyond counting.

Today young Geaad was one of the boys assigned to a lookout post. He was blond, skinny and tall for his seven summers. It was Geaad's first time to be trusted alone with this important duty. He knew the punishment for failure to keep a good watch. He had witnessed that penalty and he shivered. Yet, he was also proud to be selected for this vital task.

Both Geaad and his mother Vesa, were strangers to the tribe and far different from any of the Lipovans. Unlike the rest of the clan they had blue eyes. Also, both Vesa and Geaad were very light skinned and blonde headed. The indigenous group of Lipovans was noticeably darker complexioned. Vesa and her son were obviously much like the tribe of feared marauders of the north, yet the circumstances of arrival had made them accepted members of the Lipovan encampment.

Vesa had been born to a tribe far up the delta river near very high mountains. As a young girl she could remember seeing snow caps even in the warmest days of summer on the mountain peaks. Her unhappy life there was filled with fear. Warfare was constant among the many small tribes of her savage people.

On one bright spring day a powerful chieftain from a nearby village came to her tribe's encampment. He was called Agar. He offered bronze tools in trade for Vesa and two other young females and three boys. All six of the children were about the same pre-teen age. With Agar's fierce hunting party waiting outside the village walls, his offer of exchange could not be refused. Before the trade was completed, each child was stripped of their loin cloth and examined carefully looking for any disfigurements. If there was the slightest blemish, the youngster would be immediately rejected and another chosen.

Vesa was mortally terrified as she was traded to Agar. Now, possessed by this hideous group of strangers, she was surprised that none of the boys or girls were 'used' after their new owners hustled them away. Rather, the children were entrusted to several old women traveling with the warriors. They were well fed and warmly clothed as they travelled down river to Agar's home territory. One of the girls blurted to Vesa, "They feed us so well in order to fatten us. Soon they will eat us!" At first Vesa was alarmed. Finally she realized that this could not be true. This group of slave traders collected only perfect blonde children to be used for some unknown purpose.

More unblemished children, but only those with fair complexions and the brightest blonde hair were added to Agar's collection as they all journeyed further down river.

Eventually they left the river and came to blackish water so vast you could not see the end of it. Waves often rocked the little boat as they sailed across this sea. The motion made almost everyone sick. Eventually, after uncountable days of travel by boat, they came to a town with buildings made of stone. Vesa was amazed at the sights of this village. It was called Athens. She had never seen anything like it.

Agar traded again. This time the children were exchanged to a short swarthy man with a terrible temper for some pieces of gold. Vesa immediately noticed that her new owner's breath smelled like a pig sty. His name was Thorax. He led his newly purchased group into a large high-walled compound where each young person was assigned to a private stall with a small bed. Other older blonde children were also in the compound. Thorax warned the newcomers that he would punish any of them harshly for the slightest infraction of his rules. Vesa quickly learned that this punishment was a beating with a wide leather strap. It hurt terribly. She did not want to be whipped a second time. It was done in a way that left no permanent marks on her body.

For Vesa and the others, life in their new home was surprisingly happy, but it was also a busy time. All were schooled in the local language and customs of Mycenae. They were required to speak only this language of Athens. Thorax called it Greek. Also, in order to keep them healthy, their new owner exercised them every day with long runs through the fields and orchards surrounding his compound. The boys were trained to wrestle and throw javelins. The girls were taught to juggle and all the youngsters swam in the ocean each afternoon. Vesa learned to swim long distances in the warm salt water of the Aegean Sea. None of the young people ever wore any clothes. Their bodies bronzed in the almost constant daily sunshine. Blonde hair turned to gold. Except for the individual natural changes as each of the girls reached puberty, they all looked very much alike.

Thorax's compound sat at the edge of the village. Athens was ringed by mountains to the north and the Aegean Sea everywhere else. Since there was no way to escape this place, the youngsters were allowed at times to mingle with the townspeople. Purposely, Thorax wanted his captives to become immersed in the local culture. They needed to be accepted as the children of the colony if he were to profit. For their part, the boys and girls were fed and treated so well that all of them wanted to stay in Athens forever.

Vesa, always alert to her surroundings, noticed that the features of the local people were somewhat different from herself and the others from the north. Generally the local people were shorter of stature, with olive skin and dark eyes and coal black hair. These obvious differences apparently were not a concern for Thorax. If his fair haired group was healthy without blemish and seemed to belong to Athens by language and custom, he was satisfied. He could make a profitable trade.

Vesa became aware of the vastness of the world from the daily classes given by her caretakers. Athens, she discovered, was a small colony of Minos. This kingdom was the dominating sea power of the known world. Minos itself was located some long distance away on an island called Crete. The people both in Athens and Crete were called Mycenaean's.

One day after a very long swim, Vesa was resting on the hot sand of the beach, close to the compound. The sun was pleasantly warm and it was not yet time to return to the restrictive confinements of Thorax's handlers. A skinny young woman, wearing only a rag around her waist, came wandering up the beach. Her dark complexion said she was a native. She seemed exhausted. Nodding to Vesa, she sat down beside the blonde girl. Vesa immediately noticed that she had bruises on both of her arms and legs.

"What happened to you? Why are you so bruised?" Vesa asked.

"My master beats me almost every day," the girl replied. "He is very cruel."

"Does he take you to his bed?" Vesa asked. "Is that when he beats you?"

"No," she replied. "He does not use me that way. He has a boy for that. I have to clean and cook and tend the food garden. It is hard. Still is much better than the boy's lot and I can steal some of my master's food to stay alive."

Vesa shook her young head in disgust. "That's terrible! My owner feeds us well and treats us nicely. He is strict but rarely beats us. We have to exercise every day and learn your language and customs but we don't have to work."

The dark-haired girl almost smiled. "Yes, I know of your good life. I have heard much about it. But next year I will still be here and you will be gone to sacrifice."

"What are you talking about?" Vesa asked with a tinge of fear in her voice.

"You don't know!" Now the girl rubbed the bruise on her right arm and stood to go. Vesa grabbed her by the wrist and twisted the girl's thin arm. "Tell me of this sacrifice or I will hurt you more than your master."

The girl started to sob. Vesa would not let go, she was strong from all the running and swimming. Finally, the sobbing girl stopped struggling and pointed out to the sea, "Look blonde girl. See that big ship in the harbor. That is the tribute ship that arrived from Minos yesterday. It is here to take seven boys and seven girls from your group to the island called Crete. Minos the king has forced our little colony to send him this tribute of unblemished young boys and maidens each and every year. They are sent to his palace in a place called Knossos."

"Why?" Vesa asked. Her eyes were wide with concern.

"Because, I have been told, we here in Athens are being punished for some misdeed of long ago. I don't know what that insult was, but it offended Minos so much that he now demands seven boys and seven girls each year as a reparation for what happened. I think, I am guessing a bit, I believe that Minos' son was killed here in Athens. Still, we in our little colony are governed by intelligent men. Rather than send the children of our colony, Athens buys you fair-haired ones from the barbarians of the north and then sends you to fulfill the bounty we must pay."

"But you said 'sacrifice' a moment ago. What did you mean, 'sacrifice'?"

The girl slumped to her knees on the hot sand. In a choking voice, between new rounds of sobs, "You didn't know!" She said for a second time. "Haven't you wondered why you are treated so perfectly? Each annual payment of young men and women is taken directly to a strange half-man half-bull god on the island of Crete. This monster is called the Minotaur. I have heard that he eats his gifts from Athens in order that he can live for another year!"

With that said, the girl quickly rose from the sand to leave, but her ragged skirt-wrap stayed on the sand. Vesa had not realized that her foot was holding the girl's skimpy covering. Now naked, the girl ran wildly away without attempting to salvage her bit of a skirt.

Vesa didn't know quite what to do or think. She left the rag and returned to the compound.

The next morning at dawn dignitaries from Athens came to the compound with two strangely dressed men. Vesa had never seen such clothes or adornments as these two strangers wore. All of the young people were lined up for inspection. Seven of the oldest strongest boys were quickly selected. The girls were examined more carefully. Only older girls who had obviously reached puberty were chosen. One of the girls who had been brought to Athens with Vesa was old enough to be selected. All the others who were picked had been at the compound at least a year. Those older youths, not selected, were disappointed and on the verge of tears.

Thorax, the compound leader, praised the strangers for their selection. Vesa smirked, watching the hated overseer grovel before his guests. He talked on and on about the wonderful life that this selected group would enjoy in Knossos. Then as the local dignitaries, the Minos people, and the chosen youngsters left for the ship, Thorax turned to the remaining blonde boys and girls. "There will be a feast tonight," he said. "We will celebrate another successful year. Today no running or swimming. Only prepare for the banquet."

Under a clear sky, with a full moon, the youngsters and the compound staff feasted. Charis, a young female in charge of the girls, was more friendly and lenient than Thorax or most of the other guardians. Vesa pointedly served Charis food with much drink knowing that the wine would loosen her tongue. Soon Charis was staggering and Vesa helped her to a corner of the compound where they could sit against the wall. It took only a small amount of prompting for Vesa to learn that the girl she had met on the beach was telling the truth. They really were being fattened like cattle for the annual death payment to the Minotaur.

"What happens to the older ones who were not picked today?" Vesa wondered aloud.

Charis giggled with the wine. "They will slowly disappear. You are all too pretty to waste. Thorax will trade most of them to the brothels in town. We have many ships with sailors that come here just for you golden ones."

"Is that what happened to Wyn? She was the best swimmer in the older group."

Charis hiccupped violently. "Too mush wine," she slurred. "No. Thorax found that Wyn was with child. He beat her until she confessed that the guard at the gate, his name was...was… Hesiod, had slept with her. It is against the rules for caretakers to touch you 'bull-fodder' in that way. That's what we call you among ourselves, 'bull-fodder'! Anyway, Thorax flew into a rage as I have never seen. He sent all of you away one day on a long run through the countryside. Then the rest of us, all Thoraxes' servants and slaves were marched to the edge of the sea. Hesiod and Wyn were tied together, face to face. Next they were put in a small boat and weights were tied to their feet. Finally they were taken to deep water and dumped overboard into the ocean. Thorax told us that this is what would happen to any of us if we violate any of you. We all were terrified. It was horrible."

Vesa quivered. She fed Charis more wine to blot the exchange from the caretaker's memory. Now unexpectedly, she recognized that she was trapped in a death spiral. How could she escape? Where might she go? The coldness that flooded her heart would not go away.

As the months went by Vesa ran harder and swam longer. Perhaps she was mentally trying to escape what she now knew would be her fate. During this trying interval her body blossomed into womanhood. She was certain she would be chosen for the next shipment to Crete. Her anxieties were augmented by occasional meetings with residents of Athens. Most were only too happy to share many more lurid tales of the Minotaur. Some expressed delight that no natives of Athens had to make such a horrible sacrifice.

Vesa could only find three outcomes for herself. She would be selected to go to Crete to be sacrificed to the man-bull god or she would not be chosen and then sent to a brothel in Athens to service any man. A third possibility she considered might be to swim far out to sea until she was exhausted and quietly sink beneath the waves. She did not know what to do. She was continually troubled.

One glorious warm day Vesa met an old man drawing lines with a stick on the sandy beach. "What are you doing?" she asked. "Are you Zeno?" She knew who he was and that he had answers to many questions of life. Perhaps he might help her. Without waiting for him to reply, she explained her fate with the Minotaur.

Zeno acknowledged her with a slight nod. He continued drawing mostly straight lines in the wet sand just above the lapping blue waves. Finally, still making lines, he spoke. "At the birth of a man, the Moirai, who are the goddesses of Fate, spin out the thread of each man's future life. They follow his steps, and direct the consequences of his actions according to the counsel of the other gods. The Moirai are ugly old hateful women, some lame with strange illnesses. They are severe, inflexible and stern goddesses. They do not spin pleasantly the fates of men. But man's lot is not an inflexible destiny.

"Zeus, the king of the gods, if he chooses, has the power of saving even those who were already on the point of being seized by their worst possibilities. And the Moirai do not abruptly interfere in human affairs but avail themselves of intermediate causes. They determine the lot of mortals, not absolutely but only conditionally, every man himself in his freedom is allowed to exercise a certain influence upon himself. "

Zeno would say no more and Vesa left him on the beach. She wondered if these goddesses of fate wove their web for women as well as for men. Could she somehow change her god directed doom? Perhaps! The opportunity arrived just a few days later.

A small ship with only a single tattered sail appeared on the horizon. It was the same barbarian boat that had brought her to Athens. Could this be 'The Fates' presenting themselves? A plan quickly formed in her mind. Diving into the waves she stroked rapidly towards the incoming ship. Nearing it she saw Agar, the chieftain who had traded her, standing in the bow. There were blonde boys and girls huddled together behind him, watched by three hulking crewmen.

"Agar," she called.

He turned and looked back inside the boat.

"Here Agar," she called again more loudly from the waves.

Now he saw her in the rolling sea. He smiled. She looked to be a pretty young wench that he might add to his trade. He held out a hand. "Climb aboard before you drown," he yelled.

"No Agar. You brought me here a year ago. I will not be traded again to Thorax. You are stupid to think you can fool that evil man. I want you to take me back to my tribe and family."

For a moment Agar was angry, and then he smiled. "Don't call me stupid, girl. You are the stupid one so far out in the water. Get aboard or I will leave you to drown."

"I will not drown Agar. Thorax has given all of us elixir to make us almost immortal like the gods. If you refuse to take me back to my tribe, I will confess to Thorax that you pulled me into your boat and stole my virginity.

"Liar!" Agar roared.

"I know that, but Thorax is a hateful monster and he believes only the worst outcomes. He will accept as the truth what I tell him about you. Learn of the punishment he gave to Hesiod and Wyn when he found that Hesiod had taken Wyn. He will do the same to you. He has many men. He won't pay you. He will kill you."

Vesa treaded water as she waited for him to reply. She understood that Agar was as dim-witted as he was brutal. She did not wait for an answer. "Agar," she called again, "when you arrive at the compound, hold up your thumb to me. If you do, I will be on your ship before sunup tomorrow and you will take me back to my home. If you do not do that I will immediately tell Thorax what you did to me. He will kill us both for that. If I stay, I will die anyway so I might as well choose to take you with me"

Vesa swam hard in order to reach the compound. She got there before Agar arrived with the annual consignment of children. Her plan had worked. Agar held his thumb up to her. She had learned that by lies, coupled with the stupidity of men, she could make her own fate. She secretly sailed with Agar the next morning.

The journey was long. For days Vesa kept the four men at bay with her story of having acquired immortal powers. She resorted to telling them that she was now the blood sister of Thanatos, the god of death. To frighten the men, she gave details describing Thanatos as a son of Nyx the god of night and Erebos the daughter of darkness. She recited what she had learned at the compound about these Mycenaean gods. Charis had told them stories about the gods each evening by the fire.

"And there the immortals, dark Nyx and Erebos spawned two children, Sleep and Thanatos, also known as Death. These two are awful gods. But they have vowed to protect me. The glowing Sun never looks upon either of them with his beams, neither as he goes up into heaven, nor as he comes down from heaven. And the former of them roams peacefully over the earth and the sea's broad back and is kindly to men offering restful sleep; but Thanatos has a heart of iron, and the spirit within him is pitiless as bronze. Whomsoever of men he has once seized he holds fast. He is hateful even to the deathless gods.

"Touch me," she threatened, "and I will call upon Thanatos, the god of death to visit you." Her spell seemed to work. Frightened, they left her alone. *All men are stupid*, she thought.

As they sailed the Black Sea towards the Danube delta, a strong squall struck the small craft. One of the crewmen was washed overboard and lost. In that same storm Agar slipped on the wet wood deck planking and was knocked unconscious. Coming to, but with only part of his senses, he saw Vesa sprawled naked at the stern of the small boat. He crawled on top of her and quickly and brutally took her. Then he slumped into oblivion again. The two remaining crewmen were horrified. They believed Agar dead by the hand of Thanatos. Yet, in a few moments Agar woke again and repeated the violation of Vesa. As the seas calmed, the other crewmen two joined in the fun.

Fear was replaced by a new reason to keep Vesa. Each of the three men enjoyed her daily, occasionally beating her in the process. Vesa quickly learned to struggle a little. They seemed to like that. She desperately longed to escape but land was too far away for her to swim. Finally the delta came in sight and the small boat entered the river channel.

The wind had calmed and they anchored waiting for it to return. They would need a strong morning breeze to fill the sail to push the boat up the river against the current. As the sun set, the three men used Vesa, laughed and ate, then each used her again. She had found that they would always sleep deeply after they finished with her. Her plan was to slip over the side of the boat in the dark and swim to the delta sands. It was not to be. The fish they all had been eating had turned rancid. She became violently sick. She could barely move. During the night Agar and his two crewmen became equally ill.

The next morning was dead calm. There was no wind to push the sail. The little boat sat in the hot sunlight while the smell of vomit attracted hoards of stinging insects from the bulrushes. Vesa jumped into the water to escape the flying plague. The men could not swim and howled and thrashed at the black clouds of biting insects. Finally, they also jumped overboard and clung to the side of the boat until almost sundown. All were hungry having gone without food for a day. At last returning to the deck, Vesa was made to clean the vomit before they used her again and then collapsed into exhausted sleep.

A strong breeze woke them the next morning. It had pushed the boat to a sandbar. Using oars they shoved off and began moving rapidly upstream. Vesa was weak but saw this as her opportunity to escape. Diving off the stern she swam rapidly towards the south bank of the river. It was marshy and covered with reeds but it meant freedom from the Agar and his two crewmen. The boat continued moving rapidly upstream. The untrained sailors did not have the skills to turn and follow the swimmer. It didn't matter. They could always steal or buy another female for their amusement. Vesa was free.

The delta was a jumbling of small islands, some with stunted knurly trees. Most had reeds twice her height. These reeds had jagged knife-like edges and she was covered with tiny cuts by sundown. There was abundant water but nothing she could find to eat. At dusk, exhausted, she caught a small frog. It was too disgusting to eat. Vesa let it go.

The next morning Vesa woke to a cool drizzle. She needed the sun; otherwise, she might walk in circles among reeds high over her head. There was no way to see over them. The scrub trees would not support her weight. She could only try to walk in a straight line. For three exhausting days she struggled, angry and frustrated, against the cutting reeds. Once was she able to catch a fish with her hands. She ate it raw.

On the third night the light rain changed into a torrent and the marsh began to flood. Fatigued to the point of collapse, lashed by the constant downpour she fell into semi-consciousness on a thick mat of downed reeds. The Fates, she thought, had killed her.

When the rains stopped at last, the waters in the delta quickly receded. Two young Lipovan boys were first to check their fish traps. The clan was hungry. Instead of fish, the boys found a young blonde girl floating on a bed of reeds. They had never seen a person with this golden color of hair and skin so white. Vesa moaned lightly as the boys pulled her to shore,

"Is it Io" asked the older boy?

"The river goddess" the younger one blurted in amazement.

She could not understand the language. But in her semi-delirious state she repeated the first word, "Io."

Vesa was too big for the small boys to carry…besides they were petrified. They ran to the village jabbering for help. They told the stunned Lipovans that they had found the goddess of the river, Io.

Quickly, the tribe came to her aid and ministered to her wounds. With food and a dry place to rest she recovered rapidly. All the Lipovans came to admire her color and especially her blue eyes. They had never seen such a person…she *had* to be the goddess of their river. She was quick to regain her senses and realized that they were delighted by her, yet intimidated by her persona.

Vesa, if anything, was sharp-witted. It was time to spin a story. Using sign language, she explained that she was Io. This was a goddess she knew from stories in the compound in Athens. She explained to the simple natives that she had fallen off a raincloud into the river. The other gods were jealous of her and did not come to her rescue. Now she would stay here and protect her saviors, the clan, from evil gods. It was not clear to her if they really understood her story; still this gentle, primitive tribe seemed willing to accept her. *Better to be alive here than surely dead with Agar,* she thought.

As time passed it became obvious that Vesa was with child. Again she used sign language to explain that the father was one of the cloud gods. When Geaad was born, he was equally venerated by the tribe. As her son grew, it became apparent that he was as different as his mother compared to the Lipovans. Both Vesa and her child were lighter in color and their hair as fair as the sun. Vesa also spoke a language unlike that of the rest of the tribe. She called the language Greek, the language of the gods. She used it with her son from the moment of his birth. Eventually the two spoke in a language that none of the Lipovans understood. She never used tribal words or even admitted to understanding them. Vesa kept her secret of this perception, from both Geaad and the Lipovans. It was some small source of power for her to walk among this mild people, just listening. The tribe, in turn, felt safe saying anything in her presence, assured she did not understand them. Any small advantage was important to Vesa. Her previous life had been one of constant peril and she used all her skills to feel safe with the Lipovans.

Sometimes she also spoke still another language besides Greek, but again only to her son Geaad. She never mixed it with the idiom of Athens. She told him this was the language of the barbarians from the north. Geaad, as a child growing in the village, was easily able to speak the Lipovan language. He learned to speak it from the other children of the tribe in the communal hut where they lived. He often acted as the translator between his mother and other adults. She did not need a translator but this mystique enhanced her status among these simple folk. The tribe did not doubt that Greek was the language of the immortals.

As Geaad grew, Vesa learned who fathered her child. The boy used his left thumb and forefinger to make an un-necessary motion of sliding them down his nose to momentarily close his nostrils. Only Agar, of the four men who had taken her in the boat, had ever used this same motion. This vaguely pleased Vesa since Agar was the biggest and strongest of them.

Vesa appreciated that the goddesses, The Fates, the god Zeus, and her own actions had saved her. Now she wished to do all she could to prepare her son Geaad for life. As soon as he began his second summer she took him to the river and taught him to swim. The Lipovans smiled knowingly. This was most correct for Io, the goddess of the river.

In his fourth summer Geaad began to run distances with his mother. Soon he was stronger than any boy two or even three summers older. At night Vesa would take him outside their hut to watch the stars. She explained the patterns in the Zodiac.

One night Geaad asked, "Mother, are you really the river goddess called Io?"

Vesa was startled by the question. Was he old enough for the truth? "Go to sleep son," she said. "I will tell you that story another night."

Geaad was not satisfied. "I'm not sleepy mother. Tell me now."

"Lay back on your mat son and I will tell you.

"Io was a priestess of Hera, the Queen of the gods. Hera's mate, Zeus, the King of the gods, liked Io so much that Hera became jealous. Rather than fight with Hera, Zeus turned Io into a cow and then set a gadfly, a horrible bug, on the cow Io to chase it away. Hera now rued her jealousy and restored Io to her beauty. But then Io did fall off a cloud and became a river goddess."

Wide eyed Geaad said, 'And that was really you mother?"

"No son that was not me. I told the Lipovans that story when they found me floating on the reeds in the delta. I needed help at that moment and I wanted their protection."

"But mother, how did you get into the delta?"

"That is a very long story and we will save it for another night. Now go to sleep!"

Eventually Vesa explained to her son the hard ways of her childhood. She told him of the murderous tribes of her native land who were constantly at war. She detailed her slave trip to Athens. She explained to him that the language of the more civilized Greeks would be useful to him. When manhood came he should travel south and drink in the wonders of a larger world. She filled his mind with the sights and sounds of Athens, its warm sunlight and salt water oceans. Vesa also explained that she was teaching him the language of Agar's people in case he ever met these barbarians.

"Do you hate Agar, mother?"

"Sometimes, but he in his hard life, knew no other way."

"What about Thorax?"

"Yes son, I do hate Thorax. He is an intelligent man. He sends people to their death. He kills people. Remember how he tied the guard and the girl together and had them drown. Thorax is an evil man."

"When I am older mother, I will go to Athens and kill Thorax," Geaad said with a little boy's bluster.

As Geaad grew he learned more of the stories of Athens. He was especially intrigued by the story of the Minotaur. It was important to him because his mother had almost died as a sacrifice to this strange beast. But she had used her wits to escape from Thorax and Athens using his father, Agar.

Vesa had learned much about the panoply of the gods in Thorax's compound. She told her son that sometimes mortals could actually kill gods. With a small boy's bravado Geaad vowed privately to kill this terrible beast, the Minotaur.

Finally, he understood that he and his mother were mortals, not gods. The color of their hair and blue eyes came from their ancestry to the mountain tribes far up the delta river.

For now, he would learn from Vesa, He would run and swim until his body became like rock. Then he would go south to Athens to kill Thorax and finally go on to this strange island of Crete and slaughter the Minotaur god-beast.

He would avenge his mother.

Eleven
Geaad
Minotaur

Geaad lay back on a flat stone slab. The day was pleasantly warm. He reflected on his wanderings…no…perhaps not wanderings. It was more like a directed journey that had brought him to Athens. It was now much longer than a full year since he had found his mother dead. Following that dreadful discovery, he had taken this arduous trip south in order to kill Thorax…only to find this man also dead. All the connections which brought meaning to his life had been destroyed. How had so much change occurred? It seemed like only yesterday that he was carefree youth in the Lipovan camp.

Three Lipovan boys close to Geaad's age had challenged him to join them in a forbidden hunt. The brothers Vilk and Prut and Geaad's best friend, Buco, planned to traverse the delta, and then find a way to cross the broad river and explore its north bank. It was not really a hunt. They wanted to test their newly found manhood with a great adventure.

Geaad, now in his later teen years, had often hunted for many days at a time away from the camp, usually with these three friends. The hunts always went south, farther away from the river. This would be something new. None of them had ever been to the far side of the great flowing stream. This was exciting. Frequently Vesa warned Geaad about dangerous men traveling on that expansive highway of river water. He thought it best to only tell his mother that he was going off on another hunt. She worried too much.

Reaching the main course of the river was not a problem. They all knew the delta well, and with little difficulty they soon faced the wide expanse of the blue river water with no way to cross it. Only Geaad could swim. The four sat morosely for the day watching the waterway, wondering how they might conquer it. As dusk approached Vilk noticed an unmanned boat drifting past them. Geaad immediately dove into the moving flow and swam to catch it. The little craft was drifting away towards the vast sea of black water at the river's mouth. With great effort, and almost exhausted, he finally came close enough to grasp the side of the boat.

He quickly heaved himself over the side. There was no way for him to stop his upward motion coming out of the water. As he came down he landed with a squishing thud on a decaying corpse lying in the bottom of the boat. Shivering, ignoring as best he could the sticky body juices that clung to him, he found a paddle and rowed to his friends.

They were mildly upset about the body but laughed at the stains and pasty goo on Geaad's backside. The small boat was easily turned over in the shallows. They rocked it until the dead man's remains were washed away. All of them were accustomed to blood, bone and gore since they hunted in the forests to survive. Death also, even the sudden unexplainable death of a Lipovan, was not a stranger to this barely civilized tribe. It just happened. This great unknown of the ending of life, often an abrupt occurrence, was treated with little emotion.

At the next dawn the four adventurers paddled out towards the far north shore. The current was mild yet they drifted far down river before finally reaching the unfamiliar land on the distant shore. They were now far removed from the Lipovan territory. The river bank at this point rose quickly, and the boys, forgetting the boat, ran up a small hill for a better view of the countryside. Before them the land opened into an endless grassy plain. The only mark of variation was a cloud of dust on the horizon.

"Animals, a large drove of…of…something," Vilk said. "Let's see what it is."

With Geaad in the lead, the four ran forward through the waist high brown grasses. The mysterious herd was much farther away than they imagined. Exhausted they stopped for the night by a bubbling stream. They feasted on freshly fish caught with no trouble in the shallows.

Lazing on full stomachs, Prut turned to Geaad and said, "Tell us a story."

"Yes," the others agreed.

Vesa had filled her son's mind with legends of Greek gods; fearsome tales of forest trolls from her childhood, and still more folk tales from Athens. He learned them all as a child at his mother's knee. Many evenings the Lipovans in their encampment would gather to listen to Geaad's retelling of his mother's stories. Although secretly she understood it, Vesa stubbornly refused to speak the tribe's language.

Rather, with a mother's pride, she glowed in the attention given to her son.

Prut again spoke. "Geaad, tell us the story of the lion and the boar. I like that one."

Geaad smiled and began, *"On a summer day, when the great heat of the high sun induced a general thirst, a Lion and a Boar came at the same moment to a small pond to drink. They fiercely disputed which of them should drink first. Soon they were engaged in the agonies of a mortal combat. On their stopping to take breath before the fierce renewal of the strife, they saw some vultures waiting in the distance to feast on the one who should fall first. The Lion and the Boar at once made up their quarrel, saying: "It is better for us to be friends than to become the food of crows or vultures."*

Buco the youngest, asked Geaad, "What does that mean?"

Not waiting for Geaad, the impulsive Prut replied, "It means, stupid, that arguments or fights are often watched by others who will take advantage of the loser's defeat to benefit themselves."

Geaad was pleased. Often the tales Vesa told to him were just frightening stories. Sometimes there was a point, a reason for the story. Prut had remembered this one correctly but Geaad knew he really didn't understand it. Over and over Vesa had make clear to him that most males were dim-witted and he should always try to use this mental weakness for his personal advantage.

At the second dawn they awoke to a thunderous sound. The cloud they had chased the day before was moving directly toward them. As it drew closer they could see uncountable strange beasts stampeding in their direction. "What are they?" Prut asked. He looked to Geaad for the answer.

"I think they are wild cattle called aurochs. They are much more dangerous than anything on our side of the river. Their big horns will gore you to death."

"They are coming right at us. We'll be trampled. What can we do Geaad?"

For a moment Geaad was speechless. Then he remembered his mother's talk of the Moirai, the goddesses called The Fates. If such gods existed it would not be up to the four of them as to who might live or die. It had already been decided. They could waste the last minutes of their lives running fruitlessly away or stand bravely and wait a trampling death. "We stand and wait like men," Geaad said.

Without reason, the herd suddenly veered away from the three Lipovans and Geaad. "It is Zeus," Geaad cried. "He has taken away the power of The Fates to end our lives. We are saved by **Zeus the supreme god Lord of the Sky, the Cloud-gatherer, the Rain-god and the Thunderer. Praise Zeus my friends."** They all understood what had happened. Many evenings Vesa, using her son as the translator had told stories of the gods. Privately she told Geaad that most gods were just myths accepted by foolish people. Still, Vesa believed in the Moirai and Zeus.

As the dust cloud cleared Vilk shouted a warning to the others, "Many hunters are chasing the herd. Look, I think they see us."

All recognized the new danger. Tribes often fought over many things but hunting territory was always defended viciously. The four boys were the invaders. They would be killed.

Geaad shouted, "Run!" As they fled, the hunters divided into two groups. The larger group continued to chase the aurochs while twenty or so hunters moved towards the boys. There was little cover in the trampled grasslands to hide but their youthful strength gradually distanced them from their pursuers. By nightfall, exhausted, they felt safe enough to stop in a scrub pine area on the side of a small hill. They could see in the direction from which they had fled. There was no one chasing them any longer.

The four were still terrified. Buco could not stop shaking. He was sick to his stomach and staggered with leg cramps. Prut helped him to a small stream where he could soak his legs in the cool water. Then hungry they huddled together to sleep. With the next dawn, Vilk found some berries for them to eat while Buco again returned to the stream to soak his legs.

"We should return to the delta," Prut said.

"Yes," Geaad agreed. "But we must circle widely to keep away from those hunters tracking the herd. I think we are no longer in danger from those men. They gave up on us."

"We are stronger too. If there were not so many of them we could have fought them and..." Vilk did not finish his words. With only a slight thud an arrow had pierced his throat under one ear and the point popped out the other side of his neck. He fell dead to the grassy earth. Geaad and Prut both turned and ran away from the source of the arrow. More arrows flew at them. One struck Prut in the leg and he went down. The attackers swarmed and quickly pounced on him. He fought back momentarily with his knife. But now from a distance, Geaad quickly looking back could only see that his friend was now being stabbed over and over by this group of men.

Geaad continued to run. He was followed by just one ugly brute of a man. Occasionally he heard a word of his mother's native tongue shouted by his pursuer. The word meant 'slaughter or destroy.' The other words he could not understand except once he heard the man call the name of his father, 'Agar'. The man thought that Geaad was Agar? Why?

Gradually the man chasing Geaad gained ground. He was long legged and Geaad realized that he could not outrun him. He stopped. He knew he would have to fight. Each had knives and began circling the other as they gathered their breath. The attacker screamed words that Geaad could not understand except for the word 'destroy' and the name Agar. Geaad had the wiry speed of youth but he had never been in a serious fight. His foe was big and clumsy but was covered with battle scars.

Zeus save me, Geaad thought as the big man lunged for him. Geaad quickly sidestepped and parried the knife thrust with his own weapon. He received a cut on the arm that caused him to drop his knife.

Events moved so fast that Geaad could scarcely recall exactly what happened next. He had groped for his fallen knife but couldn't locate it. As the aggressor lunged again, Geaad threw a fistful of sand in the man's eyes. As the thug halted Geaad was able to strike him in the head with a rock. Later Geaad discovered he had apparently beaten the man's skull to a pulp with the stone he was still holding in his fist. He couldn't remember how he had done that. Sobbing he fell away from the sprawled body. He vomited. This was the first human being he had ever killed.

It was a long time before Geaad was able to stand. His legs wobbled and his mind swam with emotions of a rage he didn't recognize. Next he was flooded with regret for the lives of Vilk and Prut. Suddenly the thought came to him that Buco might still be alive. He could not desert his friend. He would return to the place where they had camped the previous night and find him.

Geaad had run wildly to escape the man who had tried to kill him. It took the rest of the day to locate the small hill where the four had stayed the previous night. Coming towards the mound from a slightly different direction he saw a walled encampment on the other side of the hill. Amazingly they had spent the night right next to a hunter-gatherer village! This had to be where the man he had killed once lived.

Buco was not at the stream. The bodies of his other two friends were still where they had fallen. Could Buco have been captured? Geaad found a place of concealment in the fading light of sundown. He would find a way to save his friend. For now he would stay hidden. Once during the night, he heard a scream from inside the compound. It might have been Buco. He could only wait.

With the earliest gleam of dawn, Geaad crept towards the protective wall. There were no sounds from inside. Then he saw it. Stuck on a pole above the rampart was Buco's head. Geaad turned and blindly ran away. He had lost all of his friends.

The journey back to the Lipovan territory was long and arduous. Geaad determined that he had to go up river, in hopes of finding a narrower crossing. He also had to hunt to continue to exist. He needed to avoid the native encampments. Once he encountered a hunter who mouthed the word "Agar" and tried to spear him. Geaad took a second life in order to survive.

Finally, able to cross the river, he made his way to the delta and the Lipovan encampment. As he neared, the absolute stillness shocked him. Had they all gone somewhere else? Then he saw it, bodies everywhere. They were all his Lipovan friends. None were wounded but all were dead. There was no sign of an attack...no strangers among them. It had happened some time ago as the bodies were decaying and many showed signs of violation by scavenger animals. In just a few frantic moments he found Vesa, his mother.

He sat by her and cried inconsolably. Vesa meant more than life to him. He stood over her body and recited the brief words that he had learned at the death ceremony of a Lipovan:

"From the land of yearning

To that without yearning

From the land of pity

To that without pity!"

He dug deeply into the soft earth and buried her. There was nothing he could do for the rest of the tribe. They were far too many to bury. He left them for the scavengers. Geaad would now follow his mother's wishes and go south. He would find the man called Thorax and kill him to avenge her. Next, he would find a way to the Minotaur and kill that horrible god-man beast.

As he hiked the long distance to Athens, Geaad found that he could easily earn the shelter of the more civilized tribes along the way. He employed his skills as a story teller. His fame began to precede him. He would tell many of the tales his mother had passed on to him about the strange gods in her childhood tribal lands. Groups were eager to be entertained. He could also perform some of the juggling tricks she had taught him.

Vesa had made sure that Geaad understood that most of these tales were myths made up by men frightened by the world around them. They needed to believe in some higher powers. Vesa herself believed only some small parts of the legends and taught her son that much of it was folktale. Still, Geaad found that the tribes he met were happy to hear of the many gods that inhabited their world and the nether world. He realized that story-telling gave him status. He was amazed that his listeners would believe almost anything.

His blonde hair and fair looks also helped. Some called him 'Agar.' He finally understood that 'Agar' was not a name but rather he resembled, especially with his long blond hair, all the men who had mistreated his mother. Agars were his tribal relatives.

Now, over and over, Geaad repeated his favorite stories to the eager but unintelligent people who traded food and shelter for the entertainment he would bring them. His very favorite story was 'The Valkyries'. He told it often.

"Valkyries are female deities with wings. After each battle they choose Lone Fighters who have died heroically in combat. They bring the slain fighters to a sacred mountain where they serve them wine to drink and give them their fill of the meat from a nightly-resurrecting beast that lives only with the gods. Then these Heroic Fighters prepare for a daily battle among the gods where many of the gods are vanquished. This battle causes various natural disasters, and it is the reason for a terrible flooding of the world with water. Afterward, the world resurfaces anew and becomes fertile, the surviving gods meet, and the world is repopulated by two human survivors."

Geaad had many legends, myths and fables to share. He learned new tales as he traveled towards Athens. His story telling skills improved immeasurably over time. He found he could almost hypnotize these simple people. Stories of strange beasts, afterlife with gods and goddesses and just ordinary myths fascinated every listener. With his nimble mind he even began to create legends on his own. Everything he said to his rapt audiences was believed as truth. Men *were* stupid.

When he finally reached Athens it had proved to be no surprise. It was as Vesa had described it. The small Minoan colony did not impress him. As he had worked his way south on his deadly mission to kill Thorax, he encountered increasing numbers of stone houses grouped in larger and larger villages. The inhabitants were generally peaceful people with small herds of sheep and patches of cultivated land. The country was tamed and civilized.

Upon arriving in Athens he found that Thorax had died months earlier. He had reached the end of his journey and his self-imposed task was impossible to accomplish. Why then had The Fates brought him here?

Sitting on a rock slab, staring at the gentle waves lapping the shore, he failed to notice a man who had come up behind him. "You, are you Geaad-the-Agar?'" the man demanded.

"Who asks," Geaad replied in an equally defiant tone. He stood to face the man and received a sudden hard blow to his stomach which felled him to the ground.

"Don't you dare challenge me slave! Now answer me, are you Geaad-the-Agar?"

Struggling to get his wind, Geaad slurred an affirmative to the man standing over him. For the first time he saw there were others with him. Finally he mumbled "Why?" to his abuser.

"Because I own you. You are now my slave and I am your new master. Now follow me. We are boarding the ship out in the harbor. I am taking you to King Minos on Crete."

On this forced sea voyage, Geaad learned several things. Someone in Athens had claimed that they owned Geaad. The man who paid for Geaad explained that he was chief steward for King Minos. He possessed great official power and was second only to Minos. His name was Acastus.

Geaad was brash enough to challenge Acastus. He demanded to know how he could be sold as a slave when no one owned him. Why was he being taken to Crete? Was he to be sacrificed to the Minotaur, a fate from which his mother had escaped? He would jump into the sea first!

Acastus roared with laughter. "No you are not to be fed to the Minotaur. I had heard about you from a number of people in Athens. They told me that you are an exceptionally good story teller and you know a great deal about the gods. My King Minos needs a person such as you to entertain him in his court. Do well and you will be handsomely rewarded. Now tell me some of your stories, Geaad-the-Agar"

Patience, Geaad thought. *The Fates and this foolish steward are taking me to the Minotaur. I will be where I want to be and kill the beast for my mother.* Geaad began to weave his story telling magic for the officers of this very large ship. It had one huge sail and many oarsmen. He learned that the Minoan power was in their vast navy. They ruled the oceans. Except for occasional pirates, who lived on the many small islands in this part of the sea, no one dared to challenge them. Crete was the center of the universe according to Acastus.

Arriving at the island kingdom, Acastus' true power was immediately evident. He had not exaggerated. The master of the port displayed a group of pirate prisoners. Prostrating himself, he asked Acastus if they should become slaves or simply hung.

"Did they pillage and murder before you caught them" Acastus asked.

"Yes my lord. And they…"

"Enough. I do not need to hear it. Torture them first with hot irons and then hang them."

Acastus did not wait for the punishments. He told Geaad to follow him. They had to take a long walk in order to reach the palace of Minos. It was called the Labyrinth in a town named Knossos.

"That is where the Minotaur lives. You ARE going to feed me to the monster!"

Acastus laughed. "No you thick barbarian. I told you the truth. I paid the slave price for you to entertain King Minos. The Labyrinth is our temple, our government house, and the home of Minos and all his court. It is the largest building in the world. You will see it just over the next hill.

Geaad chafed at the thought that he had been bought and that Acastus thought of him as a slave. *He would settle with...*

The thought was lost as he came over the rise and saw the Labyrinth. Geaad was speechless. Nothing in his travels had prepared him for the sight of this structure.

Acastus snorted. "Now you see barbarian why we rule the world."

"It is so big," Geaad sputtered. "No wonder the Minotaur is lost in such a structure"

"You are not as intelligent as I believed Geaad-the-Agar. Tell me did you ever see a woman-goddess with snakes coming out of her hair? Did you? Or did you ever see a half-man half-goat? I think not! But still you tell a story about a Satyr. Do you believe your own myths? No! I am sure you understand that you are weaving lies."

Geaad was suddenly aware that Acastus was not as gullible as most of his other listeners. This was the first intelligent man he had ever met. Still he was worried. "But the Minotaur..." he asked.

"Geaad-the-Agar, story-teller, listen and learn. There is no such beast as the Minotaur. This is an old myth started long before I was born. Most everyone believes it, even King Minos."

"But why...?"

"Because my thick barbarian, people are easier to control when they fear something. Have you not have already learned that whatever you tell the ignorant peasants they believe. Tell me is that not true?"

"Yes, that is true" Geaad sullenly replied.

"Well if King Minos can keep his people safe from this monster then he has their loyalty and obedience. Fear, especially of the unknown, makes them docile"

"But," Geaad wondered aloud with some awareness and anger, "what of the youths from Athens that are sent to you every year as a feeding sacrifice. What happens to them? Are they here?"

"Of course not, you dolt! You are beginning to make me believe that you are too stupid for my needs. These blonde Agars are ceremoniously paraded through Knossos. They are showered with flowers and honored by all the people. Then one-by-one they are taken to a ceremonial room in the temple part of the Labyrinth. There a high priest wearing a large mask made from a bull's head, slits each barbarian's throat and their bodies are buried in a deep chamber under the temple section of the Labyrinth. They are never seen again. They have been sacrificed to the Minotaur, instead of any of the people from Knossos. Only a few high priests know of this."

"Why do you trust me with this lie, Acastus?"

"On board ship I found you to be devious enough so that you will withhold such truth about the monster. You could accidently learn the reality of the beast and cause problems for King Minos. I can't have that. I brought you here to entertain, to keep Minos out of my way while

I run his kingdom. I need time to gain enough power to stop one of his sons from becoming the next Minos after that old man dies. That will be very soon. He is half-witted now in his old age."

Geaad could feel that he was gaining some power from this conversation. Again he asked, "Why trust me with this information?"

Acastus scowled. "If you betray me Geaad, I will have you killed very, very slowly. Do not doubt that. I have powers and friends that Minos and the members of his royal family do not possess. You will do what I tell you, when I tell you."

"Could you not just kill Minos and take the throne?"

"Story-teller you have yet a great deal to learn. I am a politician. I know how to make things work using other people. I know how to play one of Minos sons against another…without killing any of them or getting myself murdered. When I am ready, everyone will welcome me as the new Minos. You will help me. For that help you will be vastly rewarded. But if you betray me, then you will die painfully in a way I will not even describe." Acastus' demeanor left no doubts that the warning was genuine.

Geaad did not see the threatening steward again for a number of months. Acastus had turned him over to a eunuch named Pippo, instructing the old man to teach Geaad-the-Agar in the ways of the Labyrinth Royal Palace. Geaad was installed in a large apartment next to Pippo. He was given new luxurious clothes to wear, rings for his fingers and a young female for his use.

Pippo taught him the customs of the court and the habits of its members. He was especially keen on sharing the gossipy tidbits about the royals. Minos he learned, was both hard of hearing and could no longer see well. Many of the courtiers, plus Minos two oldest sons, were drunkards. The third son Cronus was to be feared. Pippo felt Cronus was insane. Acastus often had to step in to correct or modify a foolish royal edict that Cronus promoted. Cronus in turn hated Acastus.

The palace itself was a wonder. Geaad had never imagined a building so large. In some places it was six stories tall. The architect-builder, Daedalus, had hot and cold water somehow coming through clay pipes into many of the palace rooms. There was even a system of pipes to carry away human waste. But Daedalus currently was out of favor with the palace and had fled with his son to a large island to the west called Sicily. Cronus had somehow been a part of the difficulty.

Although only eunuchs were permitted to the royal harem, Pippo made a point to disguise Geaad and sneak him into the forbidden chambers. The style of dress of the female Minoans had initially been a bit of a shock to the barbarian. Geaad was accustomed to seeing men and women naked, but the Minoan women favored skirts of three colors worn to just below the exposed breast. It was somehow enticing. Then too, the opulence of the women's quarters simply astounded him.

"Master, I have taken Geaad-the-Agar into the harem. I disguised him as one of the queen's eunuchs."

Acastus asked, "Are you sure some of your most trusted eunuchs recognized him and can testify that he was there?"

"Absolutely, master. I have done just as you commanded me. I also perceived he was quite enamored by the women. He had some trouble keeping his youthful desires under control." The two men laughed.

On a festive occasion Pippo took Geaad to a large outdoor arena. It was filled with more people than he had ever seen in one place.

Suddenly the crowd roared as a bull with gigantic horns entered the enclosed circle. Geaad recognized the animal as the same type that stampeded when his friends lost their lives. It was an auroch.

Two men, and one woman who was dressed as a man, entered the ring and began to taunt the bull. The frenzied animal charged the woman. As the bull lowered its head she leaped upward and grasped the treacherous horns. With a natural reaction, the bull lifted its head and the woman was thrown over the back of the animal and caught by one of the male performers. The throng roared approval.

"She is one of the very best acrobats in Kenosis," Pippo said. "Many times the jumper loses his or her footing and is gored or even killed."

"I am surprised that so many people have the freedom to be here Pippo."

"We are very rich here in Crete. We have time for sport," the old man replied.

After lengthy final preparations Geaad-the-Agar was finally brought to King Minos. He had to shout to the drooling old man to be heard. Soon he learned that simpler stories were the best for the aged king. Minos could not concentrate for any length of time. Quickly Geaad became the King's favorite entertainer and hardly a day passed that Minos did not call for Geaad-the-Agar. But since he had only so many tales to tell he was gradually forced to repeat stories. Cronus began to object.

"You've told that tale too many times, Geaad-the-Agar." Cronus' tone was intimidating.

Pippo dutifully reported Cronus anger to his master Acastus.

"Good," Acastus beamed. "I knew that hot headed Cronus would bate the trap for us. Now here are the instructions that you pass on to Geaad-the-Agar. Tell him you saw this trick in a royal court in Palestine or somewhere else, and everyone enjoyed it. Have Geaad-the-Agar use it on Cronus."

As directed, Pippo told Agar what he might do the very next time Cronus complained.

"Again Geaad-the-Agar, You have told the story of the Cyclops several times. I…we will not hear it again. Either something new or we will replace you."

Minos frowned at Cronus but did not speak for the story teller.

"Yes, my lord," Agar replied. Thinking quickly of Pippo's suggestion he said, "Stand beside me Lord Cronus for something quite different."

Cronus cautiously moved beside Geaad and both faced Minos and most of the court. As Geaad said a few more words, he reached behind Cronus and tapped him on the far shoulder. Cronus turned in that direction and with a puzzled look found no one there. Minos roared with laughter. A few moments later Geaad repeated the motion and Cronus again found no one was there. The court was regaled that Cronus had been made to look foolish. Cronus, however, would not forget this insult to his royal person. Geaad-the-Agar would pay with his life for this embarrassment.

Geaad immediately recognized that he had made a grievous error and had foolishly humiliated a royal person of great power. Could Acastus protect him from the royal wrath? He begged Pippo to take him to see Acastus immediately.

"Tell him I am not available Pippo. This has gone exactly as planned. Cronus will kill the tale-teller and that will make Minos angry enough to banish his son. Then I will be free to take the crown when the old man dies."

"But lord, what of Geaad-the-Agar?"

Acastus beamed. "We can always find another story teller. They come cheaply, just like eunuchs."

Pippo smoldered at Acastus words. He had given a lifetime of obeisance to this man. True, he had lived well and managed to steal a great deal, but to be so devalued? It was a mortal blow to his ego. He also had come to like the barbarian. He would take steps to protect him..

"Geaad-the-Agar, do you trust me?"

"Yes Pippo. You have been very good to me."

"Well story-teller that was not my question. Now listen to me. You need to fear for your life. Let me explain what is really happening here."

Geaad was shocked that Acastus was simply using him as a tool to remove Cronus. Now he was going to be murdered and no one would protect him, except Pippo perhaps.

"Why are you telling me all of this Pippo?"

"I have reasons of my own Geaad-the-Agar. Now this is what you must do. I have forged papers with the Royal Seal making you an ambassador from King Minos to the Pharaoh of Egypt. Here is a satchel with enough gold to bribe anyone who gets in your way. There is a ship in the harbor leaving today. Be on it. Go to Egypt and never return to Knossos. I give you your life."

Geaad put his left hand to his nose and pulled downward. He pondered for only a few moments before leaving for the docks.

Once again The Fates had intervened in his destiny.

Twelve

Geaad Egypt

Khyan awoke early. The rose colored light of an early summer dawn was streaming into his sleeping chamber. Immediately he sensed it was going to be another cloudless and stifling morning in Memphis. Gladly, in just a few days, he and his court would be moving to the summer palace at Avaris. There they would feel some of the cool breezes of the Mediterranean Sea.

Pharaoh Khyan was the king of Lower Egypt. His tribal clan, called Hyksos, had been invited into Egypt hundreds of years earlier to labor on the many enormous monuments favored by the Pharaohs. A flood of Hyksos people came from the lands of the eastern Mediterranean. They had been nomads who tended flocks of sheep in the Levant…a land of many tribes in constant conflict. In Egypt these new settlers found servitude but with peace and security.

The Hyksos in turn dissolved many of the cultural barriers of Egyptian isolation. With natural sand and water obstructions on all sides, the Egyptians had lived in limited seclusion for millennia. The

Hyksos brought new concepts to the peoples of the Nile. They introduced better war chariots, an improved bow, horses, and even new cultural concepts...the peaceful music of the lyre. Best of all they came with an innate sense of organization to better configure the hodgepodge vassal structures of the Egyptian administrative society.

As generations passed, the Hyksos used these managerial abilities to control more and more of the Delta region's political structure. Eventually they became powerful enough to install one of their own tribesmen as Pharaoh in place of a native Egyptian. These usurpers had now ruled Lower Egypt, the Delta lands, for the lifetimes of several Hyksos Pharaohs. The fragmented political powers of traditional Egypt had no way to stop their invited guests from becoming their rulers.

Yet the Hyksos were not fools. They espoused the custom and dress of the Egyptians, even converting their ancient god Ba'al into the Egyptian god Seth. Still they were not powerful enough to rule all the lands of the Nile River. Upriver from the Delta, Egyptian Pharaoh Seqenenre, from his capital of Thebes, controlled Egypt southward from the edge of the Hyksos delta kingdom to the first cataract. There were two Pharaohs and two Egypts, both existing at the same time along the great River Nile. The native Egyptians of the Delta understood that they had been conquered by alien masters without even a fight. They called the Hyksos 'hook-noses' behind their backs. Pharaoh Seqenenre equally hated these foreigners who imposed themselves on Egypt's sacred lands. He was not powerful enough to drive them out.

Pharaoh Khyan started every morning by meeting with his Grand Vizier Menka. Over a light breakfast meal of figs and beer they would discuss important matters of state in the Delta kingdom. This particular morning Khyan complained bitterly about the lack of his favorite gazelle meat in his morning meal. Menka let him rant. It was useless to try and stop him. Menka only half-listened while thinking, *what an idiot! How did this man ever become Pharaoh? I could assassinate this fool and run this kingdom in many, many better ways.*

Vizier Menka held his tongue. It was the vizier's job to handle the daily operating details of the country. He knew he had more power than this dolt of a pharaoh. The Pharaoh, who was considered a god by most Egyptians, ignored details. You did not kill gods. Besides, his position as grand vizier provided rich rewards. He had women and slaves plus a few eunuchs. All would do his bidding in the nicest palace in Memphis, close by the Great Pyramid of Cheops.

No, it would not be worthwhile to destroy Khyan. It would set an example that, in turn, might cause others to kill me. I can easily grovel before Khyan. It is a price well worth paying in order to maintain my position. After all, we are both only Hyksos...certainly not gods.

Menka scoffed at the Egyptian gods. But secretly, he still worshiped the old Hyksos god Ba'al. He also worshiped one Egyptian deity named Bast, the cat goddess, the protector of the royal household. Bast had brought him a great deal of luck. To honor her, several cats lived in his palace, often with better care than he gave his slaves.

Suddenly Menka realized that Pharaoh Khyan had stopped talking. "What," he said. "I am sorry lord. I was lost in thought about an important matter."

"What is that?" Khyan asked, much annoyed.

Menka made noises as if he were chewing a fig. He was trying to bring his thoughts back to the present moment. "Lord Khyan," he said, "I have a somewhat serious concern this morning."

"What!" Pharaoh said a second time. This small fat man was always short tempered.

"It is about some of the Egyptians of Pharaoh Seqenenre. Those people who live at the border of our territory with Thebes. A large group of them have attacked our southernmost outpost at Cusae and killed most of our soldiers there."

"What!" Khyan exclaimed a third time, but now with a tinge of fear in his voice. "Is this an invasion?"

What a coward, the vizier thought. He said, "I think not sire. Some farmers were attempting to infringe on our cattle grazing lands. Our soldiers stopped them. The Egyptians rioted and suddenly stormed our small fortress. Their numbers were too great and we were overwhelmed. Only a few of our troops escaped."

Khyan exploded. "They ran away…Hyksos running from Egyptians who are not even soldiers…just farmers. I want those cowards punished…I want them executed. Do you hear me Menka! I want them dead!" Khyan was now screaming.

The vizier nodded in apparent agreement knowing that he would not carry out the order. The fleeing soldiers had provided valuable information. This Pharaoh was an ass.

"Menka we must respond to this violation. What can we do?"

"Sire, I have a plan. Let me tell you about it."

Geaad-the-Agar, faux ambassador of King Minos, had entered Egypt. He sailed up the Nile River using as credentials the commission forged by Pippo. The ship finally reached Memphis, the capitol city of the Delta Pharaoh. Then it had taken many weeks and several bribes of Hyksos officials before he was finally allowed to meet Vizier Menka.

Menka was immediately impressed by the size and diplomatic demeanor of this blonde barbarian from Crete. He accepted the phony credentials that Geaad presented and offered him temporary living quarters in his palace. Menka did not let on that he was already aware of the royal difficulties on Crete. He needed to know more. Several days later he arranged for a supposed private get-together for Geaad and another recently arrived traveler from Crete...Pippo. The meeting was going to be secretly monitored by a servant who understood the Mycenaean language.

"Pippo, you are here! What happened? Why? Tell me." Geaad was shocked to see a friendly face. He spoke out with almost incoherent babbling.

With a finger to his lips for quiet, Pippo motioned that they sit and talk in low tones while the servant brought fruit and chilled wine. "Master there was a terrible fight after you departed from Kenosis. I believe that Cronus tried to kill all of Acastus's retainers including me. It was punishment for the way you embarrassed him in front of the royal court. That hot-head Cronus also tried to kill Acastus. The two of them dueled with knives. Somehow, they both died from the fight. I have seen enough blood. Since I suspect there will be more, I escaped to join you here in Egypt. With my master Acastus gone, I have no future in Crete. Here in Egypt I am hoping you can protect me"

Geaad wagged his head in disbelief. The news was astounding. Yet there was more. "Pippo, why are you calling me 'Master'? There is no reason..."

With head bowed, the eunuch whispered his reply. "If you are going to live here as the ambassador then I must...I must be your servant. Please accept me in order that I may also live. I saved you, now you must save me."

Pippo took a deep breath mentally reviewing his harrowing escape from Crete and then continued, "I have been here many weeks trying to find you. I heard from a friend arriving from Crete, that the old King Minos died a short while after I left. One of his two remaining sons, the one that was almost always drunk, imprisoned his brother in the Labyrinth and took the crown for himself. I am told the Minotaur killed the brother in the Labyrinth"

"Oh Pippo, that part is a lie. There is no such animal-god as the Minotaur. It is just one of the high priests wearing a bull's mask. It is terrible for me to think that I caused all this trouble with a simple trick we played on Cronus. I caused many men to die"

Pippo move his body from side to side and made a clucking sound. "Master, remember I told you how to do that trick. It was not your fault. Acastus ordered me to tell you to play that joke on Cronus. Acastus had a plot to make himself king and you were just part of it. He is really the one to blame."

"What is wrong with these people Pippo? They are royalty and already have so much power? Why do they kill for even more of it? It must be a sickness"

The servant reported the details of the conversation to a pleased Menka. It had confirmed his suspicion that Crete was weak and not an invasion threat to the Delta. Certainly some drunken king who had killed his brother would not be able to manage it. True, he was quite surprised to learn that the Minotaur was not real. It was a powerful legend. Finally he decided, as he had often done in the past, to keep Geaad and Pippo under his control to use for some unknown future activity. The two men from Crete were given luxurious clothes, gold rings, servants and a fine apartment to share in Menka's palace.

To keep them busy, Menka sent the two out as tourists to see the nearby sights of Memphis. Because Menka's palace was hard by the giant pyramids, the first trip was but a short journey. After living in the Labyrinth in Crete, Geaad found that the sizes of the Egyptian monuments were even more breathtaking. They spent many days watching the construction process of a new tomb.

Geaad said, "It is amazing to see how they move those gigantic blocks of stone. They work so hard. These men can't all be slaves?"

"Some are slaves," Pippo answered. "The black men are captured warriors from the Kingdom of Kush from the far south. The Egyptian Pharaoh at Thebes has been at war with Kush for years. His land is trapped between that Nubian kingdom and the Hyksos Pharaoh here in Memphis. He often sells the black captives to the Delta Pharaoh Khyan. The native Egyptians are different. They work only to get a share of the eternal life granted to the god-man Pharaoh Khyan. Even the Nubian slaves work for that same reward."

"Stupidity!" Geaad spat out the word. "There is no eternal life. We all decay into the earth. I have never yet met a man who is a god."

"Don't say that to the Egyptians," Pippo sternly warned. "They truly believe their Pharaoh is a god. These are a simple people. You know false beliefs are everywhere. Was it not so with the Minotaur in Crete? Now, come and walk with me Master Geaad to the other side of this pyramid. I will show you something, a real something, to rival the Labyrinth's fake monster."

The day was particularly hot and dusty. Geaad grumbled as they strode over the burning sands. This land was un-imaginably warm compared to the cool forests of the Lipovans. Finally a new object came into sight. It was a gigantic statue that had the body of a lion and the head of a man. The Agar had never seen anything like it. "Is this another tomb?" he asked.

"No master. I have learned that this is all one piece of stone carved from solid rock. It is very old…older than the pyramids. Some say it was here before the native Egyptians occupied the land. It is called 'The Sphinx', for a reason that no one can explain to me."

"Is it one of their gods?" Geaad asked.

"No," Pippo replied.

What a strange people and a strange land, Geaad thought.

As time passed at the house of the Vizier, Geaad, always accompanied by Pippo, was encouraged to go forth and tour more of the Delta kingdom. These rich lands were formed by many mouths of the Nile River. This prosperous agricultural region was completely controlled by the Hyksos Pharaoh. As Menka anticipated, both men easily learned the customs of the districts. Geaad became fluent in the native language.

With an increasing level of confidence, Vizier Menka began to use Geaad on small political missions. Geaad carried directives to the subordinate Hyksos officials in various parts of the Delta. He never failed to impress the local leaders…his size accompanied by a startling blonde appearance made his diplomatic tasks trouble-free. Menka was pleased. He was developing someone who might be of value for future unknown assignments. After only a little more than two years, Geaad was well indoctrinated in the customs and policies of Pharaoh Khyan's lands. The forethought to train Geaad began to blossom into some possible glorious opportunity for the Hyksos.

Pharaoh Khyan spoke firmly. "We have to punish those damnable Egyptians from Thebes. They cannot be allowed to kill the soldiers of our outpost. If the deed goes unpunished, they will think us to be weak and perhaps try to take our lands. Do you have a plan Vizier Menka?"

"Yes sire, I do have a plan."

Khyan, with a look of angry impatience, bellowed, "Tell me the plan, you fool!"

Menka smiled. "Lord Khyan, a few years ago I welcomed into my palace a giant blonde barbarian by the name of Geaad-the-Agar. He arrived with false credentials to become the ambassador of King Minos of Crete. I kept him under my control until I could determine what his true purpose was here in our land. I found that he had merely escaped a vengeful death in Crete. This man is very different in appearance from both Hyksos and the Egyptians, and for that matter, even the Mycenae people of Crete. Yet he has seemed extremely skillful as a diplomat, I decided to train him in our ways. I believed he might be somehow useful to us."

"Stop prattling Menka. What would you have him do? Get on with it."

"Lord Khyan, we both know that we are not yet powerful enough to conquer the Egyptian Pharaoh Seqenenre. Thebes has a well trained army experienced in their battles with the Nubians. They are a possible danger to your delta kingdom. I believe they do not want war with us at this time. If we risked a military assault to punish them for our lost outpost, we might very well lose all we have. They might conquer us and drive all Hyksos out of Egypt."

Pharaoh Khyan sighed deeply in agreement. He was well aware that all true Egyptians considered the Hyksos as invaders, even in his smoothly run kingdom. They could not expect support from the Delta Egyptians. He motioned Menka to continue.

Menka nodded. "Sire, I will send this blonde giant to Thebes as our ambassador. He will tell those fools that he represents an army of mercenaries hired by you. He will say that all of his troops are just like him. He will demand that Thebes pay us annual tribute or face consequences."

"For the loss of our soldiers and outpost…of course. That is brilliant"

"No sire. He will not even mention that incident."

"Wh…why, Menka?" the pharaoh sputtered.

"Because our loss was only men. He will make a higher demand from the gods. It will be a claim that Seqenenre cannot refute."

"Just what is this demand that your barbarian ambassador makes, Menka?"

"He…we will demand that the Thebans stop harpooning the hippopotamus in the Nile. That animal is sacred to our god Seth. Since you yourself are a god, Pharaoh, the dying cries of these sacred beasts keep you awake at night…even here in Memphis. It is your god-like duty to protect the animal. A large annual tribute payment will ease your conscience. Geaad will demand that tribute."

"Hmmm." Khyan pondered. "Those Thebans are stupid but still will they believe this? Seth is certainly a destructive god. That is one reason why we worship him as that animal. There is no doubt the hippopotamus is very vicious. Often I hear how they upset boats and kill the fishermen. Many of those animals roam the fields and destroy crops. I can understand why Pharaoh Seqenenre allows his people to kill them."

"Yes Lord, but you also are a god and the dying sounds of Seth's animals are disturbing to your nightly rest. Tribute will comfort you. My guess is that Pharaoh Seqenenre does not want war. He is too busy fighting the Nubians to his south. This will give him a holy reason to pay tribute to mollify another god. It will also quiet the warlike factions in his court who want to invade us."

"Tell me Menka, what happens if this ruse does not work?"

"I have another plan sire. There will be no war and we will be richer for it."

That evening Menka held his annual celebration to honor Ra, the king of the Egyptian pantheon of gods. All the nobles of Memphis were invited to this celebration. Geaad was included. Menka had not seen him in several weeks.

Geaad-the-Agar always came early to these banquets. He would immediately gorge himself on milk because it soured rapidly in the heat of the day. While there were many fish dishes to choose from in this aristocratic home of the Vizier, Geaad preferred rare meat, delicious water fowl, and fruit prepared with coconuts and olives. None of this fare was available to the common folk of the land. They subsisted mainly on bread and beer. Geaad cared little for the many wines served.

Geaad was well known to Pharaoh's court. He re-told the stories that his mother had taught him and many more that he had learned in Mycenae and Crete. He never made fun of Egyptian gods or demonstrated the trick that cost Acastus his life. Pippo often warned him about that but Geaad had matured. He was no longer an unsophisticated barbarian of the Lipovan tribe.

As was his custom, Menka came to the banquet after all of his guests had arrived. When he circulated through the crowd a look of horror came over his face. He saw Geaad. He almost leaped at the Agar screaming, "What have you done to yourself? You look like an Egyptian. Where is your blonde hair?"

Geaad was dumbfounded. Menka's rage was obvious. "I…I"

"Tell me you dolt," the Vizier screamed.

A hush now fell over all of the guests. None had ever seen Menka in such rage. Worried looks were exchanged.

"I...I had my retainers color my blonde hair dark so I might look more like the Hyksos and Egyptians. I...I thought you would be pleased."

"Idiot, I have a mission for you...not as Hyksos but as Geaad-the-Agar. You will be on a ship in three days for Thebes with your blonde hair bristling or you and your eunuch will be occupying a bed of hot coals outside my door. Do you understand?"

"Yes, sire" Geaad mumbled.

"Jibade!" Menka screamed for the captain of his guard. The man came running with his hand poised on the hilt of his sword. "Jibade, escort the Agar to his quarters. Guard his door. Then prepare a bed of hot coals. He soon may be required die on it."

As soon as he arrived in his apartment Geaad woke a sleepy Pippo and related what had just happened. What had he done wrong that disturbed the Vizier to the point where he was threatened with death? Why had the Fates deserted him?

Pippo on the other hand cared not a whit for the Fates. He was concerned about the hot bed of coals. He asked, "Who made your hair black, master?"

"My three slave girls. They told me that dark hair would look nice at the banquet."

With that Pippo screamed for the slave girls. "Did you change the master's blonde hair to black?"

The girls smiled...one giggled. "Yes. He looks more as an Egyptian prince should appear in the court."

Pippo changed their smiles to tears by beating each of them with a leather thong. "You will remove the dye and get his blonde color back. If you do not do it in three days I will personally strangle each of you. Do you understand?"

The wailing girls began immediately.

Pippo using his well practiced guile persuaded the Vizier to give them seven days. It was not needed. Geaad-the Agar was returned to his original complexion in only two short days.

"Jibade you are to take a troop of your best soldiers as an honor guard and sail to Thebes with Geaad-the-Agar and his servants and slaves. He is going to deliver an important message from Pharaoh Khyan to Pharaoh Seqenenre. After the message is delivered you will have one more duty to perform before you return. Now get them all aboard the boat and go immediately"

It took many days, sailing upriver, to reach Thebes. Each day was hotter than the next. The lush fields of the Delta were left far behind and the contracted fertile strip of green along the river narrowed and was noticeably poorer. Geaad also saw that a large contingent of the southern Pharaoh 's Egyptian cavalry was pacing them along the banks of the Nile. At night they beached the ship and set guards for prowling animals. Still, everyone knew the Theban cavalry unit was nearby.

Geaad was more than tired of the ship, when at last Thebes came into view. The shore near the dock was lined with a massive contingent of Egyptian foot soldiers. A short wiry looking young man, dressed in a robe with gold trim, came forward to meet them.

"You are Geaad-the-Agar, Ambassador to Pharaoh Khyan?"

The question was obviously not friendly, but Geaad replied evenly, "Yes. I am he. I have been charged to deliver a message to your Pharaoh Seqenenre. Now take me to him!"

"You give no orders here barbarian. I am Prince Ahmose, second son of Pharaoh Seqenenre. We already know the message you were to deliver. Now order your honor guard to stay aboard their ship. You and your personal party will follow me. You are all under arrest"

With those words Geaad, Pippo and their servants were quickly surrounded by a substantial number of soldiers and forced to march away from the river. They were taken to a high walled stockade guarded by well armed men. They were roughly forced inside. Heat was trapped by the enclosure and there was little shade. No one would talk to them or answer questions.

As they sat desolately on the hot sand Pippo grumbled, "They are going to slaughter us master."

"I think not Pippo. If that was their intent we would be dead now. Something is going on that we do not understand. How could that man Prince Ahmose know of the message I am, or rather I was, going to deliver?"

"Spies, master. The Thebans knew we were coming. They had an escort following us as soon as we left the Delta. Someone in Vizier Menka's house is a traitor to the Hyksos kingdom. But still, why are they treating us in this terrible way? You are an ambassador."

They waited.

After two full scorching hot days without food or water the weakest young female of Geaad's slaves died. The guards would not acknowledge Geaad's demands for help. They were forced back from the gate at spear point.

Finally on the dawn of the third day, guards brought water and food to the prisoners. The body of the deceased girl was also removed. A short time later Prince Ahmose arrived. He was as terse as he had been in their first meeting. "Geaad-the-Agar you are alive only by the generosity of my father, Pharaoh Seqenenre. Since you are not Hyksos, but only tools of that foul trickster Menka, you and your party will stay here in Thebes. You are not free. You are under house arrest and will do our bidding or die. Do you understand?"

Pippo was shaking like a leaf but Geaad stood tall and asked, "What of my honor guard?"

"They were Hyksos. They are all dead except their captain Jibade. He is now begging for death. He is a strong man. It took a long while to break him."

"You are torturing him? He is a good man."

"Ha! You are more stupid than I believed. This is why Menka picked you to carry his message? Geaad-the Agar, your man Jibade has already told us about your mission here. Now I will give you only one chance to tell me the truth. Are you really the leader of an army of giant barbarians, like yourself? Is this army poised to invade Thebes if we do not pay tribute to Pharaoh Khyan? Tell the truth or die now on this spot."

With these words Prince Ahmose men began to draw swords.

Dumbfounded that the Egyptian Prince knew so much, Geaad uttered a quiet "No. I am the only person like myself in the Hyksos kingdom. There is no army."

With a downward motion of his hand Ahmose directed his men to sheath their swords. "I think you have been played the fool Barbarian. Did you know that Jibade was ordered to slay you here in Thebes as reason to force us to pay even a larger amount of tribute to the Delta?

"What…what?"

"I see you did not know. Fine! Now I will direct that you and your party be taken to a house where you will find all your needs for a pleasant life. You will not be allowed to leave that house unless I send for you. If you step outside the walls of the house you will be killed by my guards.

"My father believes that you might be useful to us. I doubt it. Personally my choice would be to kill you all since you come from the Delta invaders of our lands. It is not my choice to make. Instead I leave you with a gift from that traitorous Jibade." He motioned to a slave who handed a small cedar box to Pippo. Then Ahmose turned quickly and left the stockade never giving Geaad the opportunity to question him.

Geaad and his group were immediately marched through the streets of Thebes to a large walled house. A guard unlocked the massive entrance door opening into the palmed courtyard. Somewhere a water fountain was to be heard. The guards did not enter.

Inside Geaad and his party found groveling Egyptian servants, plus a feast of food and a young personal slave to entertain Geaad. Everyone was astounded at the luxury presented to them. Pippo was the first to speak. "Master, I thought yesterday that that dog, Prince Ahmose, was going to murder us all, but now…this place is as rich a palace as Vizier Menka's."

"Pippo," Geaad said harshly, "watch your words. These servants are not ours. They may report everything we say to Ahmose."

The house was extensive. Pippo noted one unique feature…there was a single entrance to the house and no windows in the outside walls. It was palatial, but it was also a prison.

Later that day they dined luxuriously on an endless variety of rich foods. Pippo was especially fond of the watermelon laced with honey. As they ate, Geaad remembered the cedar package that Pippo had been given. He asked, "Pippo what did prince Ahmose's slave give you at the stockade…you know, the package from Jibade."

"I don't know master. In the excitement coming here I forgot all about it. Wait I will get it."

In just a few moments Pippo returned to the banquet and opened the box. His eyes bulged out. All the color drained out of his face, Next he vomited. The cedar box contained Jibade's ring…still attached to the finger.

The cloud of unknown terror hung over their heads. They were certain they could be killed at any moment. As the weeks dragged into months they learned that Pharaoh Seqenenre had died. He was immediately replaced by his oldest son Kamose. Now surely they would be liquidated. Nothing happened! Occasionally they heard tales that Pharaoh Kamose was attacking the Hyksos and warring in the Delta.

No one would take a message to Ahmose…the Egyptians servants all feared him. The months of captivity dragged on into years. Pippo became quite fat on the rich food. Geaad exercised constantly to stay in shape. Servants and even the slaves were changed frequently so it was not possible to strike up friendships. Both of the men from Crete were bored to death. Pippo occasionally talked of suicide.

Apparently someone in the household was conveying their feelings to ears outside the brown walls. A new set of servants introduced them to a game played on a board. The Egyptians called it 'Chess'. It occupied their minds in their luxurious jail.

At last there was a change. News began to arrive, brought in daily by the house steward. They understood that they were purposely being informed of events. Pharaoh Kamose was finally taking his war into the strongholds of the Hyksos in the Delta. Pippo often expressed fear that no matter who won the war...when it was over...they would be killed. They would be of no use to either side. Geaad simply ignored the old man's pessimism.

One evening in the seventh year of house arrest, after an especially large meal, Pippo complained of severe pain in his left arm. The next morning he was dead and Geaad was alone. Geaad wished that he could join his long time companion in the serenity of death. Then, the very next day, shocking news! Pharaoh Kamose had been killed in the final battle that had driven the Hyksos out of the Delta and back into the Levant. Ahmose became the new Pharaoh. One Pharaoh now controlled all the lands of the Nile. Calmly Geaad waited for the dreaded Ahmose to execute him. Still, nothing happened!

Another year went by before a new Vizier to Pharaoh Ahmose appeared at the door. He ordered Geaad to gather his belongings and come with him to the docks. Geaad was being released as a messenger going to Crete as the Pharaoh's representative. Pharaoh Ahmose understood that Geaad had knowledge of Crete and the royal court. He was given a sealed papyrus and was ordered to present it to King Minos. It seemed to Geaad that his gods, The Fates, had saved him once again.

Perhaps not!

Sailing deeply into the Mediterranean Sea, far from any shore, violent storms struck the large ship. It was blown far off course. On the third evening a strong gale tore the mast from its moorings and the boat began to founder. As the ship broke apart Geaad found himself in the water clinging to the top of a large piece of broken driftwood. It already carried the helmsman of the fated ship.

"Get away," the sailor screamed above the wind. "My raft will sink if you try to climb aboard. I will kill you first!" With those words he kicked violently at Geaad. His lunge sealed his fate. He lost his grip on the wood as another large wave rolled over them. Geaad now climbed onto the empty life-saving piece of wood and rode it into the roaring windy darkness. The helmsman was gone.

"Father, father, there is a man on the beach."

"Is he dead, is it a body?" Abrix asked.

"No father. He is crawling on the sand. He is naked. He has no weapons." She knew that her father feared armed strangers. He was not a fighter but rather an artist who made beautiful objects from gold. For reasons unknown to his daughter, he hated armed men.

Abrix decided to help this intruder thrown up on his shore. It was not his way, yet he somehow felt compelled to help this stranger. Geaad was half-carried to a tiny house in the small seaside village. He was placed on a pallet. Sometimes he rambled incoherently…most of the time he slept. It was many days before he was strong enough to speak, to begin to thank Abrix for saving his life.

"Where am I," he asked of his host.

"You are in the village of Akrotiri on the island of Thera," Abrix answered.

"This is not Crete?"

"No, this is Thera. This island is a three day voyage from Crete. We are subject to King Minos. You have business with him?"

"Yes. My name is Geaad and I have been sent by Pharaoh Ahmose of Egypt with a message for the King. Now I have lost the message and I don't know what I should do."

"Geaad-the-Agar, you should stay here in Akrotiri if you want to live. If you go to Kenosis, King Midas will feed you to the Minotaur. I hear it is a horrible death. You also have no life back on the Nile. Those Egyptian animals were sending you to your death"

"How do you know my name old man and how can you tell me all of this?"

"My name is Abrix. When we found you some days ago you had an oilskin pouch around your neck. My little daughter played with it and it fell open in her hands. Do you know that it contains your death warrant?"

"No, Abrix I did not know that. I cannot read the Egyptian markings. I cannot read at all. Why do you say these things? Tell me the words."

"It says that you are Geaad-the-Agar…and that is how I know your name. You are being traded to King Minos for a peace treaty with the Pharaoh. You are the gift to seal the pact. Even here on Thera we know King Minos has long wanted to kill you for whatever you did to his father."

"I did nothing to the old King Minos. He died shortly after I fled to Egypt." Geaad stammered as he told his story. Then a thought struck him. "Tell me Abrix, why have you not handed me over to the Minoans? If all this is true then you might expect a reward."

"That is possible Geaad-the-Agar. What I have told you, is what the message you carried said. I have not given you over to those Minoan bastards because I hate them. They took me and many others living here in Akrotiri away from our families back in Greece. We work on statues and carvings to decorate their palaces. We are artists but still basically slaves. Minos controls the seas and we have no way to escape back to our old homes. I think you might be trapped here, just as we are on this tiny group of islands. You might wish to stay here with our colony of stone and metal workers. While we cannot leave, life here is not unpleasant. It certainly is better than what might await you in the Labyrinth."

Geaad decided to stay with Abrix. Akrotiri was a pleasurable town populated with cultured Greeks who had been torn away from their homes by the Minoans. Actually it was the architect Daedalus who had caused their exile. They were the secret source of the wonders of art that he used to decorate the Labyrinth. King Minos did not know that this group existed. With Daedalus exiled, they were a lost community. Yet no one stopped or changed their support process from Crete. Fearful Minoan administrators never altered the directives of the deceased King Minos.

The Greek artist colony in Akrotiri enjoyed the stories Geaad told. He also taught some of the children to juggle. In turn the village hid him from the Minoans officials who arrived every two weeks with supplies and returned with finished art to Kenosis. The steep mountains behind the town kept Akrotiri further isolated from the rest of Thera's inhabitants. No path could cross the steep sharp lava hills. Therans were barely aware of the existence of Akrotiri.

Years passed and Geaad became immersed in the community. Occasionally the ground shook with earthquakes…sometimes violently. Abrix' oldest daughter fathered a boy child for Geaad when she became of age. Life was most pleasant.

As time went by, Geaad became accustomed to the occasional earth movements. Yet one day the earthquakes were much more severe. Over the top of the ridge, the towns' people could see a gigantic white cloud rising to the roof of the world. The gold metal worker Abrix shook his head in wonder. "I don't know what this is Geaad. The ground has shaken at other times but today is the very worst. What is that great cloud over the mountains? Could it be that gods of the underworld are fighting amongst themselves? They are ripping our world apart. In your travels have you ever been through something like this?"

Geaad shook his head negatively and said, "I will climb the mountain to look over the top. I want to know if our world is dissolving into Hades."

"You can't do that," Abrix said. "The cliffs are too steep and look...look there a big boulder is rolling down the mountain. You will be killed. Who then will take care of your woman and your child...my only grandson?"

Geaad turned, without comment, and started a slow lopping run up the mountainside. It was much more difficult than he had envisioned. Tremors moved the ground under his feet. Once, a rockslide nearly carried him away. Late in the afternoon he finally reached a point where he could see over the ridge. Below him there was chaos. Clouds of steam rose from the center of a lagoon. The waters were frothing and ships were being hurled onto the shore. He could see the entire ring of islands that made up Thera. Forests and the few houses on the far side of the lagoon were aflame. The gods of the underworld were battling. There was no doubt.

Quite suddenly the steaming water changed to fire. The white steam became black smoke. Geaad could see red flowing rock in the middle of the steamy lagoon. Another earth shock knocked him to the ground. A huge crack in the ridge almost sucked him into nothingness. The sounds and the heat were unbearable. Desperately he half slid...half crawled back down toward Akrotiri. He did not think The Fates would save him this time. He had looked into Hell.

As the sun was setting, suffocating white ash flakes with occasional burning embers began to cover everything in the little artist colony. Abrix hid his current work, a small solid gold statute of an ibex, under the floor of his house. He gathered his daughter and grandson, a few belongings, and with the rest of the town, moved to the water to escape the fire. The town's people had a few small fishing boats sitting on the beach. They were soon filled and sailed into the darkness. Many sunk with the weight of the falling hot ash. A large Minoan supply ship was at the dock but the crew refused to allow any of the stranded Greeks on board. It did not matter. The ship was destroyed by a direct hit from a burning volcanic fireball of ejecta.

It was the year 1575 B.C.

A BIT OF HISTORY

The explosion of the Thera Volcano destroyed more than half of the ring of islands formed from the exposed tops of a vast undersea caldera. It was one of the largest volcanic events in recorded history. The resulting tsunami may have ruined villages on costal Crete and destroyed most of the Minoan navy. It ended the power of the Minoan civilization in the eastern Mediterranean Sea.

Some believe that the eruption also caused a disastrous climate change marked by events recorded in Exodus as Egyptian plagues. This early book of the Bible was written approximately 150 years after Thera exploded.

It is also considered by some, that the Hyksos tribes eventually were transformed by history into a group that became known as the Hebrews.

In recent years archeologists found the village Akrotiri. Much of it is intact, similar to the ruins of Pompeii which was buried some 1600 years after the Thera eruption. Akrotiri was not destroyed but gradually covered by as much as two hundred feet of ash. No bones were found, indicating that the population had escaped.

In one house, that of a metal worker, a gold sculpture of a small ibex was discovered hidden under some flooring. This sculpture is on exhibit at the 'Museum of Prehistoric Thera' on the island presently called Santorini (Thera).

Thirteen

The Amber Road

"Uncle Mark, what is this funny little thing on Aunt Julie's curio shelf?"

"Oh that…that's called amber."

"It feels like plastic or stone. But that can't be stone. Oh my gosh, there's a weird bug inside it."

"Not a bug , it's a spider and it is not plastic."

"How did the bug…I mean the spider, get inside of a stone? It sort of feels like a stone. Is it a stone? Where did you get it? Tell me about it?"

"You certainly do have a lot of questions. Yes, I guess you can think of it as piece of rock or stone. It is called amber. Years ago you're Aunt Julie and I took a trip to a country called the Dominican Republic. That is a big island in the Caribbean Sea. It is one of the most famous places in the world to find amber. Another far more historic location for amber is in Europe on the Baltic Sea coast."

"Okay, but what is amber? How did the spider get inside there?"

"The spider didn't 'get in there'. The little bug must have been sitting under a pine tree millions of years ago. Some sap dropped from the tree and covered the spider with its sticky goo. The gooey sap got hard and eventually became that rocky piece of stone we now call amber."

"Wow...wow...Uncle Mark! That's like that old movie 'Jurassic Park'. You saw it didn't you? You must have seen it...you're old.

'In the movie, you remember, this scientist used dinosaur DNA. It came from a mosquito that sucked dinosaur blood. The scientist pried the mosquito out of a piece of this amber stuff and got the blood to make dinosaurs. Gosh, maybe we could grow giant pre-historic spiders. Where can we get more of this stuff? Do other people know about this amber thing?"

Mark smiled. "More than you know nephew. More than you know. Amber has been around for thousands of years. Ancient humans got it from the shores of the Baltic Sea in an area where today Poland and Lithuania meet.

"There were tribes of primitive people living up there on the Baltic Sea coast. They existed by hunting and fishing. But they were smart enough to trade amber, which was of no use to them, to the more refined regions thousands of miles south. These Baltic traders traveled over what was known as 'The Amber Road' to take their finds south."

"There was a real road?"

"No."

"They had to walk through thick forests populated with half-civilized tribes and wild animals. They crossed lands where Germany and a few other smaller countries exist today. They needed to get very far south to what we call today, Italy. But there was no Germany and there was no Italy back then. They did their trading for metal goods in the Po River valley. The ancient people living there, in that part of the world back then, were called Etruscans.

"Nobody knows where the Etruscans came from. It is one of those unsolved mysteries of ancient history. They were a sophisticated society. The Etruscans were skillful artists and knew how use the amber to make jewelry.

"So you see, amber has been around for a very long time. It was, and can be very expensive. Ancient civilizations prized the substance. Some of the amber pieces were even found all the way across the Mediterranean Sea in King Tut's tomb in Egypt."

"Gee Uncle Mark, even if amber was so valuable how could people walk that far to sell it? I know where the Baltic Sea is and I know where Italy is. I study geography in school. That trip would take them forever. I'll bet the roads were terrible."

"No, you are not paying attention. The roads were not bad because there were no roads. There were no countries. The Amber Road would have been no more than a path through dense forests and across rivers without any bridges. To tell you the truth…I don't know how anyone could do what our ancestors did. But you know what?"

"What?"

"Somehow they did it."

Fourteen

Reijo

Shape Shifters
400 B.C.

Eeva sat at the side of a small stream flowing gently to the brackish waters of the Baltic Sea. She had wrapped her arms around herself in loneliness and despair. The chill in the woodland air did not bother her at all. Sweet smells of pine needles went unnoticed. She sobbed quietly. She felt so alone.

There was an overwhelming sadness that defeated her, now even more often as she grew older. Living had never been easy. Time and again she considered ending her life. She could not rid herself of these crushing waves of deep despair.

As a blossoming young girl her father had traded her to a stranger for a mule. She could no longer remember the man's name.

Perhaps he never told her. She bore him many children, first Miikka, and then Heikka. After those two boys several more babies were born but all seemed to turn the color blue. Each then died soon after birth.

Much later a son she named Reijo survived birth, but he, like her own life, seemed to be trailed by tragedy. When Reijo was in this third summer a band of drunken outlaws from the east had raided their tiny settlement. Eeva's man was killed in the fierce fighting. She was brutally raped.

Seppo, a village trader in amber, lost his entire family in the raid and was himself grievously wounded. He lost one ear and most of his nose in the vicious combat with the raiders. After the attack Eeva and her three sons joined with Seppo to form a new family. It was a better choice than existing alone. For Seppo, her new man, she bore two children. Again, both turned blue and died. Then she could bear no more.

Seppo taught her older sons in the ways of finding amber. As Miikka, the oldest came of age Seppo took him down the Amber Road to trade with the Etruscans in a land adjacent to a big blue warm sea. The two returned in a year with metal implements. But since that trip, Seppo's earlier wounds had crippled him so severely that he could no longer manage the long journey south. Eeva's second son Heikka clamored to join an amber caravan. In the following year he made the trip with his older brother. Seppo had no choice but to let both young men go. He had no means to stop them. Neither Miikka nor Heikka were heard from again.

Eeva had only young Reijo to cling to while Seppo continued to become more infirm each season. With Reijo now in his sixth summer, she would take him to the Baltic shore and together they would collect amber pieces in the pine forests at the edge of the sea.

"Mother," Reijo said, "tomorrow I want to hunt for amber by that huge rock we see far down the beach."

"Be careful," she told him. She worried because he was her most precious possession. Reijo was the single joy in her life. She had good reason to fear. The little boy did not return.

Each day, for years, Eeva searched the many places where she thought she might find her boy. Day after day she called his name, "Reijo, Reijo." Only the wind answered her cries. Life now became days of tending an invalid Seppo and collecting amber for trade. Her lonely hours of darkness were spent sobbing for all the children that she had lost. Often the despair was so great that she would spend days and even nights sitting alone in the pines. Occasionally she might call out "Reijo" in a loud voice. As time passed, Eeva often considered killing herself to end her misery.

One morning sitting on the rocky shore just after sunup, she saw a young boy wandering towards her. He was naked and shivering. Eeva ran towards him and could see his reddish blonde hair and when close, the hazel eyes. They were different from the colors of the son she had lost long ago, but it was Reijo!

When he saw her, the startled child stood still. He shouted words she could not understand. Suddenly he ran to her grabbing her legs, holding tight. He started to wail as he fiercely clung to her.

"Reijo, Reijo, where have you been? Why did you not come home?"

The little boy did not recognize her words. He cried back at her in a tongue that pleaded for help but not in a language that she could understand. Still, Eeva was elated. She pulled him towards her hut. For a moment he was reluctant to follow her, but then he changed his mind and grasped her hand and went willingly.

"Seppo, look here…look here! I have found my Reijo. He was walking on the shore of the sea. He has come home to me. I think he was taken by trolls. Finally, they saw my sorrow and have returned him to me."

"Foolish woman! That is not your son. Look at him. Does he look anything like your other two sons? How could he be Reijo? It was many years ago when that boy of yours disappeared and he was six or seven years old. This lad is even younger than that. He is maybe five or six at the very most. He is close to the age when Reijo was lost but that was long ago"

Seppo roughly grabbed the youngster by the arm. "What is your name boy?"

There was a sudden look of fear in the boy's eyes and he jabbered back at Seppo while reaching his other arm to Eeva. Neither adult could understand a word that he spoke. Eeva drew the boy back to herself and covered his naked body with a blanket. Rage stormed into her emotions and she lashed out, almost screaming at Seppo, "This is my son. This is Reijo. The forest trolls stole him from me and now he is returned. Dare you say no more Seppo!"

The new boy, now called Reijo, forced an uneasy peace between the man and the woman. In their partnership they needed each other to endure. It was Eeva who would seek out the amber that they required to trade for food. Seppo would do the trading. If the boy was or was not Reijo, it really didn't matter to Seppo. Survival mattered.

At first Eeva would not allow Reijo out of her sight for even a moment. She attached a long rope to his leg and would tug on it in the night to make sure he was still attached to it. It took Eeva over a year before she could calmly allow him freedom to wander from her vision for more than a short time. Gradually he learned to speak her language. Even though she questioned him often, he could not explain why he was on the beach naked the day she found him. He had no memory of any time before Eeva.

As the months passed into years, Eeva was more frequently troubled by moods of sadness. Seppo observed that if Eeva began eating very little but slept long hours, another episode of melancholy was about to occur. At those times, without reason, the woman would scream obscenities. She might tear her clothes. The villagers feared her when she exhibited these moods. They thought her to be a witch.

She might disappear for days on end. One time, after she had been gone for several days, Reijo found her outside their hut just after dark, howling like a wolf at the full moon. He approached her cautiously but when she saw him she fainted. He dragged her into the hut and laid her beside Seppo. In the morning she seemed to have returned to normal and no mention was made of the happening.

"Seppo, what occurs with Eeva, why does she act so strangely at times and disappear?" Eeva had now been gone again for five days and the boy was worried.

"I cannot tell you Reijo. It is some sort of madness that comes on her. Even the witch in our settlement can't help her. No one understands this. Some believe she had a spell cast upon her by some forest shape shifter," *perhaps it was you Reijo*, he thought,

"Are there really trolls and shape shifters and elves in the woods?"

"I don't think they exist Reijo. Then perhaps I am not sure because of you."

"Because of me?"

"Yes. If you are really her lost little boy, where were you all the years she could not find you? Who had you? Why can't you remember something about your life before you came wandering down the beach to Eeva? Perhaps you were a slave of the trolls. I have heard that it happens. How else might you come back to Eeva without aging?"

Reijo blankly stared back at the older man. "It is also bothersome to me Seppo. Every time Eeva returns from one of her cheerless episodes she asks me how I found her that day. I myself do not know."

"Let me help you Reijo. We both know that Eeva believes strongly in creatures of the forest. When she returns this time tell her that the memory came back to you. Tell her that a huldra took you."

"What is a huldra, Seppo?"

"A huldra is a forest creature that my mother told me about. My mother came from a tribe far to the east. This huldra creature is a most beautiful magical lady but she has the tail of a fox. It is forbidden to comment about the tail, even if you happen to see it hanging below her skirt. Tell Eeva that you met a huldra while searching for amber on the day you disappeared. Tell her you laughed at the beautiful lady's fox tale. In anger she made you her slave for several years. Then she tired of you and returned you to Eeva. If your mother hears a story like that it might ease the misery of her mind."

Reijo wondered if something like this could possibly be true. As he thought about it he took his left hand and closed his nostrils with his thumb and forefinger. *Perhaps that is what really had happened,* he reflected.

It was not necessary to tell Eeva the story…she never came back to the hut. A sudden severe blizzard struck the settlement during the night. Eeva's body was found by villagers the following spring, curled up in a stand of pines, near the edge of the Baltic Sea.

As he grew into adulthood, life now became a mind-numbing routine for Reijo. He tended Seppo out of loyalty to Eeva. Neither man liked the other. Eeva had been the bridge between them. Reijo longed to take their growing catch of fine amber south to the Etruscans. By chance he had located an isolated pine grove that yielded some of the finest pieces that Seppo had ever seen. Most contained small insects or colored traces of minerals. All were quite clear. All were highly prized.

Reijo was aching for adventure. He desperately wanted to travel down the Amber Road. The stories he was told of the Etruscans fascinated him. Seppo cautioned him over and over that it was far too dangerous to go alone. He had to find others who knew the way, a caravan perhaps, and join them for protection. At the same time Reijo was unaware that Seppo had warned the entire village that the young man had been cursed by forest trolls. These were the same trolls who had driven his mother insane. If the villagers dealt with Reijo they too might lose their minds. With this warning, everyone in the settlement avoided contact with Reijo. In truth, Seppo needed Reijo to support his daily needs. It was protection. If he was left alone, the old man knew he would quickly die.

Four summers after Eeva had disappeared, unexpected drastic changes occurred in Reijo's life. In the early spring Seppo had died quietly in his sleep. Very alone, Reijo continued a solitary life of gathering amber. The villagers continued to be frightened of him. They considered him a *vardoger*, a person with a double spirit…a walking omen of danger, illness and even perhaps death. Village sickness, the demise of animals and any unexplainable event were all thought to be caused by this *vardoger* living among them.

One morning Reijo heard voices on the path that led to his hut. Immediately he went outside and found two men approaching. The shorter man had the same complexion and long blonde hair of the people of Reijo's village. The other man had olive skin and brown eyes. When they neared, the blonde man told Reijo that the big man's name was Cossus, yet he failed to introduce himself.

Cossus was a tall man with an ugly scar across his forehead. Several of his front teeth were chipped. His face sagged on both sides like the jowls of a dog. He carried a spear and had a large sword strapped to his belt. He was obviously a warrior and Reijo immediately feared this stranger.

"Where is Seppo? The blonde man demanded.

"He is dead. He died two moons ago. Who asks?"

The blonde man paused for just a moment but then asked, "where then is my mother Eeva?"

Reijo was startled by the question. "Eeva is your mother? Are you Miikka, my brother?"

Now it was the stranger's turn to be surprised. "Brother? What are you babbling about? I am not Miikka. He was killed long ago by some of the enemies of those evil Etruscans. I am his younger brother Heikka. And you say 'my brother.' You could not be Reijo! You are far too young. Tell me what is going on."

"I am Reijo. Eeva was my mother as she was yours. We need to talk. It is good to find my long lost brother. Come in, come in, this is a wonderful day for me."

Reijo brought them inside and offered them food and drink. He was delighted to enjoy the company of others. Being shunned by his own kind was a living death, even the young village children ran from him.

As they exchanged stories Reijo and Heikka learned a great deal about each other. Heikka made clear that he and his brother had become amber dealers. They traded metal tools for amber from those who came down the Amber Road. Heikka lived in Veii, an Etruscan border town close to the tribes of the Latin's. The Latin's main village of Rome was about a two hour walk on the other side of the Aino River. The river divided Etruria from Latium. Another tribe, the Sabine, controlled the lands farther to the east.

Heikka obviously enjoyed talking and provided more and more details about his time in Etruria. "Our brother Miikka sailed to Corsica with a large collection of our amber. Corsica is an island controlled by the Etruscans who have many colonies. Greek pirates raided a town there where Miikka was trading. He was killed. They say he fought the pirates bravely. He is regarded by the Etruscans as a hero."

Reijo noticed that Cossus, the big man who spoke little, had pursed his lips at the telling of the heroic death of Miikka. Something was wrong? Perhaps Heikka was not completely truthful. Reijo decided that he needed to be cautious with his new found brother. "It is distressing to hear that my oldest brother is dead. Our mother Eeva tried so hard to have more children. Seppo felt she was cursed by the evil spirits that lurk in the forests."

Again the big man reacted. This time it was more than a slight facial expression. He shook himself as if taken by a cold chill. *It must be that the possibilities of forest spirits plague him,* Reijo thought. Then he said, "Heikka tell me, why you have made this long trip up the Amber

Road? You told me you traded with others who made the long journey. If you wanted to trade for more amber, why did you not return with metal?"

Heikka glared at Reijo for a long moment. Then he said, "I wished to see my mother again."

Reijo was now closely watching Cossus to see how he reacted to Heikka's words. This time the brutish appearing man showed a flash of crinkled eyes and furrowed brow. The facial emotion instantly appeared but was just as quickly gone from the big man's weather-beaten face. *What is this? Why is my brother lying to me?* Again Reijo's mind told him to be cautious. The men stared at each other. No one spoke.

Finally Heikka reached over and gently shook Reijo's shoulder saying, "Reijo now tell us about the amber and how Seppo died and also what happened to our mother. It has been many years since Miikka and I left the village. But again I must say that you look much younger than I ever expected. You puzzle me. How can this be?"

Relating his life story, Reijo dwelt long on the fact that he had been kidnapped by shape shifters. He explained in detail that a beautiful lady had met him in the pine grove where he hunted amber. He had accidently insulted her by laughing at the fox tail holding up the back of her skirt. She was a huldra, a forest spirit, a shape shifter.

In anger she had made him a slave. He had to do terrible degrading tasks. The worst was to comb the huldra's long fox tail. If he accidently pulled too hard on her fur she would beat him brutally. Strangely, the next day all the bruises and scars would be gone. She never fed him. Somehow he didn't need to eat. Also, he never aged and had no clothes, but was never cold even in winter. One day, while the huldra was napping, he escaped. Running, he met his mother Eeva on the rocky shores of the Baltic Sea.

Reijo told his story with enthusiasm because truly, his mind was a complete blank of the time before he rejoined Eeva. He had made up this fantasy. It became more real to him each year. He needed to believe that he could really be Reijo. He had gone over the possibilities many times, especially in the years since Eeva had died. Now he had come to believe the story he was telling was actually true. As he told of his adventure he recognized that the mention of a huldra made Cossus turn pale. The man was visibly disturbed by Reijo's story. Finally, hands trembling nervously, Cossus left the hut.

Heikka soon followed Cossus out of the hut. He found the big man sitting under a nearby gigantic spruce tree. He sat down beside him on the soft needle mat. He said, "Cossus that is not my brother. Look at me. Tell me, what is the color of my eyes?"

"Black," Cossus mumbled.

"And my hair?"

"Yellow."

"Yes. And those are the colors of everyone in this clan except the stranger who claims to be Reijo. His eyes are brownish-green and his hair has a reddish tint. Look at me Cossus! Do Reijo and I look at all like we might be brothers?"

"No. But then the shape shifters might have changed him," Cossus answered.

Heikka mumbled a curse. Then he said, "I want you to kill that faker for me Cossus, but wait until I find where he keeps his amber. Then we will take all of it and return to Veii. We will both be very rich men."

Cossus rose on the mat of pine needles. He towered over the sitting Heikka. "I will not do that. I am in the service of King Tolumnius. I have been ordered to bring you back with amber so you can repay the King for your evil deeds. I will not murder anyone for you." The large man's words were not entirely true. Actually he had been ordered to kill Heikka and return only with the amber.

Cossus knew that he could never harm Reijo. This possible brother of Heikka had the power of a shape shifter inside him. He could feel it. If Cossus killed Reijo that same huldra spirit possessing Reijo might invade his body. He knew this to be true. He had seen evil spirits possess others. Perhaps Reijo's mother's spirit was also inside the young man. It was obvious to him, from Reijo's telling, that Eeva's soul had been consumed by some evil forest spirit. Why else would she have bayed at the moon?

Reijo and Heikka did not get along well at all. They only tolerated each other. Heikka persisted in saying that all of the amber that Reijo had collected must be turned over to him. It was his right, he was the older brother. Reijo offered his brother only half of his collection while demanding that he be allowed to join with him traveling back down the Amber Road to the Etruscan lands. He refused to show Heikka where he had hidden most of his caches of amber.

Once they had fought about the ownership of the amber. Reijo was knocked unconscious. Heikka considered killing him while he lay there, but stopped himself. Without Reijo he might never find the hidden stores of amber.

After a time, Reijo became aware of his surroundings. He had a large lump on his head. He was dizzy and unstable for almost a week. In that time the memory of some early life events came back to him. He said words to Heikka and Cossus which they did not understand…but he did. This he realized was the language he knew before Eeva found him.

Heikka was clever. He changed his tactics. He no longer asked for the amber. Each day he surreptitiously followed Reijo hunting the pine forests for new amber. Soon he learned the location of several hidden stores. He explained a plan to Cossus. "I have met some of the villagers. I knew many of them when I was a young boy here. They trust me. I have warned them about the evil contained inside Reijo. It is no surprise to most of them. I told them that it was Reijo who killed first Eeva and later Seppo. They listened to me, as I put my thoughts into simple words. I explained his hate for all of them because they shun him. I have told them Reijo plans to curse them and finally destroy all of them."

Cossus frowned. He had come to like Reijo. "None of that is true Heikka."

"I know that, but they are an ignorant people. I have convinced them that Reijo is a shape shifting warlock. I explained that he needs new blood to grow his powers. Tonight I will prove it by getting that blood."

"How?" Cossus weakly asked. He did not like endangering spirits.

"These villagers are easily fooled. Tonight, in the dark I will go to their sheep pens. I will kill as many of the animals as I can. Then I will cut out their hearts and bring them to Reijo's hut. They will follow the trail of blood and know that my warnings have been true. I have promised them if they burn the hut with Reijo inside, they will be forever safe from his evil magic.

"And here is the best part Cossus, I know where he has hidden much of his amber. I need it all. If we took Reijo with us I might not be able to pay my obligation. But with that false brother of mine gone I will have enough amber to pay my debt to King Tolumnius and much, much more. I will share my profits with you. I will make you a rich man Cossus."

Cossus did not like what Heikka was doing. King Tolumnius had sentenced both brothers to death for their terrible crime. As Heikka had watched Miikka being publicly garroted in the Veii square, it was done slowly and painfully. Heikka pleaded with the king to let him make restitution.

Tolumnius was an angry but also prudent man. One brother's death would sooth his anger, at least for the time being, for the lost treasures.

Later, if Heikka could restore the gold by selling amber, the royal violation would be salved and he would still have his executioner kill this bold thief, unless Cossus had already done so.

Cossus was perplexed. He both liked and feared Reijo. The big man was terrified to stay inside Reijo's hut at night. It was far too frightening to sleep next to a shape shifter. He might possibly awake and find himself in the body of some animal. Cossus prudently spent his days and nights under the spruce tree. Yet the young man exhibited only friendship towards him. Reijo shared his food and had given Cossus a medicinal plant that chased away the bothersome tiny biting insects that inhabited the tree where he stayed.

Cossus deeply feared the great powers of the shape shifters. Knowing now of Heikka's evil plan, he could not allow himself to be part of a shape shifters death. Killing a man did not bother him at all. He had done that many times. Slaying a huldra was far too dangerous. He recalled the witch from his boyhood village. As a child he watched as she was burned alive. She had returned soon (*Was it the next day? He could not remember*) as a black cat. Then most of the villagers died of some sort of pox. Filled with bewildering dread, Cossus sought out Reijo.

"Reijo you are in great danger," Cossus said. He then explained how Heikka had stirred up fears in the villagers claiming that Reijo was an evil spirit. The plan was to burn him alive that night to save themselves, after they found bloody sheep hearts around his hut.

"Why would my brother do this to me?"

"He is a bad man, Reijo. He lied to you about your brother Miikka. Both he and Miikka were sentenced to die for violating Etruscan law. Heikka ransomed his life for the amber you possess."

"What crime did they commit?"

Cossus shook his head sadly and quietly said, "Your brothers were tomb robbers. The Etruscan people honor their dead with elaborate tombs filled with gold, amber and jewels. Their mausoleums walls are painted by the greatest artists in the land. Individual tombs have carved statues. I have never seen anything like that in all my travels.

"Miikka and Heikka were caught stealing from the tombs of the Vulci. The families of the Vulci are one of the oldest in all Etruria. They can proudly trace their family ancestors back to the ancient Villanovans. Your brothers would steal anything they could carry from these unguarded mausoleums. They would sell their spoils to dishonest Greek traders at the docks. The Vulci caught them in the act of robbing a tomb. Your brothers were sentenced to death."

Reijo looked sternly at Cossus. The big man trembled, fearing that he had angered the forest spirit by telling of the brothers crimes. But then Reijo's face turned to sadness. "My brother would have me killed." He said that...not to Cossus...perhaps...just to the empty sky. "I told Heikka that he could take half. Does he want all of my amber?"

"Yes. He has spent days following you and he knows where you hide your treasure. He is not satisfied with just half of what you have. That is not enough. He wants all your amber to pay his ransom and with the extra, he plans to make himself rich."

Reijo had trouble believing all of this. As he often did when he needed to mull over a situation he used his left hand to pull his index finger and thumb over his nose closing his nostrils for a moment. "Cossus, he is my brother and your friend. What can I do? I do not want him killed."

"He is not my friend Reijo. He is my prisoner. I was sent here with him to get the amber. Know too that Heikka believes you are not his brother."

"He thinks I am…."

"He thinks you are someone who…who…I think he does not know what you are."

"And why do you tell me this Cossus? Who might you believe me to be?"

"I think you must be a creature of the forest…a shape shifter…a huldra. I cannot let you be harmed or you might seize my body as your new home. I must protect you or you might steal my spirit from me."

Reijo was so shocked with Cossus' explanation that he almost smiled. *Best to keep the big man in fear of me*, he thought. He needed an ally. He also needed a plan.

"Cossus come with me, now!" Reijo ordered. The two men hurried to the largest hidden store of amber. They carried it back to the hut. Cossus was amazed as he watched Reijo set the hut afire.

"My blazing hut will ruin Heikka's plan. He now has no place to take the bloody sheep's hearts. I doubt if he will even do that tonight. Follow me now Cossus. We start down the Amber Road."

"But…"

"Do not challenge me or I will turn you into a frog. Obey me now and I will show you my power at the next sunrise. I will also reward you with a charm. Come…right now. Hurry before the villagers arrive to see the fire of my hut."

The two half-ran and half-walked south, away from the village and away from the Baltic Sea. They stopped for the night far off the beaten track in a deeply wooded dell. Reijo seemed to know exactly where he was going. In the distance Cossus could hear the rushing sounds of a cascading waterfall. The superstitious warrior did not know what to do. He had saved the shape shifter but violated the order of King Tolumnius. He did not kill Heikka and he did not have any amber. The amber they carried away belonged to the huldra and he dared not take it. If he did not obey Reijo completely he could be changed into some contemptible forest creature. His mind raced. He trembled with fear of the unknown.

At the misty dawn spread a light fog through the undergrowth, Reijo again called for Cossus to follow him deeper into the forest. There was a path which eventually widened into a well-worn trail. Ultimately they stopped where another path formed a crossroads.

"Reijo, I am afraid. Are you going to change me into some despicable thing? I have tried to follow your commands. I have disobeyed the King. He will make me a galley slave if I return without the amber. That is a slow living death. What will become of me?" The big man quivered with superstitious dread.

Reijo appreciated the apprehension of the unknown in this fearless fighter's mind. It was natural to be desperately afraid of what you could not see or understand. The same feelings of not knowing had plagued him most of his life. Where had he come from? A single memory thread of falling into the water from a sinking ship was just beginning to take shape in his consciousness. It had come to him during his time of dizziness after the fight with Heikka. At last he had understood that he was not the missing son of Eeva. He was not truly her Reijo.

From Eeva, Reijo had learned tales of giants, dragons and forest creatures. They all seemed possible, yet were never seen. From the skeptical Seppo, he appreciated that much of what people believed was completely false. He knew that Eeva had only been sick. She was not at all evil. Now he could use his new understanding to force the warrior Cossus to protect and help him. He would promote the myth that he was a shape shifter. Nature had provided a perfect example for Reijo to trick this brutish man. It might serve him well in Etruria.

"Cossus follow me," he sharply commanded. "This is my most powerful time as the sun rises." They walked for some time to a cascade. "See that you know how potent is my magic. There, look in the water of the stream that is a forest troll who tried to harm me. I changed him into a stone and set him in the cold water where he will remain forever."

Cossus knees buckled at the horrific sight. He was rendered speechless. There was the rough shape of a being immersed in the torrent of a small waterfall. Cossus could see the face with an open mouth screaming soundlessly in agony. What powerful spell might this man now work on him? He fell to the ground. A moaning sound escaped from his lips.

"Come Cossus, get up. You are my friend. I will do you no harm. We will go back to the place where the two paths cross. There I will give you a charm to protect you from every evil forest creature."

At the crossroads Reijo pointed to a very large oak tree spreading its limbs in all directions. Cossus had not noticed it when they had passed under it. Eeva had brought Reijo to this very spot many times. She explained to the young boy how the god Thor had taken refuge under an oak tree and acorns would protect anyone from lightening. She also told him that a tree like this would scream if it was chopped down.

"Cossus this is my magical oak tree. It grows at a crossroads. It has mistletoe growing on it. See that branch where lightning had struck the tree. I will give you acorns from that branch and a leaf of mistletoe. With those two charms on your body you will never be harmed by any forest creature."

The big man accepted the gifts with tears in his eyes.

"This is the spot Cossus, where I put the hoard of the best amber. Here I placed much of what I found over the last several years. What little I left for Heikka…and I knew he was watching me…what little he can find will not be enough for him. He will spend years collecting for another trip. We are rid of him.

" I will pay my brother's debts to this King Tolumnius. Then you and I will share the rich life of Etruria."

A BIT OF HISTORY

King Tolumnius of the Etruscan town of Veii entered history in the late 5th century BCE. At this time the mysterious Etruscans had spread their control over more than half of northern Italy taking the territory from the earlier Villanovan civilization. Etruscan power however was waning while Rome was ascending as a strong adversary. The Etruscan city of Veii bordered on Roman territory.

The nearby Roman colony of Fidenae revolted against the Republic of Rome. The Fidenae leaders of the revolution offered King Tolumnius control over their city, which the king gladly accepted. In return he would protect their lands from the Romans.

When Rome sent four emissaries (Cloelius Tullus, Gaius Fulcinius, Spurius Antius, and Lucius Roscius) to Veii to demand the hegemony of Fidenae back, Tolumnius had them executed.

The legendary explanation for this grievous breach of peace is that at the moment his aides inquired if they should execute the Roman ambassadors, Tolumnius, playing at dice and having just rolled fortuitously, exclaimed, "Excellent!". Thus he inadvertently ordered the execution of the diplomats and unknowingly sealed his own fate. Rome, in revenge conquered Veii. It put King Tolumnius to death and eventually triumphed over all the Etruscan cities.

Rome continued its conquests defeating the bordering Sabine Tribes and eventually controlled all of Italy.

Fifteen

Celtiberians

"Professor, now that class is over can I ask you a question?"

"Certainly, what is your question, uh…Matt isn't it?"

"Yes professor. I'm a bit confused by your use of the term 'Celtiberians'. Can you explain a little bit more about it? I thought the Celts were just early Irish people."

"Not so, Matt. Well, let me take that back. It is certainly true that the Celts migrated to Ireland. But there were many tribes of Celts. They mostly shared the same root language, physical characteristics and ferocity. The Romans sometimes called them Gaul's. The Celtic origins were probably somewhere in central Europe. No one really knows. They expanded through the countries now called France, England, Ireland and Spain.

"Since the Romans, and the Greeks even before the Romans, identified Spain and Portugal by the name Iberia, the Celts who were already settled there were called Celtiberians. Here, take a look at this map in my notes. You can see that the Celtic people traveled far and wide.

"These related Celtic tribes populated a large portion of Europe long before Rome came to power. As tribes, they looked somewhat alike. They were large bodied, usually with light skin and blonde hair. They were ferocious warriors. They commonly cut off the heads of their enemies. Another Celtic ritual occurred when a warrior died. His bones were left outside to be cleaned by the birds. They also had the custom of burying their dead children, especially those under a year old, below the floors of their houses."

Matt was startled. "Professor, that sounds just like some ancient practices that I've read about from thousands of years earlier."

"Quite correct, Matt. Men, in those thousands of years, learned how to write and count. They learned how to find and use new metals for weapons. Yet the traditional tribal customs they practiced hardly changed. For example the Greeks, Romans and the Celts had different names for their gods…but those gods were basically all the same gods for ages. Customs remained unchanged for thousands of years.

"Tribes continually fought each other for new land to feed the growing world population. A few men became rich and wanted to be even richer. Slavery and conquest of other lands was the norm for centuries…no, millennia. It has taken humanity a long long time to become somewhat civilized. Today some of that horrendous activity still goes on. Conquest and slavery still exist in our world. Rich men take whatever action is necessary to become even richer.

"By the way, the Celts often hired themselves out as mercenaries to whoever wanted to use them. They were prized for their fighting skills. The Carthaginians, the Romans and many others all employed Celts."

"Professor, I think that you are saying that much of the ancestry of European people is Celtic in origin. Why did the Celts move so much and inhabit so many places?"

"I really explained all that in class Matt, You *should* know the answer! It was primarily the increasing pressure for additional land. That stress required conquest and tribal resettlements. Certainly it was the same in our country in the nineteenth century. We populated the west while still more and more immigrants flooded into the United States. In the process we destroyed the Indian tribes using superior technology, sometimes trickery and most often, raw power. We wanted…needed their lands for farming, gold and other valuable goods, such as timber and coal. Today we call that extermination 'ethnic cleansing' and we are very moral about despising it elsewhere. Americans did it in the 1800's.

"In Europe there were enormous tribes, the Huns, the Visigoths and others. They were all farther to the east of the Celts in what is now Russia. These groups expanded westward and pushed the Celts to move their settlements farther and farther to the west. Some groups went to Spain and mixed with the indigenous Iberian tribes. We call those mixed groups, Celtiberians."

"Oh, now I understand. These wild Celtic tribes settled in Spain."

"Not wild at all Matt. The Celtiberians had migrated and lived in Iberia for hundreds of years before they, in turn, were conquered. They had built many walled towns, usually on a hilltop. They brought local tribal groups into a central jurisdiction. They began forming the rudiments of centralized government. They also excelled as metal workers. Look at this picture of a fibula, it is a broach, from around 200 B.C. It was used to hold garments together."

"Oh that is beautiful professor. But what is that round thing on the knee of the horse?"

"That is a depiction of a human head. The Celts never gave up on the concept of beheading their enemies. It is a recurring theme in most of their art."

"So professor, what happened to the Celtiberians?"

"The Romans Matt, the Romans."

Sixteen

Baetan
Spain 133 B.C.

"Grandfather Derfail, my stomach hurts so much. Please, is there anything to eat" the young boy was begging in a whispered failing voice. Even if there had been any food to give him he was too fragile to sit up and consume it. The starving boy was far too weak to drink anything but water. Little Raghnall was barely aware of his surroundings as he lapsed in and out of consciousness. Derfail saw the effects of no food on his young body. The boy had a strangely bloated stomach that was covered with an unusual rash. His eyes seemed as big as saucers. These symptoms were now common in the city of Numantia. The lad was a Celtiberian. He would not cry in his pain.

A deep sadness filled the old man's soul. He had nothing to give his grandson. All the horses, even the cats and dogs of Numantia had been consumed. Not a blade of grass was left. It had all been plucked to make a weak soup. The entire city was on the verge of collapse from starvation.

As the leader in his town and region, Derfail had been able to procure a bit more sustenance than many others. He had shared what little bit he had with his youngest grandson, Raghnall. Now everything edible was gone. The younger children and most of the women were already dead. The last of the food had been commandeered for the men defending the walls. Those few remaining fighters could barely stand. The once robust Celts were now walking skeletons shielding a lost cause. Starvation had sapped these vigorous men and their families of their physical strength, but not their moral convictions. Derfail had heard a whispered rumor that a slave had been cannibalized. It no longer mattered...he knew that the siege would be ended at the next sunrise. The suffering of Numantia would soon be over.

The Celtiberian town of Numantia with a population of about 6,000 had stood for hundreds of years close by the Duero River flowing through a high inland plain in north central Spain. A millennium later this sparsely populated grazing land would become known as Castile-Leon.

In the second century B.C., the Celtiberians, Celtic tribes on the Iberian Peninsula, had put up a 20 year resistance to everything Rome sent their way...until Rome finally sent their best Legions against the Celts. Even so, it still took eleven months of hard siege before the city of Numantia would finally fall to the Romans at the end of summer.

Just four years earlier the Celtiberians, led by forces from Numantia, had defeated a large Roman army and captured close to 20,000 Legionnaires. As was the custom of the Celts, most of the prisoners were sold into slavery. A few were beheaded by Celtiberian youths as a rite of passage. Rome had not forgotten this humiliation but licked its wounds and retreated to the Iberian seacoast. Still, the mineral riches of the uplands tantalized Rome's desire for control. The Roman Senate dispatched Scipio Aemilianus Africanus with a new army to conquer the interior of Iberia. Numantia was the key to winning the land of the Celtiberians for Rome.

Scipio arrived in Spain with a huge army and many war elephants. The animals were the same type that Hannibal had used some twenty years earlier against Rome itself. Elephants were not a surprise to the Celtiberians. The tribesmen and elephants had made up a large part of Hannibal's army a generation earlier. But elephants used here by Romans proved ineffective against the walled town of Numantia.

In the prior months the new general, Scipio Aemilianus Africanus had marched his troops into the central high plains of Iberia. The Legions had easily conquered most of the small independent tribes. The Celtiberians were quite a different challenge. They had grown beyond tribes into a regional power with Numantia as their center and Derfail as their leader.

Scipio understood the failure of his elephants against a walled town. Furthermore, the men of his Legions were not prepared for an assault against stone walls. The Legions' strength was in open field battle supported by cavalry. Scipio appreciated these special circumstances that impeded his conquest of the Celtiberians. It was wise to talk; he led a party, under a banner of truce to meet Derfail. The meeting did not go well.

"Open your gates, Celt. Save the lives of your people," Scipio commanded. "It is impossible for you to defeat my army. Surrender and enjoy becoming part of the growing Roman Empire. Resist and we will level your town and enslave all your people."

"Ha!" Derfail scoffed. "Your legions and puny elephants are no danger to us. Go away and save yourselves. Do you not remember what we did to the last Roman army led here by your Consul Quintus Fulvius Nobilior? I think you knew that stupid man. Why do you Romans believe everyone will bend their knee to you? I, in fact, have one of Quintus' centurions as my house slave. Waste not your men on our walls. Celtiberians are very strong. We are many. It is the lives of your legionnaires that will be thrown away."

Scipio clutched the hilt of his sword in anger. His eyes bulged. He had never been treated this rudely. He was a Roman Senator! But it would be a fatal mistake to strike down this arrogant Celt so very close to his own town walls. In a guttural tone Scipio said, "I hope you live through this siege Derfail. I intend to make you a slave for my elephant master. You will spend the rest of your miserable life shoveling elephant dung."

Without a look or a reply, Derfail turned and led his delegation back to the gates of Numantia. Scipio, in a rage, screamed at the Celt's back, "I will give your grandchildren to my men as play toys, Derfail."

Weeks later Baetan, the older brother of Raghnall, came running to his grandfather. The boy was barely in his teens and had never experienced combat. He carried the lance and shield of a warrior only because he was old enough to stand guard at the wall.

Derfail had only in the past spring brought the boy through the ritual of manhood. Baetan had decapitated one of the Roman slaves. Still the boy, who had not yet even grown facial hair, was tall and very scrawny for his age. This was an asset that Derfail would soon find useful.

Baetan was out of breath. "Grandfather, grandfather" he shouted, "the Romans are building a wooden wall beyond our town wall. Why are they doing that? They should be attacking us so we can kill them."

Derfail smiled, "They will not storm our walls Baetan. Roman Legions are not prepared to attack a walled town like Numantia. Our stones will hold them at bay. Their strength is to maneuver in the field. We have fought them there and won. But now they are too many and we Celts too few. I have spies who tell me that there are four Legionnaires for every one of us. We simply must wait till they tire and go away."

"Then why are they erecting a wooden wall of their own, with towers? What are they trying to do Grandfather?"

Derfail paused to choose his words carefully. He pulled his forefinger and his thumb over his nostrils, closing them for a moment. "Scipio is intelligent. While the Romans outnumber us, we are better fighters. The Roman General is going to build a wall around Numantia. He will try to starve us into submission. It is the only way he might win."

"Grandfather, you said 'might win'. Can Scipio do that?" Baetan spoke in a worried voice. "Can he make us surrender without an honest fight?"

"I think not, but the gods of war are never dependable. We must be prepared for a long siege. I have sent armed parties to gather all the livestock and grain that is movable and bring it into town. But Scipio knows what we are doing, just as I know what he is doing. Unfortunately we have already lost many men and animals to his roving patrols. We are going to need help from the other Celtiberian towns. They have to attack the Romans from the rear. I have sent messages asking for aid."

"We need help?" Worry filled the young boy's face.

"It is not simply the Roman walls that will soon surround us Baetan. As you have seen, they are digging pits in the front of those walls. They fill them with sharp stakes. They are also digging trenches protected by towers over their palisade. It will be impossible for us to break out by trying to cross all of those obstacles. *We must have help,*"

Derfail muttered this almost to himself, "if we are to beat Scipio. The rest of the Celtiberians have got to come to our aid and attack the Roman legions from the rear. We must have aid in order to retain our lands."

Baetan pondered the words of his grandfather. He had never heard him speak of anything but victory. He needed to cheer Derfail up. "We beat them the last time Grandfather."

"That is true Baetan. Romans are stupid, but they do learn. Scipio may be more intelligent than the last group we fought. After they lose badly they study how their adversary beat them. Then they change tactics and often copy the enemy.

"Like Hannibal Grandfather? You told me that you knew that great general."

"Yes, I knew him. He came into our lands when I was a boy. My grandfather, when I was younger than your brother Raghnall, joined with Hannibal over the great mountains of the north…"

Baetan interrupted, "And they brought elephants that terrorized the Romans in their own land."

"Yes. Now the Romans have learned the value of war elephants and try the same trick with us. It won't work. They can't frighten us with those beasts. So they are trying a new tactic…starving us out by siege…by walling in our town.

"Let me acquaint you Baetan as to how Romans think. It was this same learning process years ago with the Carthaginian navy. The Romans learned to be a great navel power only after losing badly to the Carthaginians. The men from Carthage were experienced sailors, the Romans were not."

"Tell me about it grandfather." Baetan was more than aware of the fact that his grandfather was a hard man. He had been beaten often for disobedience. Even little Raghnall might not escape his grandfather's violent wrath. Yet the young teen also knew that Derfail enjoyed telling stories of old. He would be at his mellowest at these times. An account of an old battle would relieve Baetan of the boredom of guard duty. It might also make him forget the pangs of hunger in his belly.

"Sit Baetan and I will tell you how the Carthaginian navy wiped out a Roman fleet just before my grandfather was born."

"Back then Baetan, Roman power was growing. They had disciplined soldiers. Carthage in turn, controlled much of the land surrounding the western half of the great Mediterranean Sea. The Carthaginians were skilled sailors and the Romans were great soldiers. The two powers warred for control of the large islands in the sea. It seems sadly, that it is the nature of man to want to control the lands, the riches, and all people. Conquest is in man's blood.

"Carthaginian General Hamilcar Barca (General Hannibal's father) was leading a successful land campaign in Sicily against the Romans. He was using a large number of mercenaries to fight the Roman forces on the island.

At the same time Publius Claudius Pulcher, the commander of a Roman war fleet attempted a blockade of the Carthaginian fleet supporting Hamilcar Barca's army at a port called Drepana, on the western end of the island.

"Is the blockade something like the wall Scipio is beginning to build around Numantia grandfather?"

"Correct Baetan. A blockade consists of ships rather than walls, but let me finish."

"In the harbor, the Carthaginians did not wait to see what the Romans intended. The Carthaginian Admiral, Herbal was his name, ordered the evacuation of his fleet from Drepana before a blockade

could be set in place. Carthage's ships thus sailed out of Drepana, passing south of the city and around two small islands along the coast of Sicily and into the open sea.

"Seeing his plan of a surprise attack fail, Roman Admiral Pulcher ordered his fleet to regroup into battle formation. By then however, everything was against him. The coast of Sicily was at his back. The Roman fleet was strung out in a long single line, and the Punic fleet was readying for battle at his front. He was trapped.

"Romans are exceedingly superstitious. Admiral Pulcher quickly performed the obligatory inspection of omens for the battle which are required by Roman religious tradition. The method ascribed for this type of situation was to observe the feeding behavior of sacred chickens on board his ship...placed there for just this purpose. If the chickens accepted the offered grain, then the gods would be favorable to the battle. However on that particular morning the chickens refused to eat...a terrible omen. Confronted with this unexpected result and having to deal with the superstitious and now terrified crews, Pulcher swiftly determined an alternative interpretation. He threw all the sacred chickens overboard directly into the Mediterranean, saying, 'Let them drink, since they don't wish to eat.'

Baetan muffled a laugh while Derfail smiled broadly. The old man continued...

"Herbal saw a chance for victory and ordered the attack. He sent his right flank to assault the rear-most Roman ships. The result was an utter Roman defeat, with almost all ships commanded by Pulcher sunk one by one. The Drepana defeat so demoralized the Romans that they waited seven years before building another fleet."

"And did they learn from their loss," Baetan asked.

"Yes they did. They captured a Carthaginian ship and took it apart. Next they used it as a model to build stronger more maneuverable ships for their new fleet. The Romans are brutes but they do learn, just as we might train a bear to do tricks. Every time Romans lose they copy their enemy or they come up with something new. That is why they are surrounding Numantia with a wooden wall. They are stopped by our stone wall. They can't use their war elephants. We, in turn do not have enough men to destroy them in the open field. So they trap us in our own town and will try to starve us into surrender."

Derfail's face turned dark. "We must have help Baetan. I have sent Taben…you know him…I have sent Taben to gather forces from the other Celtiberian towns. If they join together and attack the legions from the rear we will beat the Romans still another time."

"Good!" Baetan smiled.

"No, not good at all," Derfail growled in a voice so low that Baetan could barely hear him. "Taben has been gone for three weeks and the wall around Numantia is nearing completion. Taben has not returned and no help is in sight. Our food supplies almost gone and I was forced to start rationing. I must send another messenger for help, or it could be too late for us." Derfail audibly sighed. He did not want Baetan to know the complete truth.

These were words of defeat from his grandfather! Baetan knew they were close to starvation. A cloud of dread came over him. Derfail was pointing a wordless finger at the teenager and nodded slowly. The young man was quick. He immediately realized that Derfail might send him outside the walls alone. He was prepared to fight next to experienced warriors…but to go alone would be terrifying for the young man.

"No grandfather…not me" he cried warily.

Derfail's response was a strong punch-like slap across Baetan's cheek. The boy fell to the floor dazed spitting blood and a tooth.

"You will do as you are told grandson. Do not dishonor me, or your family or your Celtic heritage. Never show me that lack of courage again. I had enough of that spinelessness with your father." Derfail's words came slowly with a sound of rage that the young man had never before heard. The grandfather he loved and feared...the man who had raised him...now terrified him.

Wiping the blood from his chin Baetan haltingly asked, "Grandfather, how will I get over the new Roman wall? They will see me, even at night."

Derfail inhaled in exasperation. "Am I the only one who thinks," he demanded. You do not go over the Roman wall. Listen to me. Remember the narrow split in the rock where the spring water stream flows out of Numantia? I took you there once to swim"

"I remember. The water was very cold, even in the summer" Baetan replied.

"Good, you remember. That stream passes through a very narrow slit in the rock and flows far below the sides of the stone cliff. The Roman wall is high above that slit where the stream rushes. They simply bridged the crevasse. You will swim under their wall. You will be unnoticed in the stream."

Baetan gasped. "It is too narrow grandfather. I will never be able…"

He did not finish the sentence. He found himself on the floor for a second time, dazed and again bleeding. His nose pained him but it was not broken.

Baetan and Derfail waited four days until there was no moon. Each night the teenager immersed himself in the chilly waters of the shallow stream and crawled forward. For preparation, Derfail stripped the boy naked and slathered him with sheep fat to retain body warmth. Then he was allowed to wear a breech clout and take a small knife in his belt.

"If the Roman soldiers catch you Baetan, tell them you are running away. Tell them we are starving in Numantia and starting to kill and eat our children. Tell them also that your family beats you because you are a coward and will not fight. They will see the marks on your face that I gave you. Romans are generally thickheaded. They may believe you."

Baetan trembled. "What if they don't believe me Grandfather?"

Derfail took a deep breath. He grasped the young man by the shoulders and stared into his hazel eyes. "They must believe you. You appear too young to be a warrior…you have not yet even grown hair on your face. They will think you a scared beaten boy running away."

"And…and if they still see I am lying…?"

"If the Romans are not convinced that your story is true, then they will kill you. I only hope to the gods that they do it quickly."

Baetan shuddered so strongly that he could barely stand. Finally he found his voice. It was scarcely an audible whine as he said, "Then you will send someone else to get us help to break the siege?" In his thoughts he had faint hopes that another might go in his place.

Derfail was now angrier than ever, yet he knew he had to control his temper. "Baetan, listen to me. There is no other person to send. I send you because you are very tall and extremely thin. You may be able to squeeze through that narrow opening…no one else left alive here in Numantia can possibly do that. You have no beard yet and can still pass for a frightened youth. If they catch you then you will tell them how you swam under their wall."

"I will never tell grandfather," Baetan said defiantly.

"Yes, sadly you will tell everything. The Romans are skilled at torture."

"But if they catch me grandfather, what will you do next?"

Derfail realized that he had already said too much. Baetan was badly shaken by the plan. "You will succeed. You are strong and brave. Use all of your bravery and your cunning to become the savior of Numantia." Baetan thought that no savior could be as afraid as he was at this very moment.

On the night of the new moon, Baetan slipped into the frigid stream. Derfail had initiated a noisy disturbance outside the far wall of Numantia to distract Scipo's Legions. Baetan, hearing the din, had quickly immersed himself in the shallow water. With only his face above the surface he rapidly propelled himself forward. He grasped stones along the way pulling his body towards the narrow opening in the rock. Soon the water was knee deep…then just as quickly…almost to his neck. Above, barely visible in the dim starlight, he could make out the bottom of the Roman façade. With a silent sigh of relief he floated under their wall.

There was no shout of an alarm. He had not been detected. Perhaps it was possible that he could save Numantia, except now there was a new obstacle...

At this point the stream compressed suddenly into a narrow opening. He could no longer feel the stream bed below his feet in the frigid water. The water was deep and the space between the rock walls had become so narrow that he could not even squeeze his head through the opening. It was so darkly black that he could only to use his hands to feel his way forward. He was defeated! It was not possible to get his head through the opening.

The glacial water was starting to numb his body. Baetan pushed sideways with his feet and discovered that he could not touch both rock walls below the surface at the same time. *The opening below the surface must be wider,* he thought. *But I can't do this. If I go below the surface I will get stuck and drown. If I stay on the surface I will be trapped here. I will freeze to death and help no one! I must...I must save my little brother Raghnall and my grandfather.*

Without thinking, without deciding on any plan, he suddenly dove beneath the surface of the dark water. He blindly groped his way forward, getting bruised and cut as the current bashed him against the narrow, often jagged stone walls. He had not taken a deep breath to start. Now his lungs felt as if they would rip open.

With one final burst of waning energy he smashed head first into a heap of underwater brush. Baetan was instantly cut in several places. Somehow the force of his collision freed the entire mass of trapped branches. They rose, carrying his limp body to the surface. He lay there choking, coughing and spitting water. A startled Roman sentry freed him from the mass of limbs.

The soldier prodded Baetan with the blunt tip of his lance. He spoke in a language that the nearly drowned boy could not understand. The man was not a Roman, but still a legionnaire. The harsh jabbing told Baetan that he must stand. As he slowly, painfully rose he found that he was much taller than the mercenary who was a fat little man. But his antagonist was in full armor while Baetan had lost his small knife and even his breech clout. He had no means to resist. Directed by evermore severe pokes, he was marched to a small stockade. It was only a wagon with wooden bars on all sides.

"What have you got there?" asked the jailor in a language unknown to Baetan.

"Another spy! I caught him in that little stream passing under our wall," the guard replied.

"I'll cage him in with the other one. That one is almost dead anyway."

As the jailer opened the cage door the guard first prodded Baetan in the back with the dull end of his spear. Then laughing, with a swift upward motion, he struck the boy brutally between his bare legs. Baetan crumpled into the cage, moaning softly.

Before leaving the guard paused for a moment saying to the jailer, "I think you must immediately inform your superior about this new incursion. The Numantians may have found a way though our wall. I have to return to my post. We are short-handed up there. Make sure the Centurion knows that it was I who captured the spy."

The jailor, who spoke the same undecipherable language as the guard, had shoved Baetan's feet into the cage-like structure. As the pain subsided the boy discovered another prisoner sharing the very tight space.

"Who are you?" Baetan asked. A fresh wave of fear passed over him as the prisoner caught the young man's arm tightly. Only an animal sounding response came from his lips. As Baetan attempted to pull back, there was a glimmer of light from the jailer's torch as he walked away to seek out his commander.

Baetan discovered with horror that the crumpled man was Taben, the first man grandfather Derfail had sent weeks earlier to get help for Numantia.

Taben was badly beaten. Now as Baetan's eyes adjusted to the dim light he saw stripes on Taben's body. He had been whipped. "Taben, Taben, what have they done to you?" Baetan touched the man's arm and Taben let out a throaty scream. Now he recognized that much of Taben's flesh appeared to be burned. "Taben tell me what they did to you" the young man pleaded.

With a slight animal sounding cry Taben opened his mouth and pointed. The ghastly sight forced Baetan to back away as far as possible. The Romans had cut out his tongue! At last he understood why Derfail had said that he would tell the Romans everything if he was captured. The Taben he knew had been a strong Celt. Now this wreck of a man was reduced to a moaning lump of flesh. Baetan's mind swirled. What could he possibly do? Could he help Taben? Could he help himself? He had to escape. Panic made his heart beat faster.

Use your brain Baetan. Grandfather always said you were clever. Their little prison had wooden bars. It was simply a cage mounted on wheels. Baetan used all of his strength in an attempt to break the wooden poles holding them in. The close-spaced bars were far too thick to give way. With each attempt he slid backward into Taben, obviously causing the man added terrible pain. Taben's cries were pitiful moans coming every time Baetan accidently fell backward into the tortured man's body. Baetan found it was not possible to break any of the thick bars.

The young boy hung his head between his knees. *I have failed you grandfather. I let them catch me. Now they will slowly kill me as they are doing to poor Taben. I was to save Numantia and now all is lost. There is no way for me to escape this cage on wheels. If only I could…*

A sudden realization came over the young Celtiberian. The cage was mounted on wheels. It was on a hillside. He knew the place...he had been here often. That was one reason he kept sliding into Taben, the wagon was tilted on a slope. There had to be chocks holding the wagon in place. *If I can just reach them*, he thought, *the wagon might roll down the hill and smash open. The jailor has gone, I must try.*

In their confined space Baetan had to maneuver his body to stretch his full length in order to reach anything blocking the wheel. His thin arm barely fit between the bars. Then discovery! There was nothing blocking the wheel! With difficulty, again causing great pain to Taben as he rubbed against him, he found that the opposite wheel was also free. *It is the other two wheels under where Taben lays that are blocked he determined. I will have to move my friend to the other end of this cage. But I can't do that; it will cause him dreadful pain. Still, I must get our freedom in order to help Numantia.*

"Taben I must move you to the other end of the wagon in order to..."

The tortured Celt shook his head violently motioning a 'no'. He cringed with muffled screams as Baetan moved to place him at the other end of their tiny cell. Baetan was forced to ignore the grievous moans. As gently as he could he lifted Taben in his arms and moved him away from the place over the chocked wheels. Skin fell away and Baetan became be aware of an oozing slime emanating from the man's flesh. In the process of moving Taben had either fainted or died.

Baetan again stuck his long arm between the bars. This time he grasped a stone that was blocking the wheel. There was a small stick lying by the chock. He used it to dig the earth around the blocking stone. Then with some difficulty, he managed to free the wheel. The jail wagon skewed slightly to the side but refused to roll free.

Next Baetan moved to the other side of the wagon-prison. The chock blocking that wheel would not move. The weight of the wagon, plus the two prisoners, supplied far too much pressure on the stone to allow Baetan to move it.

Once again the dismayed young Celt retreated into the dark recesses of failure. He had tried his best. His fingers were raw from the effort. He had perhaps even killed Taben in the process. Now the Romans would cut out his tongue and destroy his flesh. There was no hope! For just a moment, it seemed, he shut his eyes. Perhaps it was a dream but he heard the clear voice of Derfail ordering him to use his mind. "Find a way to loosen the stone," the voice demanded.

Baetan woke from his stupor with a start. He turned to lie on his belly that he might reach beneath the stony wedge holding the wagon in place. The ground was much rougher in this spot and the stick he had used was broken. He would have to dig a hole for the stone to fall into before the jail might be freed. His only tool was his hand.

He was in agony. The hurt from the guard's blow between his legs now was shooting stabbing pains throughout his loins. In this small space his legs were bent upright and his face forced to the floor. The wood was wet and smelled of vile juices probably from Taben's body. He clawed at the hard ground. In the distance he could hear the voice of his jailer returning with someone else. Frantically he dug, with the fear of unknown tortures driving him on.

Without warning the blocking stone fell into the hole he was creating. It fell on top of Baetan's hand. The freed wheel immediately rolled forward over the rock crushing his trapped wrist and fingers. The wagon slipped quietly into the dark, first gradually, then in a rush as the hill steepened. Suddenly it jolted into the air and crashed loudly into boulder. The wooden structure splintered into kindling.

Baetan lay motionless and confused for several moments. What had happened? He was free. He could not feel his right hand that had been under the rock. Pains were shooting up his arm. Taben? Where was Taben? No time to look. Now he had to run before the Roman soldiers caught him again. *Should I hide?* He thought. *No, I must run. They will find the wagon at dawn and I must be away from here.*

The Centurion was outraged. The jail wagon holding Taben the spy was gone. The jailer had spun some tale about a second prisoner…a new spy. The wagon was located in a short time, smashed to bits at the bottom of the hill. The Celtiberian prisoner was dead.

"You let him escape and die jailer. We were not finished with him. You will get ten lashes for your incompetence."

"There was a second prisoner Sir," the guard mumbled. A guard from our wall brought him to me."

"Who is the guard?"

"I don't know. He said our wall might be breeched."

"Where did he capture this so called spy?"

"I don't know Sir. I only…"

The Centurion was livid. "Principale, (Sergeant) give this man twenty lashes. He dares to lie to me." He would not listen to the jailer's pleas or try to find the supposed guard who had delivered the second prisoner. There had been no incursions in their wall and the man had lied to protect himself because he had lost the wagon and the prisoner.

Baetan's flight had not been easy. The way was rocky and very dark. Dawn was barely breaking. He tripped often further damaging his already hurt body. By mid-day he was far from Numantia and the

Roman forces. He was lost. Exhausted, he found a small stream where he bathed his cuts, and especially his crushed hand, in the icy water.

Suddenly he realized he was not alone. On the other side of the brook was a small figure. The person was obscured by the sun behind him and the bright glare from the water.

"Baetan?" a thin voice called.

He was surprised that someone knew him. "Who calls me?"

"I am your little brother, Raghnall. I came to say goodbye."

"Raghnall, you have escaped Numantia. The Legions are gone? Is our grandfather Derfail all right?" Tell me please!"

The shape of the little boy shimmered indistinctly in the strong sunlight. "I must join Taben. We must go. Goodbye."

Baetan shook his head to clear his vision. When he looked back, the spot across the stream was empty.

During the night Derfail had continued with his plan. He had sent Baetan out of the town on a fatal mission. With real luck the boy might survive and actually escape. Derfail understood that there would be no relief for Numantia. Scipio had cohorts in every Celtiberian enclave. It would not be possible for the Celts to organize a relief party. His people's culture was doomed…they were conquered!

With the dawn he returned to his house to find little Raghnall dead. It was a great relief. He was not forced to kill his own grandson.

A BIT OF HISTORY

In 133 B.C. after a long and brutal siege, the city of Numantia was finally taken and destroyed by Scipio Aemilianus Africanus. As a final act of defiance, the starving Numantians committed mass suicide rather than surrender and become Roman slaves. It marked the end of formal resistance of the Celtiberian cities to Roman domination. The Romans then submerged the Celtiberian culture into a Romanized province.

In Spanish society Numantia has a tradition similar to that of the Alamo for Texans. Miguel de Cervantes (author of Don Quixote) wrote a play about the siege, 'El cerco de Numancia', which stands today as his most well-known dramatic work.

Publius Claudius Pulcher managed to escape the terrible defeat of his fleet at Drepana. He returned to Rome in shame. There he faced charges of treason. He was brought to the court accused of sacrilege due to the sacred chicken incident. He was convicted and sentenced to exile, his political career finished.

Seventeen

Britannia

"Grandpa, you sure do like maps, don't you? You have them all over your house"

"That's right Matt, I do. I've got a bunch more of them in my bookcase."

"What's this one on the wall behind you grandpa? Hold it. I know. Don't tell me. It's England. You went there didn't you? Dad told me."

"Yes, with your grandma. Your folks gave us a trip there for a wedding anniversary present."

"I heard about that. I'll bet the lines on the map are all the places you visited."

"No. That is an old, old map. It represents what Britain looked like to the Romans after they conquered the country. The dark lines are the roads that the Romans built all across what they called Brittany. It is the way the roads looked in the year the Legions abandoned the country.

"They built all that stuff and then went home to Rome? How come Grandpa?"

"Well the Romans were a tough bunch of people. They had spent about 800 years conquering everybody. They controlled most of England for about the last half of those 800 years. Seems like they never had enough territory. The Romans were always fighting…even among themselves. Everybody wanted to see who could be the Roman

Emperor...the boss of it all. If a general could conquer a big chunk of territory for Rome, he might be able to get himself appointed Emperor."

"No elections?"

"Correct my boy. Many of the Roman generals came from rich families. They would form their own Legion and personally pay the troops by using the riches they took from the tribes they conquered. But often the generals were better politicians than good soldiers. Their idea was to make a name for themselves by conquering somebody. Then, because they were now famous, they could possibly get the job of Emperor. They were not concerned about the people or territories they conquered. They cared more for politics and more power.

"Anyway the Romans got so spread out that they couldn't control everything. They had too much territory and not enough soldiers to hold it. Barbarian tribes kept pushing into their frontiers. It was not a nice time to be a citizen of the empire during those last days before the empire fell apart.

"But you asked about the map. The Roman army had been in Britain for about 400 years. That is a long time. Those tribes who lived in Britain, even before the legions arrived, were somewhat civilized. They had farms and towns but those tribes had never united as a nation. It was easy for the legions to defeat each small group and take over most of the country."

"I'll bet the Romans picked them off one at a time...right Grandpa?"

"Smart thinking Matt. I don't know for sure what happened but what you suggest sounds reasonable to me."

"I play a lot of computer games and I've learned about tactics."

"Well to get back to the map, after almost 400 years of occupation the Romans suddenly left England...I mean Brittany as they called it, in the year 407 A.D. The borders closer to Rome needed to be defended. As they were leaving, the British Legions had decided that their general, Constantine, should become the new Roman Emperor. That is the way things sometimes happened back then. If you controlled a large military force you might be able to force yourself into leadership.

"Constantine took all his troops to Gaul, which is now France. There were no legions left in Britain to keep order and defend the rich Roman landlords. For the first time the Roman citizens in Britain, and there were lots of them, had to fend for themselves. The ancient people of the land, the Celts, had been tamed by centuries of Roman law. Still, the Celts wanted their original tribal lands back. At the same time less civilized groups from Ireland and Europe were landing in Britain and pushing back the native Celts. It was a mess. No one was in charge any longer. The little Roman towns bricked up their gates and built higher walls to protect themselves from the native tribes. The rich villas in the flat countryside couldn't be defended and the people had to move into hilltop forts. Village officials turned into warlords and eventually made themselves kings of their area."

"That sounds like what happened when we left Afghanistan!"

The old man laughed. "You are a smart boy. I guess you get that from me."

"That's not what mom says grandpa."

The old man smiled and continued. "The Romans had developed civilization, new towns, and an amazing system of roads and waterworks, all in what had been a mostly primitive land. They had even built a wall across the entire island to hold back the barbarians from the north. They couldn't conquer a wild people called the Picts."

"I learned about that in school Grandpa. It was called Hadrian's Wall. I even read about it in the National Geographic magazine."

"That's right. Grandma and I visited part of the wall on our trip to England. Not much of it remains …but it certainly is there. It was built almost two thousand years ago.

"But in only a hundred or so years, after the Legions left, there was very little remaining anywhere of what had been part the great Roman Empire in Brittany. Civilization and the rule of law crumbled into anarchy. England, like the rest of Europe, slowly dissolved into what we call 'The Dark Ages'.

"Okay, grandson, enough about the maps and England and Romans. All of those inhabitants are long forgotten. It is such a long time ago that it is hard to even think of them as people.

Come on, let's get the dog and go for a walk."

Eighteen

Ruga

Flight into Darkness 411 A.D.

Dosia was delighted that her older sister Janae was coming for a visit. Janae was accompanying her husband Quadratus Cinna on the long trek to Villa Magnus. This villa was Dosia's splendid new home. Quadratus, for some reason, needed to see Dosia's husband Gaius. Dosia did not know exactly the reason. It was not her nature to pry into the affairs of men.

Growing up, Dosia always felt that Janae appeared to get the best part of everything. Then when their father had arranged for Janae's marriage to rich Quadratus Cinna, it had made her sister even more insufferable. In turn, that made Dosia even more jealous of her sibling.

If Dosia had been bothered in their youth by her elder sister's dominance, Jaene's marriage made it far worse. Janae had wallowed in her impressive married home. True enough, younger Dosia had been astounded by the richness of the Cinna Villa. Often she visited there accompanied by Titus, the girls' father. But she tired quickly of Janae's endless bragging about the appointments of her new villa home. It was certainly true that Janae had many servants and seemingly endless slaves. Their father Titus was unquestionably prosperous but not on the scale of Jaene's new husband.

There was one bright feature of the visits to see Janae. Cinna Villa was close by the warm thermal baths of Aquae Sulis. Long ago the Romans had constructed a wonderful spa around these natural springs of western Brittany. Even though she despised Janae's constant boasting, she would suffer it for the pleasure of a trip to these warm mineral waters. She loved to bath in their relaxing pools.

When Dosia's father finally gave her in marriage, it was to Gaius Magnus. He was a much older man, a bit too portly with balding gray hair and a constant wheezing. Dosia often thought that Gaius would collapse from a lack of breath. The man had no energy at all.

At first she sobbed about her father's choice for her, but then there were advantages. Gaius tired quickly in bed and had never beaten her. Then, wonder of wonders, immediately after the marriage Gaius took her to her new home on the south coast of Brittany. It was the original family home of Sallustius Lucullus, the first governor of Roman Britain. It had stayed in the same family for over 300 years. Gaius explained to Dosia that it was the largest villa in all Brittany and rivaled some of the Emperors palaces in Rome. Dosia burned with invidious desire to take Janae through this amazing villa. It would stifle her sister's snobbish mouth.

Upon arriving the previous evening Quadratus and Janae had retired immediately to a luxurious guest apartment. Dosia anxiously now awaited her sister to join her for breakfast in the large atrium.

Gaius was already entertaining his brother-in-law guest Quadratus in the sun-filled courtyard. As two of the richest men in Brittany they would start the day with a breakfast of cheese, olives and honey. Being Patricians, they enjoyed the finest bread which they dipped into their wine filled cups.

"Quadratus, did you sleep well. I know you had a long journey. That is why I suggested last evening that you retire immediately." Gaius could see dark circles around his brother-in-law's eyes. The man looked very ill.

"Thank you Gaius for asking. I must tell you the truth. I did not sleep well at all. It is not the fault of your wonderful accommodations. My mind has been anxious since Constantine took his Legions to Gaul. But of course that is almost five years now. In the past months though, I have started to sleep very little. It is strange. I have consulted a doctor and even Jaene's Priest. You know don't you, that she has become a Christian? It is very disturbing to me. But then I don't intend to blame that for my sleeplessness. I'm not sure what is wrong. In any event the doctor helped me not at all and neither did the priest. If you hear me scream during our stay, it is because I feel things crawling on me in the night. It is not a dream that I am having...I am not even asleep."

Magnus did not know how to respond to this revelation from his brother-in-law. He only nodded.

Quadratus gave a weak smile and continued, "I was much relieved to see Legionnaires stand guard here. I had not heard that the Legion had come back to Brittany. Is this an advanced guard or has the entire Legion returned to protect us and restore our peaceful life?"

"There is no legion Quadratus. Those men you saw last evening are not even Romans. They are hired Spaniards that I have purposely dressed as Roman soldiers. I do this to control my slaves and frighten the local Celtic tribesmen."

"Oh," Quadratus responded with a low mournful sigh. "For a moment I had great hopes that the Legion was back. Things are getting bad...very bad. Let me tell you, if I may, about the trip I took with Titus, our father-in-law. I believe we both have anticipated a large inheritance from the man since he has only the two daughters.

"Titus and I took a trip to inspect his gold mine far to the north. It is close to Hadrian's Wall. The expected ore shipments from the mine recently stopped."

Quadratus suddenly discontinued talking. He was obviously caught up in a deep memory. He stared upward at the deep blue open sky above the roofless atrium and drank heavily from his cup of wine. Gaius noticed that the man's hands trembled.

"Please continue," Gaius finally urged after a long silence.

"Yes. Well, it took us two days travelling north on the Fosse Way to reach Ratae. Titus has...had a friend there named Sulla who owns, I mean to say owned, a large villa about three miles from the town. We found the villa in ruins. Everything was burned or smashed. The slaves were gone. Worst of all we found Sulla's head stuck on a pole. It was horrible. Sulla was a hard man. Titus told me that Sulla crucified a slave or two every year just to keep the rest of them subdued."

"Sulla had been brutally murdered? And you say he crucified slaves? The Emperor outlawed crucifixion as a punishment many years ago. He capitulated to those Christians who seem to be flooding the Empire. They feel that it dishonors their God."

"I am aware of all of that Gaius, but Sulla was a most powerful landowner and he was not obviously challenged by anyone about what he could or could not do with his property. Years ago Sulla told me that Rome was too far away to be bothered with him. He especially felt that Christians were all fools. He decided Rome would not be allowed to control how he treated his property. A few of the local retired Legionnaires from Ratae were more than happy to keep the slaves frightened. A crucifixion was like old times for them.

"In any event, we immediately continued on to Ratae and surprisingly found the whole village in disarray. That place is a veritable stronghold of retired Legionnaires. You would think there would be some order, some discipline, among people of military training, yet all were in panic. A few of the villagers thought we had come to save them from...I don't know exactly what. Most of them were in the process of building a protective wall around the town." For a second time Quadratus suddenly lapsed into a deep silence.

"So Quadratus, get on with it. Tell me who destroyed Sulla's villa?"

Quadratus shook himself. "The people of Ratae don't really know. Some of the townspeople told us it was a slave revolt, especially since Sulla was such a violent slave holder. Others claimed that it was the Celts or a raiding party of Anglo-Saxons. No one was sure of anything."

"This is terrible. Yet I can't believe that old Roman soldiers would be frightened by the destruction of just one villa. The Celtic tribes around here have not been troublesome. They have long been tamed. But perhaps a raiding party of Anglos or Saxons or..."

"Wait, Magnus. There is more. We learned that other villas in the outlying valleys have also been destroyed. It was not simply a slave revolt only at the Sulla Villa. There is something larger and more sinister happening. Some of the people at Ratae have decided to move to a nearby hilltop and erect a strong stone fortification. They are building it on the foundations of a Celtic fort that existed before Rome ever conquered this province. There is great dread in the land. The villas, the farms, the mines are all being destroyed."

Gaius could hear the fear in Quadratus' voice. He asked, "Your journey was to go farther north to Titus' gold mine. Did you get there?"

"Titus was alarmed by what he saw. Honestly, I was too. He inquired about his gold mine but received no answers. He did learn that the Picts, the ones called 'The Blue Men' have been raiding south of Hadrian's Wall. They cross without impediment since the Legion has left Brittany. Titus decided it would be best that we should return south to safer lands. He told me that he expects that his mine is now lost."

Magnus shook his head in disbelief. "I have been to Ratae. I know some of the people there. They are a tough bunch of old Legion veterans. If they are withdrawing to defensive positions, then I truly suspect that a lawless time is coming to Brittany."

"That is exactly why I came here and brought Janae with me," Quadratus said. "I am beginning to fear for our safety. I tried to bring Titus along with us but the old bull says that there is no danger around Aquae Sulis. He told me that everything will return to normal as soon as the Legions come back to enforce order. Tell me Magnus, when do think our Legions will return?"

Magnus put his hand to his mouth and rolled his eyes upward in a gesture of hopelessness. He inhaled deeply which caused him to cough for a brief time. Finally, he found his voice. Slowly he wheezed a reply. "It will not happen Quadratus. It will never happen! The Empire is crumbling around us brother-in-law. There will be no Legions returning to Brittany. Have you not heard about the situation in Italy?"

"No." The single word rolled slowly out of Quadratus' mouth. A chill of fear ran through his body.

"Well Rome has been attacked by the barbarian Visigoths led by their king Alaric. Someone, they say slaves, opened the gates of the city after a long siege. The Senate and other government offices had been moved before the siege. They went to the old Etruscan town of Ravenna. This was the action of our heroic young Emperor Honorius. He ran away! Still, I hear that the sack of Rome was mild because the Visigoths are now Christians."

"Rome is gone," Quadratus whined. "Then what will happen to us?"

"There is more. Remember that Constantine took his Legions across the channel as his troops declared him emperor. For a time we had two Emperors."

"Yes, I certainly remember that. But without his forces we cannot defend ourselves against the local Celtic tribes or invasions of others. We just barely fought off that Saxon incursion two summers ago. It is becoming more and more difficult to maintain Roman control over our lands."

"That is correct Quadratus. Now hear this. Constantine is dead. Currently there is massive fighting all over the Empire. No one seems to be in charge any longer. Finally just two days ago a boat arrived with a reply from Emperor Honorius about our request for help."

"I think I can surmise what it said, Magnus."

"You are probably correct in your thinking. It said we must look to our own defenses."

Magnus was suddenly caught up again in a spell of wheezing and coughing. He had talked too much. His face turned purple for lack of breath.

Quadratus watched helplessly, not knowing what to do. His head hurt gravely. He was not sure if it was the bad news or simply his recent lack of sleep.

Janae finally arrived in the atrium. She was accompanied by two of her maids and led to the breakfast by one of Dosia's slaves. The sisters embraced. Dosia noticed that Janae's strong hug represented more than a greeting. Something was wrong.

"Dosia, your villa is unbelievable," Janae said as the two reclined, waiting to be served their morning meal. "You must take me on a tour of this splendid place. The marble and tile works are the finest I have ever seen. Who has done all of these floor designs? I must have him come to our villa for some work."

Dosia laughed. "This is a very old villa my sister. My husband Gaius told me that a master craftsman named Matteo of Bartolotta came here all the way from Italy in his grandfather's day, to do most of the tile work. That was long ago. I'm sure that Matteo must be dead by now.

"But tell me Janae, what news of father…and of course yourself? Are you feeling well?"

"No, Dosia, I am not at all well. But you must understand, it is not me, it is those around me. Our father Titus has been in a deep depression ever since he and Quadratus returned from their trip to father's gold mine. Neither of them will tell me what is wrong. Worse yet, Quadratus has insomnia. He has slept very little for several months. The sleeplessness is getting worse. If there is a loud noise, even when he is awake, he panics. He tells me that sometimes he feels snakes or bugs are crawling all over his body."

"Do you think the trip to the gold mine caused him so much worry that it would affect his mind?"

"It is not possible Dosia. This insomnia started a month or more before he traveled there with our father. It has to be something else. I don't know how to help him"

"I can see how this would worry you, but you said you did not feel well. Could you be with child?"

"Definitely not! Quadratus has been most disappointed in me. Still, I am sure it is not my fault. He has had many children by his slave girls, but none in several years. I think his organs are dry. He wants a son very badly. He needs one to inherit our villa and properties. You know of course, that when father dies his estate and ours will become one of the greatest in Brittany."

Dosia held her tongue. Her sister had never lost her imperious nature. She could almost see the wicked smirk of superiority on Janae's face. They ate for a few moments without speaking.

Janae broke the silence. "What of you, sister? Has Magnus managed to get you with child yet? You have certainly been married long enough."

There it was again. The haughty personality of her older sister could not remain hidden for very long. Janae knew full well that Magnus was impotent. They had coupled only a few times since marriage, and never to completion. Magnus had never had a child, even by a slave girl. It seemed that the sisters had been married off to unhealthy men.

Dosia, as she had done all her life, swallowed the bile of Janae's remarks. She did not answer. Instead she said, "Come Janae, let me show you the marvels of Magnus' villa."

The sightseeing was arduous for Janae. Dosia insisted on pointing out every luxurious feature of the villa. There was hot and cold running water in every bedchamber. The floors were all heated to ward off the chill of winter. The gardens, statues and mosaic work were exceptional. Dosia was delighted by the envy she detected in her sister's responses to each rich appointment. It felt so satisfying.

Finally Janae called a halt to the exhaustive tour. "Stop Dosia," she complained. "I must rest," she lied.

The two sisters sat down in a in a quiet sundrenched alcove. Slave girls served wine and fruit. Although the slaves were the property of Magnus and Dosia, Janae ordered them away. It was a breach of good manners, but Janae explained, "I don't care to have them hear us talking."

Dosia was miffed. "They are *my* slaves' sister. You know slaves don't think."

"Things are changing Dosia. It is not as it was when we lived with our parents and mother was alive. Listen to what I tell you. As we traveled here we met several groups of Celts on the highway. They failed to get off the road so we might immediately pass. Once we actually had to stop while a farmer drove his herd of sheep across our path. He did it purposely. He had seen us coming. Then he turned and made an obscene gesture towards us. If it had not been so late in the day Quadratus might have chased the man and punished him. I expect he would have killed the scoundrel. Quadratus slips suddenly into violent anger in a way I have never seen before. I believe it is his lack of sleep."

The younger woman mused, "That sounds possible."

"But more than that Dosia, the Celts are getting more unruly ever since the Legions departed. We have had trouble with many of them. They are becoming less docile. In Brittany we have civilized the tribes, stopped their incessant warfare, and what do we get for thanks? The Celtic tribesmen are acting like it is their land. The example they set is so bad that it is spreading to the slaves. Just a few weeks ago I had a slave look me directly in the eye. Can you imagine? I had Quadratus blind the slave in one eye as punishment for doing that.

"What of the Legions Dosia? What news do you hear? When will they return?"

"Oh Janae, you have had so much trouble. Now, I can understand why you might not feel well. "Gaius told me just last week that the Legions will be back shortly. He and some others sent a delegation to the Emperor demanding that the Legions return. Everything will be going back to our old ways in just a short time. It has to happen. Quadratus will be able to sleep and the Celts and slaves will return to their proper places. You need not fret so Janae. Gaius explained to me that because we have controlled Brittany for some many hundreds of years, nothing will change."

Ruga felt as if he had parts of himself in two different worlds. He was not sure exactly where he belonged. His father and grandfather had long served the villa of the family of Gaius Magnus. Ruga in turn followed in their footsteps. For many years now he had been the overseer of Villa Magnus. His sons, and this spring also a grandson, earned their living from work at the Villa.

Yet, much was different compared to the old days. Starting late in Ruga's father's time of stewardship, the Romans began to lose control over the civitates, the client native kingdoms of Brittany. These political territorial distributions, made hundreds of years earlier, had only vaguely followed tribal lines. The old boundaries, earned with much blood by competing tribes were never forgotten. As control weakened because of the departed Legions, old tribal wars were being renewed. So too, vast lands that had been under the control of Roman villas for centuries, were being gradually reoccupied by native tribes. Ruga and his sons could not stem the tide. Much Villa Magnus' land was being repossessed by Ruga's own tribe.

Gaius Magnus was equally aware of these incursions but did not have the manpower to hold back the land-hungry Celts. Local Roman magistrates were powerless without the army. Gaius had hoped that Ruga could negotiate with the nearby tribes. It had not worked.

Ruga was a typical Celt. He was very tall in stature, with rippling muscles under clear white skin. His hair was blond, but not naturally so. He, as others in all of the Celtic tribes, bleached their hair, washing it in lime and combing it back from the forehead. To Gaius he looked like a wood-demon, his hair was thick and shaggy like a horse's mane. While some of the Celts were clean-shaven, others like Ruga shaved only their cheeks and left a moustache to cover the whole mouth. It was a symbol of authority among the natives. In the Roman way of cleanliness, Gaius often prodded Ruga to bathe and shave more often.

Yet in many other ways Ruga was almost Roman. He had adopted many of the Roman customs. One prime benefit of his position was his ability to eat and drink as a Roman. He especially enjoyed their wines.

From his father, Ruga had been taught the ways of the Villa. Now that he was chief overseer he controlled all of the servants; the freemen and slaves of Magnus Villa. He would punish any of them as Gaius commanded. Often he meted out discipline completely on his own.

Ruga, even his name was Roman, had learned to walk a fine line between tribe and villa. He provided his tribe with income as he purchased cattle and grain from them. Yet he had to be careful when a Celt was punished for infractions. This split of loyalties was becoming more difficult each season.

On one occasion Ruga was in an adjoining room and overheard a conversation between Gaius and a visitor from Rome named Brutus. As was Ruga's custom, he had entered the Villa after the noontime meal to finish off any lefPover wine. The words he heard between Gaius and Brutus stiffened his dislike…now bordering on hatred… for all Romans. Listening, he better understood how he was valued by this arrogant man.

"Brutus, I am at a loss as to what to do. I am master of this vast Villa yet I have no heir to continue it."

"Your wife, Dosia?" Brutus asked. "Is she…?"

Gaius almost blushed. "No Brutus. The problem is with me. I am sure of it. Ever since I came of age I have coupled with a variety of slave girls…all to no effect."

"Well then, you might think of adopting a boy. I'm sure there are many healthy lads who would be quite willing to become your son. As a matter of fact you might consider adopting one of those big vigorous Celtic boys. The countryside abounds with them."

Now Gaius turned angry. "That is foolish…no more than foolish…it is stupid Brutus. I do not mean to insult you but I could never adopt one of those coarse smelly Celts. Just look at my overseer Ruga. He does his work well but he is a loutish brute. He has this especially vile habit of pulling his nostrils. Then if there is any fluid in his nose, it remains as a sticky mass on his beard. I could never have someone like that inherit Magnus Villa! He, like all the Celts, is little more than a dirty animal."

Ruga was stunned. He had never realized how he, his family and his tribe were absolutely undervalued by this imperious Roman. He would not forget the insult. Unconsciously he pulled his nostrils shut with his left hand.

Ruga's tribe was another matter. Times were also changing for them. Some of the finest, almost indestructible pottery in Brittany was made by his tribe. It was shipped all over the Roman Empire. Unfortunately, political upheavals had recently ended this lucrative trade.

More and more border clashes were happening among the tribal kingdoms. His clan was looking for alliances to battle the Iceni...the once very powerful tribe to the north. There was need for revenge. Recently the Iceni had captured a hunting party of his clan that had strayed into their territory. A chief had been in that party. All the hunters had been killed. In true Celtic tradition the chief had been beheaded and the head taken away. Every Celtic tribe accepted as true, that the human soul lived inside the head. They believed that capturing someone's soul gave you extraordinary magic. It was therefore proper to collect the heads of important enemies killed in battle. With waning Roman control, it was becoming possible once again to assert tribal custom and try to reestablish old boundaries.

Each of Ruga's sons was agitating to go to war. Fighting was a condition in the Celtic psyche. Bloody battle...to clash and even die in glorious conflict was good. Only Ruga, now an old man, counseled peace to his tribe. It did no good. The life he led at Villa Magnus was excellent...why jeopardize it with uncontrollable warfare? Ruga was mocked by his own people. He was called a coward. Worst of all, he was sometimes called 'Roman.' Ruga was unsure of what he was or where his loyalties belonged.

Jaene's planned visit of three weeks with her sister Dosia had now stretched into nearly three months. Her husband, Quadratus, had advanced from insomnia to almost complete sleeplessness. His eyes were sunken black orbs, almost holes in his head. He was losing weight and had serious problems making connections with reality. He was far too sick to manage the long journey home. Everyone understood that.

Gaius Magnus was lost about what to do. He felt that his brother-in-law was on the verge of insanity…or perhaps already there. Late one evening, the night watchman found Quadratus destroying statuary in the atrium. A week later he accosted a slave girl, screaming that her name was Dosia and beat her badly. These events were taking a toll on everyone. Now a guard was assigned to watch Quadratus full time. He was no longer to be left alone. The strain of these events caused Gaius' breathing problems to worsen.

Janae made every effort to excuse Quadratus' behavior to Dosia. The sisters now quarreled frequently. There was friction almost every day. They were particularly angered with each other over a rare blue glass cup that had belonged to their mother. When Dosia had been given in marriage to Gaius, her father gave her the cup as a parting present. Both girls treasured it as a remembrance of their mother.

"I am the oldest Dosia. That blue cup belongs to me."

"You can't have it Janae. Father gave it to me. You have always received the very best from mother and father and I only got what was left. The blue cup is mine!"

They called each other names and the problem of the antique cup was never resolved. The pressure of the difficulties caused by Quadratus seemed to give Dosia some backbone. Previously she had always given in to Janae's demands, no matter how petty. She did not like to fight. Together they found peace only in the heated waters of Dosia's relaxing bathe. Janae was especially fond of the tile designs on the walls. She remarked over and over about the excellent tile work.

"Yes, that work of two women with a ball is also one of the many in the villa done long ago by Matteo. I think the man was a genius."

The warm waters of the bathe calmed both sisters. They recalled games they played as girls and giggled over a boy they had both liked.

Unexpectedly this day, both exchanged looks of concern. There were screams outside the bathe. It was obviously Quadratus. He was shrieking his wife's name, "Janae, Janae," in an almost unintelligible voice.

Both women rose out of the bathe, one on each side of the pool. Quadratus entered the room carrying a long knife. He hoarsely screamed, "Dosia you have killed my wife. Now I will kill you."

Both sisters and even the slave attendants all screamed. Quadratus could not be stopped. In his crazed state of mind he flew at Dosia and stabbed her in the heart. Both of them fell into the bathing pool. Janae fainted. One attendant dashed out bawling loudly for Gaius.

Gaius heard the clamor and ran as quickly as his lungs would permit. When he entered the bathe he found a sight that made him instantly sick. Dosia was face down in the bath water which was now blood red. Janae was slumped on the floor, perhaps dead too. Quadratus, standing at the side of the bathe, was stabbing the two women ball players on the decorated tile wall using his bloody knife.

Gaius did not think. He leaped at his brother-in-law and caught him in a choke hold. Gaius was no longer strong but he had been a wrestler in his youth. Quadratus could not free himself. They tumbled backward into the bloody pool on top of Dosia's body. In his raging anger, Gaius could not, would not, let go. Both men drowned in the shallow pool.

Ruga, running, finally arrived at the crime scene completely out of breath. The carnage overwhelmed him. He was accustomed to blood on the field of battle, but here in the Villa? The attendants were now reduced to sobbing. "What happened?" He asked. No one seemed able to answer him.

As a man of action, Ruga pulled Quadratus from the pool. He was shaken to find another body...it was his master of the Villa, Gaius Magnus under Quadratus. Then he realized that below Gaius there was still another body. It was Dosia, the now obvious source of all the blood filling the water. *What had these foolish Romans done to each other?*

Ruga was now bloody himself. He became aware of the shrieking directly to his rear. It was Janae. He hadn't even noticed her as he burst into the room. She had risen from her faint and now started to pound on Ruga's back. "You killed him, you killed my husband you Celtic barbarian," she wildly cried.

Other horrified household servants had now entered. All were stunned by the three bodies and the wailing handmaidens. Blood was everywhere. Janae was still erratically flaying at Ruga while he held her at a distance with one arm. He needed time to think. He ordered two of the men to take the unstable Janae to her quarters. He stopped her maid servants from following.

"What happened here?" he demanded.

Through heaving, halting sobs one girl was able to explain that Quadratus had assaulted Dosia and Gaius then apparently strangled the man.

"Did Janae see this?"

"Yes," the girl replied, "then she fainted."

Ruga suddenly asked, "Did you see the man who was supposed to be watching Quadratus?'"

All shook their heads. One girl stammered, "Quadratus was alone."

Ruga took several deep breaths to think. Everyone stared at him and waited. It dawned on him that he was now the master of Villa Magnus. He drew himself to his full height, found his deep commanding voice and gave orders. Janae's women were returned to her. He ordered others to prepare the three bodies for cremation. Next he commanded slaves to clean the bathe. Finally he sought out Quadratus' missing attendant. Why had Quadratus got away from his guard? Quickly he found the answer in Quadratus' chamber. The guard was dead drunk. Ruga roused the man and then beat him badly. Next he ordered the man to be buried up to his neck in the sand where the crematory fire would be built. The guard would be roasted alive beneath the burial blaze.

In the weeks that followed Ruga acquired a fuller appreciation of his position. All formal Roman authority had departed Brittany. He was now master of this huge structure and vast farmlands. Trade with Roman possessions had stopped. There was little reason to maintain anything. There was no authority to challenge him.

Ruga brought his sons and their families into the villa to live. Many of the tribe followed to enjoy the more substantial accommodations. The new arrivals built fires on the tile floors and tore open beautifully decorated walls for ventilation. Some farm animals were stabled in the villa proper.

Ruga saw Janae only one more time. She was evicted from her apartment and given a room in the villa rustica, the out building where the staff and slaves of the villa worked and lived.

As she left Janae looked at Ruga with penetrating hate in her eyes. She screamed at him as she was dragged away, "Where is my blue cup, I want my blue cup."

A BIT OF HISTORY

Fatal Familial Insomnia (FFI) is an extremely rare disease. It starts with a sudden and inexplicable onset of insomnia, causes panic attacks and unfounded phobias. This early phase lasts for about nine months. It then develops into total insomnia causing rapid weight loss and limited mental functioning leading to dementia and agonizing sleepless death.

Nineteen

The Unicorn's Horn

CHILDREN'S STORIES

It was bedtime and Madeline wanted to hear her favorite bedtime story. Her twin brother Dan was already asleep in the other bunk bed. They were six years old and had school the next day. Their cousin Matt was babysitting.

"Matt, read me the story about the Unicorn."

"Oh Maddy, I just read that last night. Why not a different story tonight?"

Maddy pouted and started to fidget.

Matt sighed. He said, "Oh all right, but then you will go to sleep, just like your brother. Understand?"

Maddy didn't answer. She smiled, just a little, as her cousin read the story. Once again she had got her way.

One fine afternoon when Lion and Unicorn, were play wrestling in the forest, Lion said to Unicorn: "I'm weary of this, let's stop. My paws are tired, the topknot on my tail has got quite dusty. My mane is full of knots and needs combing. I think we should stop and rest."

Unicorn smiled and replied: "That's a good idea. I am getting worn-out too. My swirly horn is getting chipped and my hooves need repainting."

So they both sat down in the shade of a big mulberry tree. Unicorn took a comb made of carved bone and gently combed all the tangles out of Lion's matted mane. Then Unicorn brushed all the dust out of the topknot on Lion's tail and fluffed it prettily.

When he was tidy again, Lion reached behind the tree-trunk and found a pot of gold paint with a bristly brush by its side. Dipping the brush into the paint, Lion said: "Hold still, Unicorn. If you fidget, the paint will go into your eyes." So Unicorn sat without moving while Lion carefully touched up the chipped parts of his swirly horn with gold. Next he made Unicorn hold out each hoof one after another while he repainted the hooves until they glistened in the bright yellow sunshine.

"I'm hungry," Lion said, "let's go and have some tea."

So they found a tea-shop and forgot all about wrestling each other. Lion ordered brown bread and butter sandwiches with mustard and watercress, of which he was very fond. Unicorn had lettuce with cocoa, his favorite dish. Together they enjoyed their meal, and strolled into the forest just as the pale moon was coming up over the hillside. It was time for bed.

INUIT STORY 1050 A.D.

"Mother, please tell me the story about the Narwhale horns," the little boy whined.

The mother sighed. She was very tired but this was her only living child, so she began...

A wicked woman lived with her daughter and her son. He was born blind. The mother hated her child for his blindness. As the boy got older, his sight improved, yet the mother tried to convince him of his useless condition. One day a gigantic pure white polar bear came near their house. The mother told the son to shoot an arrow at the bear to strike him down. The boy pulled back the arrow and the mother took aim for him. The arrow struck the heart of the bear. Although the boy could hear the groans of the dying bear, the mother laughed scornfully at him, telling him he had missed the bear. That night the mother and the daughter had fresh polar bear to eat. The mother cooked dog meat for her son. Later the boy's sister told her brother that his shot was successful and secretly gave him some tasty polar bear meat to eat.

Time passed. One day an old Inuit man came to the house for a visit. Before he left, he told the young girl how she could help her brother regain all of his sight. In the spring, he said, the children should watch for a red throated loon who would swim trustingly toward them. Once the loon was close enough, the blind brother should wrap his arms around the loon's neck and the loon would take him to the bottom of the ocean. Once they came up for air, his sight would be returned.

It all happened just as the visitor had said. The loon then told the young man not to tell anyone about his regained sight until later in the summer. At that time he would send a pod of narwhales to their campsite that the boy could see and harpoon.

When summer came and the ice started to break, the narwhales began to move. On one occasion, a pod was closer to land than usual. The young man grabbed his harpoon and told his sister to accompany him to help him aim. They went to the shoreline, and the mother, seeing the son with a harpoon, became concerned and followed him.

Once she was close to them, the son gave his mother the end of the line from the harpoon asking her to tie it around her waist to hold the harpooned animal. The fearful mother told her daughter to make sure he was after a small animal as she was tied to the harpoon. The son instead aimed for the largest narwhale and harpooned it. The mother was cast into the sea. As she submerged she spiraled around the line, with her long hair twisting into its extended lance like horn.

This is how the narwhale-unicorn horn came to be.

Twenty

The Saga of Haagan

1020 A.D.

I need to tell you about my life. It will be over shortly. I will be dead by the time the sun rises. It is my hope that you will remember me for all that I have done and all that I have been in the days of my life. I was a hero! I was a raider. Never, *never* was I a Viking pirate. For this I will be welcomed in the Halls of Valhalla. Vikings steal. They are thieves. We raiders are honorable men. We fight for everything we take. Yet, by the morn I will die. These Christian savages insist on calling me a violent Viking. It is not true. I am not a Viking.

Let me tell you about my cousin Egill. It will explain the difference.

When raiding a coastal farm on the northern shores of Scotland, Egill and his men were shamefully captured by the farmer and his family and his many retainers. They bound my cousin and all of the raiders with ropes. In the night that followed, Egill was able to slip his bonds. He and his men seized their captors' treasure and headed back to their ship. But along the way, Egill realized he was acting like a thief. That was the shameful trait of Viking's. So he returned to his captors' house, set it ablaze, and killed the occupants as they tried to escape the fire. He then returned to the ship with the riches, but this time as a hero. Why? Because...he had fought for the treasure and won it in battle. He could justly claim the booty. He was an honest raider.

Now listen to the story of my life as a raider and adventurer...would you have done differently? Am I not an honest raider? I am not a Viking pirate. Listen and judge me fairly, for shortly I will die.

You may have heard of my great-grandfather, Ásvald Úlfsson. As a young man he was on a raiding party that sacked a large monastery on the English Coast. The raid went well. But as they rowed and sailed away in their dragon boats a violent storm rose on the sea. My great-grandfather was washed over the side. Someone threw him a rope, but as he grasped it, Thor sent a thunderbolt down from the heavens directly striking the mast of Ásvald Úlfsson's dragon ship sending Thor's power surging throughout ship. Everyone aboard died except my great-grandfather who was in the water still holding the rope. The other dragon ship picked him up. His hands were burned badly. A metal amulet that he wore around his neck, shaped as a hammer to honor Thor, had seared its outline deeply into his chest. It was a sacred scar. Also, his beard suddenly had a white streak added to it. Immediately he was honored as an apprentice of Thor. Still, some of his family said that he was never completely sane again. He became a man with an instant fiery temper.

He was to be feared. The gods had endowed my family with that same hot blood.

Thor the Thunder God is our family god and protector.

After that raid, Ásvald Úlfsson returned to the family farm in Jaederen. That is a full day's walk from the sea. The land there is hard with high craggy mountains surrounding deep green valleys. On his farm he raised cattle and grain with his five sons. It was generally a peaceful life. Yet Ásvald and his sons were often in conflict with neighbors. One day his eldest son Thorvald got into an argument with another farmer over a cow. It led to a fight and Thorvald savagely killed the man. To maintain some measure of peace Thorvald was forced to leave the valley and the country. He took his family to a new colony called Iceland.

One of Thorvald's sons was named Eric. He had red hair and as he grew older, a small streak of white in the middle of his beard. Eric was only ten years old when they moved to Iceland. As the young man grew it was obvious that he had the same violent temper that Thor's bolt of lightning had pummeled on his grandfather. Just out of his teens Eric killed two men in a stupid fight and was banished from Iceland. As his father had done before him, he gathered many of his relatives and sailed west to a land discovered years earlier. It was still unexplored. Eric called their new home Greenland.

With his small fleet he had found a deep fiord on the southwestern coast of the great island. The land held lush grasses and was much like Iceland...perhaps better. Because Eric named the place Greenland, it sounded much more pleasant than Iceland to colonists. Soon thousands of settlers began filling the new land.

I was born there in the first town of Greenland...Brattahlid. Eric-the-Red is my uncle. He is part of the reason I die today.

Best I start at the beginning of my troubles.

The late spring winds were milder than usual this day as I sat outside my Uncle Eric's large house, waiting for his return. The grass was turning from the gray color of winter to a more promising green. The sod on the roof of his dwelling was especially lush with the warmer winds of the new season. One of Eric's slaves told me that his master was in a low valley just over the ridge past the house. He was expected to return soon. The slave brought me bread and beer.

After a short wait the older man came tramping down the hill. When he saw me he broke into a trot. "Haagan," he shouted from a distance, "how long have you been back?" He held a big smile on his face. He was always happy to see me.

"I just returned uncle and I needed to talk to you first," I said in a low voice when we were close.

"There was trouble?" the older man read in my look. He was no longer smiling.

"Much trouble! Six of my men are dead. It was too long of a trip to return them from the place where they died. And we could not leave their bodies to be defiled by those little yellow men, the Skraelings. We put their remains in one of our three boats, towed it out to sea and set it afire. We gave them a proper Norse funeral."

"Explain to me how all of this came about. Your undertaking was just a simple trading mission with those loathsome natives. Trade is good for them and it is very good for us. What happened?" His tone told me I was still a little boy in his eyes.

I trembled a bit. I needed to choose my words carefully. My uncle Eric had the same fearful temper that had troubled our family for generations. Some of his very good friends had been killed in our battle. "Uncle, let me tell you what I know. I can do no more.

"As you remember, we took three small boats, each with ten oars, and rowed to the normal trading site. Only two Skraelings were awaiting us there and they had no trade goods at all. We beached our boats and Joachim took his Skraeling slave woman to talk with the two savages. We needed to find out what happened and where we were to meet, if we were to do our exchanges of goods."

Eric nodded his head. "I always thought that Joachim was foolish to waste a good metal axe to get a Skraeling slave, especially a female. She was useless. But he told me he bought her in order to learn the language. Perhaps I can understand why he did it."

"That was his foolish act, uncle. I am sure his slave cost him his life."

"I will kill her then," Eric angrily replied.

"No need uncle. I took care of her myself."

Eric moved his left hand over his nostrils and closed them momentarily. He snorted and said, "Haagan, explain to me what happened. How could these vile little savages kill Viking warriors?"

"Yes uncle. I will explain. When the slave woman and the two male Skraelings met they jabbered noisily for a long time. Joachim could not follow the conversation. The words came too fast. His slave told him that we had to travel to the north one more day to arrive at the exchange site. After talking, the two males quickly departed; each of them, in their funny little one man boats. It was late in the day so I decided that we should camp at that rocky place for the night."

"You set a night watch?"

"I did...I am not a fool."

"Go on."

"The next morning we again started northward rowing along the coast. There was no wind to use our sails. Rounding a rock outcropping we came upon the Skraeling encampment. There were many men waiting for us. We could see the usual piles of trade goods: white polar bear furs, two beautiful live white falcons and a large pile of narwhal tusks. We were so intent on the treasure in front of us that we never noticed the twenty or thirty one man boats that suddenly came out of a hidden cove to our rear. We had rowed right past them. They swarmed Joachim's boat just as we reached the beach. At the same time the mass of Skraeling men to our front charged at us. These hideous small men intended to rob and kill us.

"Using our swords, shields and protected by our metal armor we killed ten or more for every man we lost. There was blood and gore everywhere. It was a good fight. Myself, I used my double headed battle axe. I had never killed so many in such a short time. I love that weapon. The cowardly Skraeling's finally ran from us. I used the axe one more time on Joachim's slave. She was kneeling, sobbing by one of the native bodies. With an enormous swing of my axe I split her completely in two. It was glorious.

"Joachim and five others had been killed in the fight. Then, as I said, we took their six bodies out to sea and set the boat on fire. The vile Skraeling had disappeared. They had tried to steal our trade goods. But instead we took their narwhal tusks and white bear pelts without trade. The white falcons had somehow been killed during the fight.

"With only the two boats left to us, we dumped our trade goods of iron tools, raisins and cloth into the ocean to make room for the Skraeling's materials. We did keep the wine and drank it on the return trip. We left the savages only their dead in return."

Eric smiled. "You did well Haagan. I know you dislike the word, but still, you and your men fought like Vikings."

"We went as traders uncle, not thieves. We only fought because we were attacked. I do not like to be thought of as one of those villainous Vikings. We did what we had to do to survive. We did not steal."

My uncle Eric was reflecting quietly for a few moments. Then he made some disgusting bodily noises as he told me that he would meet with the council of the settlement to decide how we might divide the spoils from my expedition. I did not think this was right. I had already agreed with my men about sharing the treasure from our adventure. Eric was still treating me as a child. Yet Eric-the-Red was many things. He was my elder, my uncle and quite famous in Greenland. I could not disagree with him. Also, there was much more going on in the settlement than I knew about at the time.

I was a close friend to my cousin Leif, Eric-the-Red's son. Just three years earlier Leif had taken a trade voyage to Norway. There, King Olaf had persuaded Leif to join him and many of the leaders of his court in the Christian faith. It was the King's wish. Leif really had no choice. He returned, first to Iceland and then Greenland with Missionary priests. Our colonies were expanding rapidly. At the same time the people were seemingly deserting the old ways of our traditional Norse Gods. Now, most of the newcomers were Christians. There were also raiding parties of Vikings attacking our settlements. This forced battles between Christian and Viking settlers. It was a trying time.

In the midst of all this, Leif had bought a boat from Bjarn, the man who had discovered new lands to the west of Greenland. Bjarn had not explored them. Cousin Leif had sailed west to investigate and had not returned. His father Eric feared for him.

All these events were very upsetting to my uncle Eric. His old gods were being destroyed. He was not a Christian but rather a true Norseman. His favorite son was gone. Everything was changing too rapidly for him. He was not the same man.

I met Uncle Eric again three days later accompanied by Bjarn. They were heatedly arguing about the land that Bjarn had discovered earlier. When they saw me they suddenly became quiet and both frowned. I sensed this was not going to be a happy meeting.

"Haagan, come to Bjarn's house. We must talk." As we walked to his dwelling an icy wind blew the heavy early morning fog out of the bay. A large iceberg became visible offshore. It was drifting slowly to the north. This was not normal. For me, these were two sudden dark omens. Something was not going right? We settled by the central fireplace of Bjarn's house to talk.

The large single room held only a slave woman who was suckling a baby while at the same time milking Bjarn's goats. All of the straw bedding had been cleared from the sleeping benches to be aired. Even the animal manure from the pens at the end of the room had been cleaned. That was the section where the animals wintered and slaves normally slept. Bjarn's house smelled spring-air clean. Yet it was shared each night by almost fifty people.

I looked quizzically at my uncle and his friend as we sat. We simply stared at each other for a few moments. Finally I said, "Tell me uncle, is there a problem?"

"Yes Haagan and it is you. Your actions cause difficulty and perhaps put our family in danger."

"I don't understand?"

"You divided the spoils of your raid…"

"Of course! And it was a mission to trade not a raid," I exclaimed angrily.

Bjarn spoke up, "Don't use that tone with us boy."

I smoldered. There it was again…treating me like a child. My axe had slaughtered many contemptible Skraelings. The year before, I had killed Viking raiders who had attacked our rich settlement of Brattahlid. "I have bloodied my axe often as a man. Don't call me a boy. I deserve some respect."

"That is true nephew. Still you put me in danger with your foolishness!"

"What did I do that is foolish, uncle? How can it be that I put you in danger?"

"You killed Joachim's slave and you are not willing to pay his family the price for the deed."

"Uncle, I know the price for killing another man's slave is equal to the price of a good cow, but the Skraeling slave woman led us into a trap."

"Can you prove that? Wait, it doesn't matter! You killed Joachim's slave. That is all that matters. You must pay his family the traditional agreed upon price for that act. It is our custom."

I shook my head violently in anger. "No I will not pay. She deserved to die. Joachim was already murdered by those stinking savages. He could not take his revenge. I did it for him."

Bjarn spoke, "Haagan you know the laws of our community. If you kill another man's slave you must give him the value of one good cow to make up for his loss. If you fail to do this, Joachim's family can take revenge on you at any time…even years from now. It is a legitimate debt that you have to pay; else they believe you are cheating them. They will have the right of revenge."

I stood up quickly, anger boiling my insides. At that moment the slave women, with her child, were passing behind me. My quick movement sent her flying across the sleeping platform. In my rage I turned and struck her hard across the face as she tried to get up. She spilled the container of goat's milk and her child fell from her arm. I ignored her wail and turned back to my uncle and Bjarn.

"I will not pay the slave price" I shouted. "It was an honor killing. She deserved to die."

"That is true Haagan, but still you bring shame on our family. If Joachim's kin are not compensated then they have the right to take vengeance and kill you. That in turn, will obligate me to kill some of Joachim's family. It will be the start of an endless feud. You have only two choices. You either pay the slave price or you move away out of their reach. Your grandfather fled to Iceland for somewhat the same difficulty. I in turn, was forced to leave Iceland and come here to Greenland to avoid the wrath of the local settlers. Neither situation was the same as yours, but still, you must leave. Each of us must do what is best to keep peace in our community."

I was stunned by their lack of consideration for me. I had returned from an honorable battle with two boats loaded with highly valuable goods. I couldn't accept the judgment of these two pessimistic elderly colonists. Both had, in their own ways, committed acts far worse than not paying for the price of another man's slave. Eric-the-Red and Bjarn were both famous adventurers. Now they were acting like sniveling old men. I would have none of it. Angrily I stepped back…directly onto the slave's child still lying on the floor behind me. The slave woman dared to scream at me so I hit her again. Then I stormed out the door of Bjarn's house. I would not yield my principles. I was right in my refusal to forfeit the slave price. As I left I heard Erik say to Bjarn, "I will pay you for the spilled goat's milk." I had no idea what milk Erik was talking about.

As the spring moved into summer the three of us met again and again to argue that I should pay for the slave or leave. I refused both choices. Finally they had arranged a voyage for me. I understood something of what they were doing. I was to take the season's cargo of narwhal tusks and polar bear skins from Greenland to a trader named Lars at a major commerce center on the eastern shore of Denmark called Hedeby. It was made clear to me that I should sail directly to Hedeby, avoid Iceland, and that I should never return to Greenland. Their arguments had tired me…so I agreed to go.

It was late in the day when our dragon ship arrived in the harbor at Hedeby. Ours was the last ship admitted to the calm port waters before a massive chain was raised across the narrow harbor entry. The quays held several merchant ships and two other dragon ships. The town behind the wharfs showed me streets running straight away from the docking area. These streets were paved with logs…you did not have to walk in the mud. This was a marvel I had never imagined. The houses were close knit and there were other buildings on each side of the walking lanes. I also noted a high protective earthen wall surrounding the town. Later I found that this wall, called Danevirke, extended from Hedeby westward all the way across Jutland to the Northern Sea.

I had been told that Hedeby was the largest trading center in all the lands sovereign to the Vikings. Yet it was ruled by a Danish king who often fought with Olaf, the King of Norway. The whole place was certainly not like anything I had ever seen as a child in Iceland or Norway.

The directions Bjarn gave me were true and I quickly located the house and workshop of the man named Lars with whom I was to trade. I brought a bundle of the best narwhal horns to show Lars. As I entered, I immediately saw a well fed older man with long blonde hair hanging down to his shoulders. He was sitting at a wooden bench carving on a narwhal tusk. His beard and hair seemed to flow in a rhythm as he stroked the giant tooth-tusk of a narwhale using some sort of smoothing device.

"Are you Lars?" I asked.

"Who wants to know?" He replied in a rasping voice. He did not raise his head to look at me. I was annoyed. After a long, often freezing sea voyage, I expected some courtesy. Perhaps this man was only a slave or lowly serf, yet he had the traditional look of a Viking warrior. I struck the work bench with my fist. The blow was hard enough to make all of many loose tools fly into the air. Now the man looked at me.

"I am Haagan. My uncle Eric-the-Red sent me to find Lars. I have a boat full of narwhal tusks and some polar bear pelts. Now, where is Lars?" I fumed.

He grinned. "So you are Haagan. I have heard much of you. I expected you weeks ago. Where have you been? I was sure your ship was lost. How many tusks have you?"

I could feel the anger raging in my brain. My hand was on the hilt of my knife. With guttural tones of wrath I moved closer to him and whispered, "Where is Lars?"

"Ha! You are a hothead, just as they said. I heard that from several who came before you. Now sit and tell me of your battle with the Skraeling. All of my raiding voyages were to Ireland and once…I went to France. I have never been to your home colony of Greenland or met any of those yellow savages. And, yes…yes…I am Lars."

I relaxed, took a deep breath and sat down. As I told him my tale, a servant brought me some beer, bread and delicious cooked fish. The food was warm. I had not had hot food in weeks. I talked at length between bites while Lars continued with his carving. The servant kept filling my cup. My tongue became very loose. Occasionally Lars prodded me with a few questions. It was a pleasant time.

Then there was noise at the doorway. A man in strange dress entered, smiling and calling Lars by name. Lars stood for the first time and I was astounded. Standing, the top of Lars head could not even reach my chin. He was a short rounded little man. I have rarely seen a fat man. Seldom is there sufficient food. Lars was plump. He had to be rich to eat so well.

Lars waved me out of my place so that the newcomer might have the stool. Again, another shock as he moved to accommodate the stranger. I saw, for the first time, that Lars left foot was missing. He hobbled slightly on the stick of wood that replaced his missing limb. He was not a whole man.

Lars was obviously interested in this man. He made a great fuss over him and offered him much food and drink. I was ignored, so I leaned back against the wall and listened.

"Al-Tartushi, tell me about your travels. You have seen most of the world, have you not?"

"Not quite all the world, my barbarian friend. However this past year I was in the city of Rome and was granted an audience with the Holy Roman Emperor, Otto the First."

"What! You are a Jew. You live with muslins in Cordova. You, with a Christian Emperor! How can this be? I myself have just joined the new Christian church here in Hedeby. The priest is telling us every

Sunday that it was you Jews who killed our Savior. I may have to spirit you out of town to save your life...after, of course, we do our business."

Al-Tartushi roared with laughter. He slapped his knees and tears came to his eyes. "Why you...you old Viking rogue...a Christian! I thought all you Danes worshiped Sirius. I see you still hang part of a slaughtered animal on a pole by your door for that god. You still throw babies into the sea as offerings for that god. When your people sing, it is the sound of a pack of howling dogs. I tell everyone in my travels that there is no culture in Hedeby, only unicorn horn. That of course is why I am here."

I watched Lars redden in mild anger from Al-Tartushi's criticism of Hedeby. Yet he uttered no argument except to say that as a new Christian he no longer worshiped Sirius. This surprised me. I thought that most older *true* Vikings and Norsemen still worshiped Norse gods.

I had never heard much of Sirius. My god was Thor and I proudly wore his hammer on the chain around my neck. Were the gods changing? It seemed that Christians were appearing everywhere. King Olaf had given up the old gods and Christian missionaries were now in Iceland and my home in Greenland. They would not get to me. Thor is my protector.

After much banter, Lars and Al-Tartushi bargained over the tusks. They also agreed on a price for the powder shed from Lars carvings. As I listened, I found that both men called the narwhale ivory 'unicorn'! How could this be? I had never seen a unicorn. I heard that they were magical forest creatures with a single tusk in the center of their forehead. It was a common belief that unicorns might be captured only by a young virgin girl sitting quietly alone in a deep wood. A unicorn would find the maiden and lay its head in her lap. How she got the horn I did not know. But Lars and the Spanish Jew were trading my narwhal horns as unicorn ivory. Those tusks that I had just brought to Lars still smelled like fish. Was Al-Tartushi so easily deceived?

Al-Tartushi left after completing the bargaining. He promised to return on the marrow with gold and men to carry the goods. I returned to my seat across from Lars. He picked up his work tools and a piece of horn. He explained to me that he was hollowing a tusk to form a drinking cup.

"You have a query Haagan. I can see it in your face. Is your issue why we both talked of the narwhal tusks as unicorn or are you just discovering that the old slimy trader Jew is paying me five times what I pay you for the same quantity?"

"Both," I replied in a somewhat angry tone.

Lars laughed at me, but his smile quickly turned into a frown. "Haagan, I will give you the truth. You must never reveal this secret to anyone. Our very profitable ventures, yours and mine, would be destroyed if the facts became known. Many tradesmen and men in powerful positions as healers, advisors and others would be killed if the real source of the horn was learned. Do you understand?"

For the very first time since we had met, the Viking was looking directly at me. His dark blue eyes flashed a fierceness I had seen only when engaging in mortal combat. I nodded agreement to his stern demand for secrecy.

Lars bobbed his head in return and said, "Haagan there is no such thing in the world as a unicorn. These are animals of legend that never have existed. Tell me Haagan, have you ever seen a dragon?"

Not waiting for my answer, Lars continued. "Dragons don't exist. Yet most of the Norsemen sail 'dragon ships'. Why? I'll tell you why. They do that to frighten and deceive the stupid weaklings living in the lands where we raid. When we arrive at their shores or sail up their rivers, the sight of our ships often panics them into immediate submission. We don't even have to fight for their treasures."

"I like to fight!"

"I know you do Haagan. That is not what I am trying to say. Now listen to me and try to understand. Again remember, there is no such thing as a unicorn.

"There are many kings, princes and other royalty that live in the endless lands south of Hedeby. They are rich and have many luxuries. Younger brothers of these rulers, and many others, want to usurp the positions of those in power. Men are greedy. They desire all the riches and all the power of control but only for themselves. Often, the leaders are poisoned by their underlings. They can't be murdered publicly as that would cause too much internal strife. They are poisoned so their deaths appear natural. Because the danger of poisoning is so common, many nobles take steps to protect themselves from anyone attempting to kill them this way."

"How can they protect themselves?" I asked.

"It is the magic of the unicorn. In the hands of a skilled conjurer, unicorn powder will heal anything. Some say it will cure rabies or plague. A few claim that unicorn powder will even raise the dead. Al-Tartushi loves to brag about the superiority of the peoples to the south, but I think they are dolts to believe in these wild tales of animals that don't exist and a magic that does not work."

"Tell me about the narwhal…I mean…unicorn cup that you are making by hollowing out the horn. I believe I understand that Al-Tartushi pays you a great deal more in gold for a cup than for just plain horn"

"That is the truth Haagan and I'll tell you why. The unicorn cup is believed to destroy any poison that is put into it. It is a legend that charlatans such as Al-Tartushi have promoted for generations. This cup I am making right now is supposed to be a magical vessel formed from the horn of a unicorn."

"But Lars, what if the person who drinks from the fake unicorn horn-cup dies?"

"No matter! If the drinker dies it had to be from some other cause. It could not be poison. After all, the person who expired was drinking from a unicorn cup. You see Haagan, people suddenly die all the time. Who knows why? This is a good business for everyone. You bring me horn. I carve it into cups and sometimes I make spoons for eating. Traders such as Al-Tartushi travel the world selling magical unicorn materials to brainless rich royalty."

"Would a real unicorn cup stop the poison?" I asked.

"Haagan, are you as stupid as the rest! There is no such thing as a unicorn. Haven't you listened to what I have been telling you? The world is full of fools who believe anything that is told to them. It is not necessary to make a Viking raid to get royalty gold. We just trick them with these narwhale horns and they give us their wealth."

"I would rather raid, I enjoy a good fight to get my riches" I said. For some reason Lars seemed to shake his head at me in disgust. He would no longer talk to me. A strange man.

I stayed with Lars for almost three years. We did not get along well but he paid me much gold to protect him from the scoundrels who sometimes came to Hedeby. I used most of the gold Lars gave me to buy a house and a woman in the town. Lars wanted me to become a Christian and marry the woman in the new church. I refused. My god is Thor. I will not change.

Once, a drunken group from a dragon ship came to steal Lars' carvings of the unicorn. I killed three of them with my double axe. Lars was happy with that. Later he became very angry when I accidentally killed a servant of another of the merchants who came to trade with him. I mistakenly thought the servant was stealing.

Lars told me that he was selling fewer cups and horns. Traders were going elsewhere because they were afraid of me. He finally demanded that I leave, but I refused. I had no other place to go. I was not welcome back in Greenland. I would stay with Lars and protect him.

Just days ago a large raiding party from the east, with many ships, attacked Hedeby. The entire town, even Lars with his one leg, turned out to repel them. They burned ships in the harbor and stormed the town's fortifications. It was a wonderful battle. I used my double axe to slice the invaders to pieces. I had never felt so strong. I sliced arms and legs and I cut off one invader's head. My mind was buzzing but I was filled with a greater strength then I had ever known. The wounds I received in the battle meant nothing…they only made me stronger. There was blood everywhere. I felt I had already entered Valhalla.

I could not stop my blood lust. As the raiders withdrew I hacked their wounded to pieces. I killed the already dead time and again. No one could bring me to a halt. Finally shaking violently I collapsed.

Days later I woke in my own house with only my woman attending me. She fed me broth and explained how the entire town of Hedeby was now terrified of me. They thought me insane. As I fought I had been screaming Thor's name over and over. I couldn't remember doing that.

One morning soon after the raid I was shocked when Lars came to visit me. Previously he had made it clear that he no longer wanted me around him. Now he came and offered me work. I was to follow the River Schlie from Hedeby until I came to a short portage spot and then follow the Eider River to the north ocean. I was to meet a group of dragon ships and guide them to Hedeby. He wanted me to leave on the marrow although I was still weak from my wounds.

"Why do they need a guide? I asked. "The two river route across Denmark is well known."

Lars answered, "These Vikings are from the Shetland Islands and have never been here. They are very cautious. I understand that they have a great deal of plunder from the monasteries in Ireland. I want to treat them respectfully and also be the first trader to accept their cargo in exchange for my gold."

This seemed strange to me as Lars had only dealt in unicorn horn. Still, if he was willing to offer me work I would go. I left the next morning, after smiling down upon my two boys asleep in the same bed. Their golden hair was as bright as the sun.

The trip up the River Schlie, across the portage and then down the Eider River was miserable. It rained constantly and the dampness made my still healing wounds pain me. Arriving at the docking area, my porters put me aboard the only dragon ship there. As I climbed over the railing they quickly departed. Then a distressing surprise! I was face to face with a group of Joachim's relatives. I was no match for them in my weakened condition. Besides, I had only a short knife to defend myself and I quickly lost that.

"What do you want?" I demanded as they held me prisoner.

"You owe a debt of honor Haagan. You killed Joachim's slave woman and never paid the price of her loss to our family."

"I owe you nothing," I shouted."I would never pay for that slave."

"No matter, Haagan. Lars and the people of Hedeby arranged for us to wait here for you. They fear you and your great axe and your blood lust. They do not want you to ever return."

So now you see me here waiting to die. Joachim's kin chained me to a gigantic log at low tide. The tide is rising now almost to my head. I cannot move. They also nailed my feet to the log. In a short time I will drown.

Remember me. I was a warrior and a raider but never a thieving Viking. I will be welcomed in Valhalla.

Remember me.

A BIT OF HISTORY

Greenland, in the year 1000 had as many as 5,000 inhabitants in several settlements. Additionally, as Europeans put aside their pagan roots, there were churches, a monastery and a convent on this northern island. All this happened, during an exceptionally warm climate period in the northern hemisphere.

The unicorn material, in the form of cups and powder, was considered a source of healing for millennia. Until the 1800's the unicorn was part of the crest of the Royal British Medical Society. Even today there are over 400,000 therapeutic references for unicorn horn listed by Google.

Hedeby was plundered and destroyed by the Slavs in the year 1066. It was never rebuilt on that same site.

Twenty-one

Epigenetics

It was a family party. It was a celebration for the younger brother of the family. After many struggling years, Matt had finally earned his PhD in biology. The party was equally an occasion for Matt to see his older brother Chris. Their varied careers had made it ever so difficult to see each other.

"Well Chris how is the career going?"

"Better than I expected, Matt. As I'm sure you heard from dad, I drifted for quite awhile trying to find just what I wanted to do with my life. Now I think I have a handle on it. But first, tell me about your world travels. How was England? How long have you been back?"

"Only a couple of days Chris. As I'm sure dad told you, I just got back four days ago from my year at the University of Bristol. I had to fly directly across the country to the University of California at Irvine for a job interview with the Epigenome Center. There were big flight delays in New York and again in Chicago. I'm kinda frazzled. I'm not complaining. Certainly going to California was worth it for me. It was astounding to meet so many of those genius-type people that I've read about. I had to do much of my doctorate work based on their research and their publications"

"How did all this happen with you? England first, and now California. We all believed you would stay in Omaha and teach at UNO or maybe KSU. Did you get the job in California?"

"Yes I did." Matt produced a big smile.

"Tell me about it. All I remember from biology is cutting up frogs. I hated that."

"Chris, I don't cut up frogs. This work is in a very new field called Epigenetics. True, I was originally aiming for a teaching job at Kansas State. But my professor-mentor there, Doctor Feig, is a world-famous scientist and deeply into biochemistry. He encouraged me saying I had a profound aptitude…that was the word he used…'profound'…for work in epigenetics. He was the one who arranged for me to study in England. That in turn, led me to the University of California."

Chris frowned. "Matt, I don't know much at all about this epigenetics thing. It sounds weird. What is this career field you are talking about?"

"Sure! Sorry Chris, I do get carried away. I think everybody knows about this stuff. Do you remember years ago when dad got that map from something called the Genographic Project…well maybe you don't. We were both really kinda young to notice. Using dad's DNA that map showed how our ancestors moved out of Africa to Europe. Now recently, we have found a gene variant called DRD4. It occurs in about twenty percent of all humans. It apparently drives us to explore and maybe was the catalyst that made our ancestors wander."

"I guess, I forgot all about that," Chris replied. "I sure don't remember that DRD4 at all."

"I can understand that. We were just kids. As I remember, the DRD4 was not even mentioned in the results that dad got. This field is moving at warp speed. What we have also found is that some physical conditions or even the life processes of a parent, can modify the DNA of the generations that follow. It doesn't take thousands or tens of thousands of years for these changes to take place. Circumstances can have immediate effects on sperm and eggs that will then alter the DNA strands of humans.

"I learned when I overseas that there was a huge study done in England in the 1990's with over 14,000 pregnant women. It was designed to show how an individual's genotype would combine with environmental pressures to influence health and development. Years later this study was able to determine that the sons of those fathers who smoked had significantly higher body mass and will continue to be at greater risk for health issues all through their lives. This was a change in just one generation caused by a smoking father.

"My new job will be to help map the human epigenome. The potential is staggering. We had thought DNA, based on Darwin, was an ironclad code. It was assumed that we and our children and their children's health and other factors could not be altered by any short term changes. That's wrong! Soon it will be possible to tinker with the DNA and bend it to our desires. We will be able to cure a lot of diseases. I'm going to be part of that revolution."

"That is just great little brother. Tell me, when you were in England, were you any part of the people who found and identified King Richard III?"

"I wish I had been. There were a lot of 'heavy-weight' professionals in on that one. I heard a lot about it but I was only on the fringe."

"Well Matt at least your DNA studies have definite results. By the way, I did get a grant, not a big one mind you, to examine why we humans continually fight, have wars and kill one another. Do you think it could be in the genes? Maybe we can alter genes to stop this endless human aggression in the world"

Twenty-two

Rogaard

Egeskov Slot 1200 A.D.

Rogaard had always been lucky. Most often, because of his youth, he did not realize the circumstances of his good fortune. As a youngster he had won the freedom of Egeskov Slot...the Danish castle where he was born. This freedom was unusual for the child of a servant. An accident during his sixth summer established his special status.

Rogaard had been sweeping the floor in the guardhouse where he lived. It was at the end of the moat bridge as you entered the castle proper. As he swept the floor Rogaard heard a piercing scream. He dropped the broom and ran to the doorway. The sound came from the direction of the long bridge from the castle to the mainland.

The nurse-maid for Adalena, the only daughter of Baron Haakon, had been walking her four-year old charge on the bridge. Adalena had scampered away trying to catch a pigeon. She slipped off the bridge and plunged into the lake. Both Olaf, the duty guard at the castle entryway, and the nursemaid, were far too fat and far too old to move quickly enough to save the little girl.

Rogaard saw all this and shouted into the castle for help. Then he ran the length of the bridge to the drowning girl. Without a thought, he jumped into the water and the girl's her head up. Rogaard could barely swim himself. Adalena, in her terror, scratched him badly. Still, he held her tightly until help arrived and pulled them both out of the cold water.

Adalena's father quickly stormed onto the scene. He was furious that he had almost lost his precious only daughter. "Did this boy push you in the water?" he demanded in a wavering angry voice while pointing at Rogaard. He did not know Rogaard's name. As a matter of his station, he knew few of his servants' names and none of their children's names.

Adalena could only wail in fright. She could not reply to her father's irate question. The nursemaid also did not respond. She was sobbing hysterically while trying to straighten the little girl's clothes. Rogaard cowered before the livid adult. This was the feared master of the castle. In the excitement the young boy did not even notice that he was bleeding at the neck.

After no one immediately answered. Olaf, the old guard, finally found his voice. "Sire, your daughter pulled away from her nursemaid to catch a bird landing on the bridge. Before we could reach her she fell into the lake. Young Rogaard jumped into the water to rescue her. He did not push her. He was not even on the bridge. By running out of the castle gate and across the bridge he managed to hold her up until we could get them both out of the lake."

From that moment Rogaard was recognized by the Baron as a person worthy of a name. He was awarded permission to go anywhere in the castle. To sooth his whimpering daughter Barron Haakon told Adalena that she could have the boy as a playmate.

The Danish Castle Egeskov was constructed in the center of a small lake. Its only access was over a long bridge. In addition to the protective lake moat, Egeskov was further defended by a contingent of huscarls. They were professional full-time soldiers employed by Baron Haakon, the Lord of the Manor. Rogaard's father was the captain of these guards. The captaincy was a position his family had held for generations while serving the masters of Egeskov.

Rogaard, by his actions this day had earned favor with the master of the castle. With his quick achievement saving Adalena, Rogaard's father felt assured that the son would follow him in years to come as the next captain of the huscarls.

Rogaard was filled with wonder as he toured the family quarters of the Castle Egeskov. Most of it he had never seen. Adalena had an entire room to herself with a bed raised off the wooden floor and with heavy material covering the drafty windows.

"This is all just for you Lady Adalena?" The awed boy asked.

"This is my room," the young girl replied. "Don't you have a room like this?"

"No my lady. I live in the guard barracks with my mother and father and all the huscarls. But my father is the Captain so we have a room to ourselves at one end of the barrack."

Adalena did not bother to listen to his answer. She didn't care. "My father said you can visit me anytime and be my playmate. What do you want to play?"

Rogaard did not have a response. He had no idea how to play with another child, especially a girl...perhaps more importantly, someone who was part of the master's family. Most of his waking hours were spent in performing menial tasks for his father and the huscarls. There was little play. No other children of his station lived in the castle. He wasn't really sure what it meant to play.

Day after day he was sent by his father to entertain Adalena. At first he was quite shy, and she in turn, treated him like her personal toy. At her tender age she already perceived her privileged status. Her favorite game was to make him get down on all fours. Then she would ride him like a horse. The young girl taunted him mercilessly because of his rough clothes. Neither child had the slightest idea that the age in which they lived was dominated by a Feudal System where clothing provided an immediate way of distinguishing 'Who was who'. Fashion, like almost everything else, was dictated by a dress code in the Sumptuary Laws. Only the wives and children of nobles were allowed to wear velvet, satin, sable or ermine. Adalena was always richly dressed. Rogaard, as the son of a servant, wore class defining simple brown trousers and a tunic made from wool. Adalena would laugh at him as he pulled at the scratchy material.

Baroness Ingeborg, Adalena'a mother, was not at all happy that Rogaard was allowed to spend the days with her daughter. She considered him a rough, ill-mannered servant's boy. Certainly he was not bred well enough to spend time with the daughter of a Baroness. Still, since the Baron allowed it, she could not protest his wishes. Her only other living child, Jerrik, was a mother's worry. Four years older than Adalena, he was brutish to the servants, rude to his little sister and perhaps a bit less than intelligent. She had arranged with Father Vilfred, the priest in residence in the castle, to start teaching her children fundamental morals, religion, reading and writing. Jerrik pouted and Adalena whined…neither wanted schooling. Adalena demanded that Rogaard go to lessons with her. She had come to enjoy his time with her. He was certainly nicer than her sibling, Jerrik. But she was not above using some of the nastiness she had learned from her brother on her new friend.

Rogaard had often been angered by Adalena's haughty treatment and would refuse to visit her. At these times Adalena missed her only playmate. She soon learned that he would return to play with her if she offered him a sweet. "What is this?" he would ask as he greedily consumed a honey roll. Never had he tasted anything like these treats she offered him.

Adalena giggled, and as usual and did not answer him.

"Tell me a story," she would demand.

He found that she loved stories about knights and dragons. He had learned these fables by listening to the huscarls. "Did you ever see a dragon Rogaard? Are they in the wood around the castle?"

"Yes, my lady," he lied. "My father and his men fought a big fire-breathing dragon two winters past. It was a terrible battle. The dragon ate two of the huscarls before he was driven off."

"Is the dragon still there in the wood? Could it eat me?" Her eyes were wide with fear.

"Yes Lady. But we huscarls are here to protect you."

Somehow this story that Rogaard had weaved drew Adalena closer to her friend. Now every time he told the tale, adding gory details, she would shudder and sometimes cry. But he repeated, again and again, that he would always protect her from this fierce beast.

When Father Vilfred started his little class of three children he straight away discovered that the younger Rogaard was much quicker than Jerrik. Rogaard knew his place, he never answered first. Sometimes he delighted in whispering responses to Adalena so she could appear to be the better student than her older brother. Jerrik caught on to Rogaard's little game and sometimes would beat him after class. Rogaard could only ward off the blows and not fight back. He knew he would be severely punished if he struck anyone of noble rank. He managed the beatings since his austere life in the huscarls barracks had toughened him. His father had also started the boy in military training. Daily, after class, he learned the art of hand-to-hand combat with weapons and fists. His strength grew.

Father Vilfred watched as Rogaard developed in class and hoped he might someday guide the lad to the priesthood. Baron Haakon also watched Rogaard learn to fight and ordered the same training for his son. Again Rogaard had to play the fool and lose the mock combats to Jerrik. He quietly vowed that someday Jerrik would be made to pay for all the hurt Rogaard was forced to accept.

By the time Adalena turned ten she had tired of most of their childish games. She insisted Rogaard bring wooden training swords to her quarters and teach her how to fight. She learned well. Soon, with her quick movements, she became a challenge to Rogaard.

"If you let me win I will beat you just like my brother Jerrik does," she goaded him.

"You will never beat me. I am a huscarl and you are a weak girl…my lady" he shouted back at her as he delivered a blow. But in his boisterous eagerness, he slipped and then tripped. Adalena's wooden sword was immediately at his throat. She laughed loudly and stepped on his stomach. Rogaard saw a fire in her eyes. Adalena was someone to be reckoned with.

"Don't ever call me a weak girl again" she said. "Now if I spare your life you are required to do something to please me."

Rogaard saw that the glint in her eyes had turned to mirth and readily granted her wish, if only to get her off his stomach. He was forever sorry that he agreed to do this nameless task. The next day he found Adalena in the company of several of the ladies of the castle. As a group they forced him to learn to dance…even to dance with Lady Adalena. He was so embarrassed that he told no one what had happened…not even his father.

As time passed, Rogaard became more of a companion bodyguard rather than a playmate to Adalena. The two made excursions outside of the castle. They would ride the Baron's land holdings. The peasants would bow as they passed. Adalena relished her position of power and privilege. But Rogaard remembered how Father Vilfred talked long about pride being the worst of the seven deadly sins. It was the sin of Adam and Eve who wanted to be as great as God. *I wonder if pride is a disease of the nobility, they always want more then they have,* Rogaard thought while watching Adalena let her horse carelessly trample over a serf's meager vegetable garden.

Rogaard's sixteen years had shown him the hard life of Baron Haakon's serfs. His father's huscarls were the Baron's tax collectors. They demanded for the castle a share of everything produced: crops, animals, cloth. The nobility enjoyed their life of privilege while the serfs and peasants barely survived. Adalena observed none of their misery.

She did not think of peasants as human beings…if she thought of them at all.

On an especially hot summer's day the two were riding over an un-familiar wooded pathway and abruptly came to a wide stream. The warm still air of the forest bothered Adalena enough that she stopped and dismounted. Slipping off her sandals she cooled her feet in the blue water. Rogaard also dismounted and held the reins of their mounts as Adalena waded into the stream to grasp a water lily. Suddenly she slipped and fell backward into the still water. She was soaked from head to toe. She sat on the bottom of the stream. Rogaard could only laugh at the angry girl.

"You help me out of here Rogaard…Now!"

"Are you cool enough my lady?" he continued to laugh as he dropped the reins of the horses and waded to help her.

Adalena was prepared to snarl a response but instead, grasped his outstretched hand and pulled him past her into deeper water over his head. He came up sputtering.

"You, you…" he never finished as she stood and pushed his head under the water again.

This time he rose to a giggling girl who turned to run. He caught her in three steps and tossed her with ease back into the pond. Now she came up out of the water splashing him and flattened him on the bank of the stream. He hit the muddy bank on his back with Adalena falling on top of him. He was momentarily dazed.

"Rogaard, I killed you. Oh Rogaard speak to me" she cried.

His eyes fluttered and he let out a small groan. For the sheer joy of the moment she kissed him. Rogaard, now aware, reached his arms around her waist and kissed her back. Instantly they were both conscious of the impropriety of their actions. "Get off me you lout," Adalena screamed even though she was on top of him. They both stood, wet, muddy and red faced with the primal awkwardness of youthful passion.

"I am so sorry my lady," Rogaard apologized over and over.

"You just wait until I tell my father," she snapped. They were both covered with mud.

They returned to the castle without another word. Yet both of them felt something inside that was completely new and warmly satisfying. It almost transcended the gulf between nobility and servants. Almost!

It was late in the afternoon of the same day when Rogaard got the dreaded call to see Baron Haakon. He could not imagine his punishment. He hoped that he would not be sent to the dungeon. Rogaard had seen serfs sent there for failing to pay their taxes to the Baron. They had entered the dungeon as strong healthy men. Those who lived to be released came out of that black airless hole as staggering vermin-ridden skeletons. Whipping or the pillory would be better than the dungeon. His only hope was that his father might be able to save him.

Slowly, with head down he approached the Baron. He started to mouth another apology but was cut off before he could get the words out. "Rogaard, my daughter tells me you saved her life a second time today. I don't know what gets into that girl about water. She told me that you managed to pull her from a muddy grave after she lost her balance and fell into the stream. I thank you a second time for her life and I want to give you this brand new sword as a reward."

Rogaard was astounded. He did not know what to say. With his right hand he took the sword while involuntarily with the other hand he pulled down on his nose closing his nostrils. At that moment he caught a glimpse of a coyly smiling Adalena standing behind her father. He bowed to them, turned and left. He was not sure he was breathing. Now he knew he was lucky.

Adalena's emotions roiled her thoughts. She became even more impolite than usual to the servants and was especially ill-mannered to her mother. She wanted nothing to do with Rogaard yet could not forget how he had held her tightly and kissed her. She somehow hoped he would kiss her again. Finally she confessed to Father Vilfred the yearnings that she had for an un-named servant youth. The Priest knew it was Rogaard. He too had visited Father Vilfred and in the confessional exclaimed his passions for Adalena. Custom forbade a bond taking place between such disparate social classes. The Priest was conflicted. He could not violate the seal of the confessional. Yet in the confines of Castle Egeskov it would be impossible to keep these two heated youthful lovers apart. He sensed that their secret infatuation was burning like a double sun. Soon they would discover that the other carried the same smoldering desire. It would lead to disastrous consequences for each of them. In general terms, without revealing names or details, he counseled with his wife about the situation. She had guided him many a time, in far more difficult situations.

"Baron Haakon, I need to speak to you about your son, Jerrik," Father Vilfred said.

The Baron smiled and at the same time shook his head in disgust. His only son and heir was often in trouble. "What did the boy do now Father? Is another maid pregnant?"

"No Baron, not that. I am concerned that I have failed you with your son. I am only a simple parish priest with limited learning. I cannot impart to him the wisdom that you possess. He needs additional education to ably fulfill his future role in the Barony."

"Father, you are too diplomatic. I think my son is plainly stupid."

The priest sighed. The Baron was right but he could not openly agree. Instead, "Baron, your son needs more than I can give him. I offer the suggestion that you would consider sending him to Paris for additional learning. I can arrange for him to be taught by some of the most learned men in France at the new university there."

Baron Haakon immediately liked the idea. Jerrik had very rough edges. Perhaps, away from the protection of Castle Egeskov, his crudeness might mellow. *I will do it*, he thought. *Yet he is my son and heir and I must protect him. I will send two huscarls with him.*

"I will do as you suggest Father. I will send two of my huscarls to accompany him and keep him out of trouble."

Happily seeing the Baron warming to his suggestion, Father Vilfred diplomatically continued, "Perhaps something else might serve your purpose better Sire. Jerrik tends to be a bit of a bully. We want him to learn to reason. He needs to appreciate tact and diplomacy. The simple uneducated huscarls guards will not be able to help in many social situations. Jerrik will only order them away. He needs a strong companion to guide him."

Baron Haakon pondered for a bit and again had to agree. "What else can I do Father. Do you have a recommendation?" he asked.

"Why not order Rogaard to accompany him. He is close in age to Jerrik and a good fighter. He is also intelligent. He understands morals and everything else I have tried to teach. I have seen him give into Jerrik in the mock combats when he might have beaten your son badly. He has often guarded and saved Adalena from harm. Rogaard knows how to treat the nobility with strength and diplomacy. He will keep Jerrik on the proper path to God. If you command him, he will watch over your son. Tell Rogaard that he is not bound to obey Jerrik. I am confident that Rogaard will help guide Jerrik to a richer understanding of life."

That said Father Vilfred watched as Baron Haakon considered the proposal. He was delighted when the Baron finally said, "I will do just as you say." The priest thumbed his Rosary beads with gladness. A great deal of difficulty had just departed from his spiritual jurisdiction. The troubling Jerrik, with all of his ghastly behaviors, would leave Castle Egeskov. At the same time the impossible romantic dangers brought on by his sister and a servant would be no more. *I must thank my wife profusely for her wonderful plan,* he thought. *She is, and always has been, a brilliant helpmate.*

Both Rogaard and Jerrik were shocked by orders to travel to Paris. Confronting them together, Baron Haakon directed Rogaard to protect Jerrik in all things. They were to treat each other as equals, while Rogaard would also hold their purse. Rogaard was further directed to ensure that Jerrik maintained the moral code of mother Church as taught by Father Vilfred.

"Father are you commanding me that I, the son of a Baron, must obey a common huscarl? I won't do that," Jerrik stormed.

Baron Haakon flushed crimson. "Son, you are telling me you will not obey your father's orders and the teachings of Holy Mother Church" he screamed. "I do this for your protection. Disobey me in this and I will see you never become the next baron of my lands."

Jerrik was shaken. He had never seen his father this angry. Rogaard was wide-eyed with concerns. How could he...

"Jerrik, do you understand? You are to follow Rogaard's directions for safety and morals." Haarkon's face was only inches from his son's. As he shouted some spittle struck the young man's face. "If I hear that you fail me, you will not like your punishment. Do you get through your thick head what I am saying?"

All Jerrik could do was to nod in agreement. They stood together in silence as Haakon regained his composure. Then he turned to Rogaard. "Young huscarl, you may use whatever measures necessary to keep my son out of trouble. If you succeed, you will be richly rewarded when you return."

The pair left Castle Egeskov a few days later. Rogaard was totally absorbed in the wonder of a brand new adventure. Jerrik was sullen but made no attempt to thwart his father's orders. Adalena was heartbroken watching them leave. She stayed in her room for days crying for her departing first love. Father Vilfred felt a new lightness in his step as two difficult problems had disappeared over the horizon. Baron Haakon continued with the usual affairs of his lands. He had no additional thoughts of his son.

Paris France, in the early 1200's was one of the largest cities in Europe with some 50,000 souls. Like other cities in these times it was polluted by innumerable vices and all kinds of criminal activity. In their first week in the city Rogaard and Jerrik were attacked twice by small bands of ruffians who attempted to rob them. Standing back to back the young men successfully fought off the muggers both times.

The prostitutes were a different story. They would drag any male, even a cleric, practically by force, into their brothels. Almost no one in Paris thought of fornication as a sin.

Rogaard discovered that it was a common practice for learned educational classes to be held in houses where the second floor was devoted to scholarship. At the same time whores practiced their profession on the first floor. Jerrik found this arrangement quite satisfactory and often spent considerable time on the lower level…against the wishes of his protesting companion. Thoughts of the beautiful Adalena drove Rogaard deeply into his studies…almost always successfully driving away temptation of the available females below.

The world of knowledge opened endless vistas for Rogaard. He learned of mathematics, music, astronomy, philosophy and ethics with the eagerness of a parched man seeking water in a desert. Jerrik however was generally bored. He could not concentrate sufficiently to grasp fundamentals. He did well only with mathematics, but cared little for any other subject. "I can use this learning to count and collect taxes when I am Baron. I will not be cheated," he boasted.

Both young men enjoyed the minstrels and troubadours who traveled to Paris from the south of France. Jerrik found that he could hire these entertainers, group them together and charge admission for their performances. Well-to-do men would bring their mistresses to be entertained. It was an opportunity for them to demonstrate their positions and wealth.

At first, only for the rabble, Jerrik offered a new entertainment…a performance of cat burning. Here a cat was hoisted in a sling and slowly lowered into a fire. This became a popular amusement. Soon much of the Paris nobility came to see this spectacle. They would shriek with laughter as the animals were singed, roasted and finally carbonized, Rogaard did not enjoy this form of entertainment. He thought it stupid.

As the months passed into a year neither man talked of returning to Castle Egeskov. Rogaard was excited almost every day by the deep wells of new learning experiences. Jerrik was equally energized with his new found riches earned by his entertainments . Now with his earnings he could buy all the drink he wanted and pay for the choicest women. He did need Rogaard for protection. Paris was a dangerous place with little law and no order. Jerrik could buy his own guards but knew he would never be able to trust them. Rogaard was an indispensable bodyguard.

One warm summer afternoon, during their second year in Paris, Jerrik demanded that Rogaard follow him to what he believed was the most prominent brothel in Paris. "Here you are huscarl. I have purchased a good bottle of wine for you while I enjoy the pleasures of the finest courtesan in France. Her name is Abrial. I met her at one of my shows. She shyly approached me and requested my visit…without charge she said. Can you imagine that! She is the lone woman in her house and services only nobility." Jerrik was obviously overwhelmed with this rare opportunity. "She must have heard of me."

Rogaard took the wine to a bench in the courtyard behind the stately stone house. A slight breeze was moving the leaves of the blooming horse chestnut tree in the center of the small walled yard where he sat. A maid of the house came and sat beside him. "Are you also here for the pleasures of my lady?" she asked.

"No, I only accompany the son of my master, Baron Haakon. He has been told that your mistress has exceptional talents."

"Indeed she does. But I am amazed that your master was allowed here. She is sworn to the service of only the King's Royal family. I have never heard of your Baron Haakon. Does your friend know there is a death sentence placed on any who share Lady Abrial's exquisite talents?

Two...no three men have died for being with her. Sometimes I think she entices men just to see them killed. It is much like a sport with her. She will claim that your friend forced her."

Rogaard was shaken. He recalled that this Lady Abrial had talked briefly with Jerrik two weeks earlier at one of his cat roasting. She had appeared to enjoy the spectacle in a most demonic way. She had screamed over and over for the cat to be raised from the fire so it would yowl longer. She laughed and laughed at the charred animal. She apparently enjoyed death and now she wanted to take Jerrik's soul.

Leaping to his feet, breaking the wine bottle, Rogaard ran to the house. He found Jerrik adjusting his clothes while the smiling nude woman lay supine on the divan. Quickly he blurted out what he had just learned.

The courtesan laughed at Jerrik. "Your friend does not lie, Danish barbarian. I sent my maid to tell your friend what I do so that I could bask in your anger. The King will have your head for what you have enjoyed with me today. I get great pleasure from watching men die, just as you do from burning cats. Perhaps I will have the King set you ablaze for my entertainment."

Jerrik yelled, "You are a bitch Abrial." He moved to hit the women but was restrained by Rogaard. "Stop, Jerrik. You don't have time for revenge. We must leave now." It was just as well. Two burly men with clubs had quickly appeared behind the unmoving Abrial. *They must have been in this room all the time,* Jerrik realized.

Wisely Jerrik agreed to leave. If he valued anything, he valued his own skin. Suddenly there was a new danger: he might be killed, perhaps in a most unpleasant way by the royal family of Paris. *These people are really foul,* he thought. *It is time to depart.* Gathering their belongings Rogaard and Jerrik found a ship at the docks preparing to sail down the Seine just before sunset. Both young men, for very different reasons, would miss Paris. It was time to return to Castle Egeskov.

By the ninth century, Europe had degenerated into many small counties and fiefdoms. In many of them local lords and knights frequently fought each other for power. The lands of Denmark were controlled by three separate kingdoms. There, and throughout central and northern Europe, various segments of nobility were involved in constant violence against one another.

The "Peace and Truce of God" movement was one of the ways that the Church attempted to Christianize and pacify these feudal structures of society through non-violent means. In times such as these, when a region was suffering from disorder due to frequent conflicts, the local clergy, such as abbots, heads of monasteries, and bishops, would hold a town council meeting. Invitations would be issued to nearby nobles demanding that they attend. Assuming the nobles showed up, the clergy would bring all the saints' relics they had available. These relics could include bits of bone, vials of blood, and clothing from the saints; anything that had at one time come into physical contact with a saint. These relics were often heaped in a pile or displayed dramatically at the meeting.

The clergy would use these sacred items to induce fear of the saints, fear of spiritual retribution. All this was done to intimidate the nobility, to persuade them to promise to obey the Peace and Truce of God and reduce the violence. The belief in the power of saints' relics was very strong. The Truce of God extended the Peace by setting aside certain days of the year when violence was not allowed. Whereas the Peace of God prohibited violence against the church and the poor, the

Truce of God was more focused on preventing violence between Christians, specifically between knights.

In 1076, the Muslims had captured Jerusalem...the most holy of holy places for Christians. There was no more important site on Earth than Jerusalem for a true Christian. Christians called Jerusalem the "City of God".

In 1095 Pope Urban II authorized a religiously-sanctioned military campaign known as the First Crusade. This and later Crusades were fought mainly against Muslims, although campaigns were also waged against pagan Slavs, Jews, and even Russian and Greek Orthodox Christians. In 1193, nearly one hundred years later, Pope Celestine III sanctioned a Northern Crusade. The Nordic nobility was generally too far removed from Palestine to fight the Muslims. The northern Crusade was an extension of the desire to Christianize pagans and Russian Orthodox peoples of the eastern Baltic.

Kings, major and minor nobility and even peasants of the Nordic countries were overjoyed at this opportunity for a Baltic Crusade. The benefits of a holy war were well worth the risks. All assets at home were protected and could not be seized for the payment of debts. All sins and crimes were forgiven: even those committed before the crusade or while on the crusade. After tithing to the church, loot taken on the crusade could be kept by the crusader. It was quite a proper reward for fighting the enemies of the church.

Jerrik and Rogaard had returned to Castle Egeskov. They found Baron Haakon in wild turmoil, organizing for this new crusade. Almost every segment of royalty with their serfs and servants were also preparing. For the peasants it would be a way to escape the grinding poverty of their lowly classes. They would attack, defeat and Christianize the Livonian peoples on the eastern shores of the Baltic Sea. They would return with gold.

Learning of the crusade long before reaching home, both young men were excited. Jerrik sought the adventure and the occasion for plunder. He had been forced to leave much of his recently earned wealth in Paris. Rogaard only wanted the opportunity to expiate his sins…those committed in Paris and the dim remembrances of his lust filled nights with thoughts of the Lady Adalena.

There was a noisy commotion in the great hall of Castle Egeskov. It woke Adalena from a sound afternoon nap. Rushing to the top of the stairway she was surprised to see her brother Jerrik, now older and more mature. He was being roundly greeted by their father.

"Jerrik You have been gone a long time. We are going on a crusade."

"I heard father. It will be a wonderful quest. I am happy to return in time to join you."

Baron Haakon suddenly frowned. His son's return was a surprise. It disturbed the arrangements he had made for his wife, Baroness Ingeborg, to supervise his holdings. He had very little confidence in Jerrik, yet this young man was his son and heir. "Bring the Baroness here," he commanded a nearby servant.

Mother and son greeted each other…but not warmly. Ingeborg realized that her son's presence changed a great deal. Jerrik had no idea as to what change was to take place.

Haakon looked sternly at each of them. "Jerrik, you cannot go on this crusade. You, as my sole male issue will be inheritor to this Barony. You are here. You must stay here to preserve our right of possession."

"But father..." Jerrik whined.

"Don't disagree with me. I have spoken. Your mother will guide you in your decisions. She has the wisdom that I suspect you still lack. You will accept her advice or if you do not, I will disinherit you upon my return." Baron Haakon was obviously irritated with his choices as he forced his words though tight lips.

Ingeborg had to nod in agreement but she knew it would not be easy to control her untamed son. She could see the anger forming in his young face.

Strong bile of disappointment rose in Jerrik's throat. "Father, I have learned much in Paris. I am older now and a better fighter. I want to kill infidels as much as you do."

"You have never been a good liar Jerrik. I have not been unaware of your drunkenness and whoring in Paris and your entertainments. You are greedy and I think you just want to reap the riches of warfare. You will do as I command, until I return. Disobey the Baroness, and you will reap consequences from me that you will not like."

Jerrik put his head down to hide his anger. He thought, *why does this old man always threaten me? I hope he gets killed on the Crusade. Then I will be the Baron and do anything I please. Perhaps this is better. I can easily control my mother. She is only a woman. I will be the master of Castle Egeskov.*

"Mother, they are back from Paris?"

"Yes Adalena."

"Did Rogaard also return? I saw my pitiful brother, but what of Rogaard?"

Ingeborg was surprised that Adalena's girlhood crush was still with her. "He is a servant my daughter. You should not be concerned about the likes of him."

Adalena was apprehensive. She instructed one of her maids to inquire after Rogaard and quietly order him to visit her. Yet, because of the chaos of the crusade preparations, it took two days for the maid to locate Rogaard in a place where she could covertly relay the message from her mistress. But now the huscarls and men of the Barony were streaming across the bridge to join the invasion fleet. Rogaard had failed to receive the message in time to visit Adalena.

She however, from an upper window of the castle was able to spy him in the marshaling area below. She felt that her heart had stopped. Rogaard was taller and no longer appeared the youth she remembered. He was man, a man she was still falling in love with. Yet, how could she, a member of the nobility, possibly love a servant. It was terribly wrong. Her passion for him burned in her breast much like a hot undying ember. She knew it was a sin. Eyes brimming with tears, she turned away.

Adalena never knew that his return to Castle Egeskov had immediately rekindled a passion in Rogaard such as he had never experienced. He desperately wanted to visit the Lady Adalena. The demands of preparation from Baron Haakon and his father had forced him to remain away from her.

A BIT OF HISTORY

Pope Celestine III (born Giacinto Bobone) authorized the Northern Crusades. He was elected Pope on March 21, 1191 at the age of eighty.

Because he was only a cardinal deacon (essentially an administrator) before becoming Pope, he was ordained a priest on April 13, 1191 a month after his election to The Chair of Peter. He reigned for six years until his death.

Twenty-three

Rogaard

The Northern Crusade
Haplogroup M343

Rogaard's mind was alive with a zeal known only to young men. It was to be another adventure in another land. His life could not get better. He was finally free of the forced companionship of that vile Jerrik. Next his father, with Baron Haakon's approval, had promoted Rogaard to second in command of the huscarls. Finally, he had been given control of five of the ships transporting the peasant Catholic Crusaders. They sailed as part of a vast fleet to convert the pagan Livonians on the far eastern shores of the Baltic Sea. He would fight gloriously to convert the heathens, amass booty and at the same time have all of his sins, most of them from his adventures in Paris, forgiven. Adalena was all but forgotten.

Rogaard's ships, with many others, were separated from the main fleet by rough seas. They finally landed on the shores of Latvia two weeks after the main body had arrived. Rogaard was immediately summoned to Baron Haakon's headquarters tent. It took him a day's travel to finally locate the Baron. Rogaard saw no signs of combat as he journeyed inland. He was surprised at that.

"You are finally here Rogaard," the Baron said with his usual snarl.

"I am sorry Sire. We were blown off course."

"No matter Rogaard. I have sad news for you. Your father is dead. For three days those abominable infidel Livs simply backed away from our forces. We pressed forward and spread out taking much of their lands without incident. A few of the Russian Orthodox heretics living among the Livs surrendered and came forward to be baptized. We had some conversions! But at dusk on the fourth night we were attacked. Unfortunately your father was killed in that surprise assault. You will now be captain of the huscarls and my personal bodyguard."

Rogaard was saddened, but not overwhelmed by the loss of his father. They had never been close. Deaths were expected in warfare. He was now a captain.

The Northern Crusade marched eastward through the summer and fall. On many of the small hills, the pagan Livs had erected insignificant forts to protect their territory from traditional warring neighbors. The Livs had been invaded many times, especially by the Germans from the south and the Rus from the east. As a people, the Livs were sorely divided into many local tribes and could not or would not put together a combined force to resist a major attack by invaders. They had been conquered many times. Fighting and disorder was common in this land. With ease, this large crusading army overwhelmed every small garrison. Pagan or Russian Orthodox populations were easily baptized into Roman Catholicism as the army of Danes and some Swedes continued to move farther inland.

Rogaard was almost immediately disenchanted with the Crusader battles. Each was a violently bloody occasion. Every skirmish was a melee of noise, confusion and gore. A few nobles and many peasants lost their lives earning each Crusader victory.

The weather was turning colder. Mud and misery were slowing the advance. Prince Valdemar of Denmark, the leader of the Crusader forces, called a halt to the advance. He gathered the nobles and warrior priests to discuss actions for the future. Rogaard, as a bodyguard, accompanied Baron Haakon to the meeting. It was not pleasant. Several of the noble attendees were upset.

"We have lost many of our peasant soldiers, Prince Valdemar. Our army is no longer as strong as when we landed here," one noble spoke plainly.

"True," said another. "But we have conquered much of the pagan Liv lands and brought Christianity to this sorry people. There are fewer heathens to fight and convert. This land is now part of The Holy Roman Empire."

Count Aalholm shook his head in disagreement. "That is not quite accurate," he said. "We have military victories and our priests baptize each conquered tribe but the priests warn me they will go back to their old pagan ways as soon as we return to Denmark."

"Count Aalholm speaks the truth," a warrior priest added. "Their leaders will submit to Rome now. It is prudent for them to do so. If we become exhausted and leave them, they will revert to their old pagan rites and practices. We cannot leave! We must stay and build churches and fiefdoms. Our nobles must rule these lands"

"We cannot leave," many shouted. It now became a chant.

"We cannot stay either," Count Aalholm continued. "This poor land has not given our peasant soldiers the riches they expected. They will not fight the infidels much longer just to please the Church."

"Our crusade is not for gold, it is for God," one angry priest bellowed.

Prince Valdemar allowed the dissension to roll through the meeting. Finally he spoke. "My nobles," he said in a firm voice, "we are here in this land for several purposes. Our most important mission is to convert those who are not of the Catholic faith. We must amend the heathen's beliefs to allegiance to the true faith of Rome. But we are not here just too spread our religious beliefs. We also desire to open safe trade routes for the merchants who are the sponsors of this crusading endeavor.

"They hope for trade and profit from our successes. You nobles will share in those riches. And for myself and our King, I wish to add these conquered lands to our permanent control. Latvia will become a part of Denmark. There will be new Baronies awarded to many of you.

"Still, our dedicated purpose is to honor God. We have won the Livs for Rome. Next we have the opportunity to push eastward and conquer the Orthodox heretics of the Novgorod Republic. These separatists must come back to the proper true faith of the Church. This is why this crusade was authorized by Pope Celestine. Prince Alexander Nevsky of Novgorod and his people must be returned to the one right faith either by choice or by force. Then our crusade will be successful. Only after that will our crusade be completed. Tell your soldiers that when we get to Novgorod they will find all the riches they seek. It is their reward for returning these wayward people to the proper worship of God and our Pope.

"Now hear me, when the ground freezes we will push on to Novgorod. The heretics will be no more." The rousing cheers from his nobles told Prince Valdemar he had won the day.

As they rode back to their campsite, Rogaard puzzled over what he had heard. He asked, "Baron, may I pose a question?"

"Yes Rogaard. What is it?"

"Well sire, I believed that this crusade was to convert the heathen and the heretic to our one true faith. Of course many Crusaders came only to rid themselves of their sins. I am one of them. I am a sinner. Others, perhaps most of the peasants, also hope for gold. But today I heard that we are also here for the merchant classes?"

"That is true huscarl. How do you imagine we are able to supply this vast army with food and other goods? It is the merchants. They don't do it for God. They do it to enrich their purses. Our victories open new trade routes for them. The royalty gains by taxing them for the use of the ports and toll roads. Everyone achieves something from this venture."

"Even the nobles? How to they gain sire?"

"Many of the nobility are here in hopes of enlarging their holdings. We expect to retain sovereignty over the lands we conquer. It is my hope to build a castle here in Latvia where Jerrik can become its master. He is a difficult son and I am anxious to be rid of him."

Rogaard had never imagined such sentiments from the Baron. He was stunned by the older man's frankness. Perhaps Jerrik's father disliked his son almost as much as Rogaard despised the young noble.

They rode in silence for a long while. Finally Rogaard asked, "Sire, is it then only the priests who seek to convert the heathen Livs and return the Eastern Orthodox to our one true faith?"

Baron Haakon laughed so hard he nearly fell out of his saddle. "Rogaard, you are as unaware of the workings of the world as my foolish daughter Adalena. The priests with us are as greedy and ambitious as any men I know. Each seeks to build a church, but only to control the peasants and to tithe them. You will never find an underfed warrior priest who does not seek his personal wealth. You need to learn more of the world Rogaard. All men seek to ever increase personal power and wealth. It has always been so."

Unknown to Prince Valdemar, his meeting with the nobles was attended by a spy for the Sovereign of Novgorod, Prince Alexander Nevsky. In less than a week's time the spy had reached Novgorod and was reporting the events to the Prince.

"Sire, Prince Valdemar has declared that his Crusaders will storm Rus. He calls us heretics since we do not give our fealty to Rome."

"Ivan, are the soldiers and leaders supporting that contemptible Dane? Are they willing to bring his crusade to our homeland?"

"Yes sire. They have destroyed the Livs. The common soldiers seek more riches in Novgorod. Prince Valdemar has a powerful army with many heavily armored knights. His rabble of peasants is healthy and well led."

"Are they marching here at this moment?" Prince Alexander asked worriedly.

"No sire. They are encamped waiting for colder weather. Their horses and heavy armor cause them to sink into the wet bogs. Valdemar cautioned his forces to hold position until the ground freezes. Only then they will advance on us."

"Excellent, Ivan. You have done well. Now we have time to prepare. We will repel these evil invaders trying to despoil the blessed earth of Mother Russia."

As the weather grew colder, the Crusaders found that they were being opposed by small detachments of swiftly moving Rus light cavalry. Rapid pursuit was not possible because of the makeup of the Crusader forces. The heavy armor of the mounted knights and the chain mail of the average soldier slowed them. Still they were marching closer every day to Prince Nevsky's city of Novgorod.

Eventually the Crusader army reached the shores of immense Chudskoe Lake. It divided the lands of the heathen Livs from the lands of the heretic Rus. The annoying Rus cavalry had led them to the shores of this very large lake and then seemingly disappeared? Novgorod lay some distance on the far side of the lake.

"Prince Valdemar, what are your orders? Should we go around the lake? It is quite large. That will take time. We could soon cross directly on the ice…perhaps."

Always cautious, Prince Valdemar replied, "We will wait here until I can see a troop of mounted knights move on the ice without it cracking. I see islands in this lake. Send a scouting party to look for that vanishing Rus cavalry. We need not fall into some sort of trap. I will not be ensnared by these heretics. Our scouts will also test the ice."

Baron Haakon was furious with the halt. He hated the deep Rus cold. If the Rus had only the fighters that they had encountered, the Crusade would overwhelm Novgorod within the next week. "Our Prince Valdemar is a goose," he said to no one in particular. "I want to finish this crusade and return to Castle Egeskov." Others in the army felt exactly the same.

The scouts returned to Prince Valdemar and reported that the islands were deserted. The Prince then sent some troops and several wagons of supplies onto the ice. The ice held. At a council that day he ordered the Crusaders to start the move across the lake toward Novgorod on the following morn. Alexander Nevsky heard of the planned crossing even before the directive reached all the elements of the Crusader Army.

By noon the following day a major portion of the Crusaders were on the ice of Lake Chudskoe. Suddenly a large attacking force of Rus cavalry, larger than any they had seen previously, appeared from one of the islands. As the battle ensued, the Crusaders were forced to alter their direction, but only towards another large island. Suddenly that island erupted with massive units of pike men and other infantry. It was not possible to quickly form defensive lines and the crusading knights fell back. The ice thinned behind them. The weight of their heavy armor doomed a large portion of their most powerful weapon…the mounted knight. Prince Nevsky had cleverly defeated the Crusade. It would not return.

"Rogaard, I have been grievously wounded," Baron Haakon screamed.

The Rus cavalry had first charged directly at the Baron's troops. They were overwhelmed. Every man fought for his life. First the Baron lost his horse. Next he was surrounded and grievously wounded by the charging infantry. By the time Rogaard reached him, the Baron was gushing blood from two separate wounds. The two were now close to a small island and Rogaard dragged the Baron across the ice in hopes of finding some shelter from the warring parties.

"Sire…" Rogaard said in a subdued tone. He knew such wounds were fatal.

"Rogaard, listen to me. I will die soon. Take my ring. It is the seal and symbol of my barony. You must deliver it to Jerrik. Also take this bag of gold that I carry. If I had died directly at the hands of an enemy it would have shown him that he had killed a great man. Now take the gold and convey it to the Baroness."

The Baron abruptly slumped into unconsciousness. Rogaard thought him dead and removed the bag of gold. He put the ring on his finger for safe keeping. Then he was shocked as the Baron opened his eyes and weakly grasped the young man's wrist.

"Rogaard…?"

"Yes sire, what else can I do for you?" he replied in a trembling voice.

"Protect Jerrik. You must save him from himself. Promise me."

Before Rogaard could reply he heard the death rattle of the Baron. He sat with the corpse for a few moments with tears streaming down his face. There was nothing more he could do. Suddenly his whole body shook with an emotional coldness. He picked up the Baron's blood stained cloak and wrapped it around himself. He rose and marched out through the trees towards the screams of the ongoing battle. He hated warfare; it was not at all glorious as he first imagined. His father was dead. Now the Baron was also dead. A vengeful fire began to burn inside his chest. He would kill Rus. He would kill them all.

Suddenly everything went black.

"What is this Captain Borya? Here we are celebrating a great victory…did you see allof those Crusader Knights sink into the lake…and the rest of their army ran away…did you see it Borya?"

"Yes I saw it all Prince Alexander. You have a great victory. It will be remembered forever in the histories of the Rus."

"So why now do you bother me, Borya?"

"Sire, we have captured a Crusader, I think he is of noble rank."

Prince Alexander Nevsky put down his cup of fermented potato water. He thought, *a hostage, a high ranking member of the Crusade…his prisoner. This could be profitable.*

"Bring him here at once," he ordered.

The still unconscious body of Rogaard was thrown at the feet of the Prince. The man's face was covered with dried blood, as was his cape. The Prince noted that the garment was rich material, trimmed with ermine. *Yes, he would be of some royal rank, perhaps even a king. This certainly was a good omen.*

"Borya, who is he?" the Prince demanded.

Captain Borya replied "I do not know sire. But I have sent for Ivan. He was in their camp for weeks as our spy. He may recognize him. He must be of some importance. He is wearing a ring that carries the same heraldry as you see on his cloak. I also took possession of this bag of gold tied to his waist,"

Prince Nevsky smirked. "Borya take two pieces of the gold for yourself as a reward. Give me the rest of the purse. We must now find who he is. Where is that scum Ivan?"

Captain Borya pocketed the two gold pieces. He smiled politely. Inwardly he was overjoyed. He had already taken six pieces from the pouch for himself and one more for each of the two Rus soldiers who had captured the Crusader. They would all be quiet. This deed was profitable for everyone.

Prince Nevsky anxiously paced the floor of his battle tent. *Who was this man? Where was Ivan?* He took another large quaff of fermented brew. It burned his throat but warmed his body. "Where is that idiot Ivan?" He screamed in a now slurred voice. His retainers were well aware of the unhinged decisions made when the Prince drank too much. They were all in peril at times like this.

Ivan came running into the tent, breathless. "Sire you called for me?"

Prince Nevsky pointed to the still unconscious Rogaard lying in the middle of the tent. "Who is he?" the Prince demanded.

Ivan was wide-eyed with fear. He knew of the Prince's erratic drunken behavior. You did not disappoint the despot at times like this. "Sire, may I look closer at the man?"

"Look you fool. You were in their camp for weeks. Who is he?"

Ivan turned Rogaard over so he might see his face. It was smeared with matted blood and there was considerable swelling. He had never seen this person before. But then he observed the ring and the matching coat-of-arms on the cloak. "Sire, yes I know this Crusader. This is Baron Haakon. That heraldry design on his cloak is the same as was flying over his tent. He also wears a matching ring. It is Baron Haakon"

Nevsky spat! "Only a Baron! I was hoping he might be a King or a rich Prince that I could hold as a hostage for ransom." The Prince was now close to a drunken rage.

"Prince Nevsky," Ivan said, "I learned, when I spent time with the Crusader Army, that Baron Haakon is one of the richest men in Denmark. He has more lands and gold than many princes. You have a very wealthy hostage"

Nevsky, in his drunken state, began to snigger. He thought, *this...this is then a profitable opportunity. I will ransom this Crusader*

Baron. I will build a new palace using his money. He said, "Throw water on the Baron. Wake him up. I want him to see his captor."

The icy cold water brought Rogaard to a low level of consciousness. He recognized that he was surrounded by armed men…enemies jabbering in a language he could not understand. One voice, somewhere in the group, said "Baron Haakon" and Rogaard turned his head towards the called name before he slipped back into blackness again.

"See that. He acknowledged his name," Ivan said.

Prince Nevsky smirked and gave orders. "Captain Borya, take this man to my castle."

"To the dungeon, Sire?"

"No you fool. He is valuable only alive. He is no good to me dead. Lock him in one of the tower rooms. Let him keep his clothes and especially that ring. It is all the proof we need in order to ransom him. And Captain Borya…"

"Yes Sire."

"Keep him alive or his fate will be your fate!"

Rogaard's journey to Prince Nevsky's citadel was nightmarish. Many times he lapsed into unconsciousness. It took four days of being dragged or stumbling in an erratic walk to reach their destination. Often he fell into the slushy snow. But he attempted to use the fall as an opportunity to bathe his badly bruised face. The cold slush helped ease the pain. One eye was swollen completely shut. He was fed very little and realized a weakness overcoming his body.

Finally the stronghold loomed ahead. It appeared massive against the dark early winter sky. Strangely the ground here was bare of snow. Still, Rogaard was so cold from his loss of blood and lack of food that he almost welcomed the sight of his prison.

In the fortress the Rus guards roughly pushed Rogaard up a narrow flight of winding stairs. He was prodded with batons from behind by the laughing men. Finally they arrived at a landing opening to a small room closed off with a barred metal door. "Here is your home Crusader," one of the guards said with a laugh.

Rogaard did not understand the language, but he heard from the ear not damaged a word that sounded like 'kresaater'. He was pushed into the tiny cell-like room with such force that he slammed into the opposite cold stone wall. He struck it with the wound already on his head. The gash bled severely anew as he lost consciousness still another time.

When he woke he felt a blinding pain in the side of his head. His vision was blurred but he could make out his surroundings as he lay on the floor. He was too weak to force his aching body to rise. He saw a large pile of filthy straw in one corner of the room. It contained the dried human wastes of the previous cell occupant. Past the iron door gate locking him in, he could see the narrow slit of an opening in the fortress wall. It provided a dim light and some air. Yet he wondered why they were keeping him. *Why am I still alive*, he thought?

After a time he heard voices. The guards were coming up the stairway towards his isolated cell. He could not understand any of their words except 'Baron Haakon.' What was this? He began to understand. He saw that he still had the Baron's ring on his finger. *Why hadn't they stolen it? They must think I am the Baron. They are holding me as a hostage or better yet they hope to ransom me. I may live yet.*

Now the two men had cleared the stairs and were looking in on Rogaard. One man was obviously an officer while the other was the guard who had shoved him into the wall.

"Have you fed the Baron," Captain Boyar demanded.

"No sir. He just got here and we only put him into this cell," the nervous guard replied. "We treated him well just as you commanded Captain."

"I can see that you did it with your usual boorish brutality. The fresh blood on the floor gives you away…liar. Get this man food, fresh straw and water to clean himself. If he is harmed further you will personally answer to me and later directly to the Prince. Do you understand? The Prince is not as kind and forgiving as I am." Captain Boyar was holding the guard by his neck, choking him.

Rogaard understood none of what was spoken. But as they returned down the stairway the guard looked back at Rogaard with hatred in his eyes. He somehow would find ways to make this prisoner pay for his humiliation at the captain's hands.

Day after day Rogaard sat alone in his locked chamber. Each day the winter weather grew colder. He wrapped himself in the single outer garment that they had let him keep…the Baron's cloak. It was not enough to keep him warm. Occasionally snow would drift into his small confined area. The little toe on his left foot was turning black. Running in place helped to keep him warm but he was not fed enough for sufficient energy to run frequently.

Usually, once a day, the guard would deliver a bowl of something edible. There was no conversation as they did not speak each other's language. At first he could barely swallow the vile mixture. It was purple green with tiny specks of some type of plant. Gradually, as his days lengthened into months, he began to wait with anticipation for this meager meal. His ribs were becoming noticeable as he lost weight. He began to expect that he might die in this cell.

Now the vicious guard began to torment Rogaard with the daily gruel. At times he would set the bowl just barely out of Rogaard's reach. Then he would laugh as Rogaard tried to get it. Occasionally he would dump the bowl inside Rogaard's cell. He would howl with glee as Rogaard would be forced to lick the floor to salvage some of the meager nourishment. The guard would bark like a dog as Rogaard licked the stones as his only way to survive.

On a warmer afternoon in the spring the guard was again accompanied by his superior. The captain took one look into the sunken eyes of the emaciated prisoner and without a word struck the guard with his fist. Then the captain kicked the crumpled man down the stone staircase.

A short time later a tattered slave scurried up the stairs. Reaching through the bars he passed Rogaard some bread along with a bowl of sweet smelling soup containing a piece of mutton. The little man said, "Here, eat." Rogaard tore at the food. He gulped down the stew meat barely taking time to chew it. His shrunken stomach could not accept the large chunk of food in the middle of the rich soup. Rogaard vomited it back out into the bowl. For just a moment he stared at the piece of lamb. Then he picked it out of the bowl and chewed it slowly, consuming only bits at a time.

Finished, he turned to the waiting servant and smiled broadly and said. "Thank you. That was the first real food I have had in many months"

"You are welcome Baron." The man replied.

"We are talking," Rogaard almost shouted. "You can understand what I say!"

"Yes Baron."

"I have not been able to speak to anyone since I was captured. You must have been on the crusade with us. You are a Dane too."

"No Baron. I was part of a merchant's expedition to Novgorod many years ago. My master sold me to the Rus as partial payment for some narwhale tusks. I am not a Dane. My great-grandmother was captured in a Viking raid many years ago and we have been slaves in Sweden ever since. My name is Pehr."

"Pehr, do you know what happened to the guard that fed me every day?"

"Yes Baron, I do. Captain Boyar had the man whipped and sent to the dungeon. You are a very valuable prisoner. I have been ordered to bring you food twice a day and other necessities to return you to good health."

"Thank God," Rogaard whispered, "thank God." He took his left hand and pulled down on his nostrils, tightly closing his nose.

As spring passed into longer days Rogaard slowly regained his health. Pehr brought him something to eat even more frequently than twice a day. Most often it was the same purplish gruel that he at first despised. Now that watery porridge seemed not so bad.

Pehr often stayed to talk with Rogaard. He spoke of his early life in Sweden and his duties in the palace of Prince Alexander Nevsky. Pehr learned that the Prince was frequently drunk. At these times everyone feared for their lives. Rogaard was sensible enough to not reveal his true identity to the slave. If by chance the Prince learned that he was only a common huscarl he would be in great danger. Since he had grown up in Castle Egeskov it was not a problem to fabricate tales of life in the Danish nobility. Yet many stories brought back his fond memories of Lady Adalena. He knew that his soul longed for her while at the same time his body lusted to hold her again. The lust was a sin but he was a Crusader and all would be forgiven.

Life was getting better. He felt lucky again. At the stairway wall, in the slit to allow light and air, a small pair of birds had built a nest. Soon he spied hatchlings begging their parents for food. At first he thought there were three young birds but now he knew there were four. He watched them grow and knew they would soon be able to fly away. The nestlings entertained his solitude waiting for food and a chance talk with Pehr.

One afternoon Rogaard heard footfalls coming up the stairs to his chamber. If it was Pehr, the slave was not alone. Captain Boyar appeared first followed by a humbling slouching Pehr.

The Captain did not smile but he appeared to be pleased. "Pehr, you have done well. Baron Haakon looks much healthier. Trim his hair and wash his clothes. We have to present him to an ambassador from King Valdemar and determine a ransom."

"Yes Captain. I will immediately do as you order."

As Captain Boyar turned to leave he noticed the bird nest resting in the window sill. The small birds were not yet old enough for flight and hid quietly in the bottom of their nest. Boyar, as he passed the sill, pushed the nest outward to crash on the rocks far below.

For a moment Rogaard was stricken at the loss of the birds. He swiftly recovered and said to Pehr, "What did the man say to you? I can't understand the language. The only words that I understood were Haakon and Valdemar."

"He ordered me to make you presentable for the ambassador of King Valdemar who is coming to ransom you."

"Wait, wait Pehr. You said 'King Valdemar'. He is a prince not a king."

"No Baron. He is now a king. I heard in the court that your Danish King Erik III has abdicated. No one seems to know why he gave up his crown. Valdemar took his crown but there are two other pretenders for the throne. That is all I know. I suspect that King Valdemar desires powerful rich Barons, such as you, to help defend his title."

The Baron's ring, still on Rogaard's finger, was accepted by the ambassador as proof of his true identity. Before leaving, Rogaard shocked Captain Boyar by demanding that Pehr be allowed to accompany him to freedom. Prince Nevsky laughed at the stipulation while he poured the ransom coins through his fingers. In his alcohol induced stupor he simply nodded agreement to Pehr's release.

Rogaard, with Pehr, sailed directly to Denmark on the ambassador's ship. The huscarl was vexed. He thought, *how can I explain to King Valdemar that he has paid a huge ransom for a simple warrior? I will surely be sent to a dungeon to die for my deceit*.

A BIT OF HISTORY

The "Ice-Battle" between the Crusaders and the Rus took place on Chudskoe Lake in the year 1242. It is depicted in an old Russian film titled "Alexander Nevsky."

Twenty-four

Rogaard

Love and Deception

Screaming exuberantly, Jerrik ran wildly through Castle Egeskov. He had never felt such a joy in his entire life. He vaulted up the stairs to his mother's quarters and exploded through the archway into her rooms. The startled baroness, having her long tresses combed by a maid, rose facing her son with a look of confusion.

"What is the matter with you Jerrik?" she demanded.

"He's dead, he is dead. My father is dead! I am now the Baron and the complete master of all the lands of Castle Egeskov."

Jerrik started doing an uncontrolled dance in front of his mother. Ingeborg moaned fearfully as she slumped into a nearby chair. "How do you know your father is dead?" she murmured

Barely able to catch his breath, Jerrik replied gasping, "Because, old woman, the crusaders are returning. The one single huscarl left alive from the Baron's contingent reported to me. He told me there was a terrible battle on some ice covered lake. The Rus somehow managed to surprise Prince Valdemar. Father and his men took the brunt of the first assault. This surviving huscarl saw Rogaard drag the Baron to a nearby island. He could see a trail of blood from my father's many wounds spurting across the ice.

"The huscarl told me that the charging Rus infantry passed right through the baron's formation and on towards the main army of the crusaders. After they had rushed past, he thought he spied the Baron coming out of the edge of the island to rejoin the battle. But the huscarl quickly realized that it was not the Baron. It was Rogaard wearing the Baron's cloak. Rogaard is a stupid ass, but he is a loyal stupid ass. He would only take my father's cloak if the Baron was dead."

Baroness Ingeborg winced, but she held back tears from her offensive offspring. "That is not proof enough, Jerrik." She spat the words at him.

Jerrik grinned wickedly at her. "There is more my dear mother. Our huscarl saw Rogaard attacked by a number of Rus. They knocked him down. Next they pulled him away instead of killing him. I don't know why they didn't kill him. But still, they are both gone." Again, Jerrik began his frantic little dance.

"Stop that Jerrik. How can you be happy when your father might be dead?"

"I will dance. I will do whatever gives me pleasure because that old man *is* dead. I am now the Baron and master of Castle Egeskov. All this is mine to do with as I please."

"This is not true, Jerrik. I have not heard enough to believe you". Baroness Ingeborg began weeping as she uttered those words. She bent her head to her knees and clutched her tear filled face in her palms.

"Listen woman, I am now done with your constant meddling in my affairs. You and your brat of a daughter are confined to your rooms. Go elsewhere in *my* castle and I will put both of you in irons in the dungeon. You are finished…I need you no longer! I want never to see you again." Jerrik slammed out of the room snorting in a wild laughing rage.

Ingeborg was stunned beyond grieving. She called Adalena to her side and explained, between wrenching sobs, what had just occurred. Adalena also wept, but she was wise enough to call for their priest Father Vilfred. She repeated to him what had transpired. Father Vilfred immediately summoned the returned huscarl to come to the Baroness's quarters.

"Yes, my Lady," the soldier said nervously.

"Tell me what happened out on the ice. Tell me why you believe that Baron Haakon is dead," Ingeborg angrily demanded.

The guard, for a second time related the struggle on the ice. It was just as Jerrik had described it. Her son had not lied. Adalena asked, "Are you sure that it was Rogaard and not my father that the Rus carried away?"

"I am positive my Lady. I saw that it was Rogaard who dragged your father to the shelter of the island. It was his duty as Baron Haakon's body guard and captain of the huscarls."

"You are wrong soldier. It is Rogaard's father who is your captain," Ingeborg challenged.

"True my Lady, except Rogaard's father had been killed almost on the day we arrived in that heretic land of the Livs. The Baron made Rogaard our new captain."

"Alright! Tell us more. What happened next?" Adalena sharply demanded.

The huscarl nervously continued, "The battle had carried far beyond us by this time. I ran across the ice to the wooded area on the island to see if I could locate the Baron. I found him. He was dead from two very grievous wounds. I was as close to his body as I am to you at this very moment. There is absolutely no doubt that the dead man was the Baron."

Baroness Ingeborg fainted at these words while Adalena dissolved into tears. Later she wondered why Rogaard had been captured. *Might he still be alive?* She pondered.

Father Vilfred was severely apprehensive as Jerrik assumed the title of Baron. The young man was obviously depraved. The priest had heard about Jerrik's deeds in Paris. He had discounted those actions as the folly of youth. Still he felt that Jerrik's sins were only a precursor for his actions as a tyrant. His worry turned out to be true.

Peasants under Baron Haakon had been required to work two days for the manor. Baron Jerrik increased their workload to three full days. Freemen, who had no ability to pay new higher taxes, were publically whipped. Village maidens, who caught his eye, were brought to Castle Egeskov to serve Jerrik's personal pleasure.

Father Vilfred pleaded with the young Baron for some degree of temperance, but his pleading fell on deaf ears. Jerrik would not even participate in the sacraments. He ignored the priest. "Close your mouth priest or I will end your service here. I am Baron! You and your stupid church rules have no control over me!"

On one occasion Jerrik boldly attempted to bring one of his mother's youngest maid servants to his bedchamber. Baroness Ingeborg confronted him by going there herself and shaming him. While Jerrik did not respect his mother he still held some fear of her. She was the only person who could defy him and not be brutally punished. Peasants, freemen and servants of the manor were all equally terrified of the erratic young nobleman. Father Vilfred was besieged by members of his flock seeking relief from Baron Jerrik's cruel treatment. There was no relief.

As the harsh winter departed the land, Jerrik made plans for a cheerful occasion at Castle Egeskov. When King Erik III abdicated the Danish throne, civil strife had erupted among three strong contenders. Each was a relative of King Erik. Each of the pretenders for the crown sought support from the lesser nobles of the land. Jerrik strongly favored Sweyn, son of Eric II. The new Baron planned a festive banquet at Castle Egeskov for all supporting nobles of Sweyn. Jerrik schemed to find a way to strongly unite himself with the House of Sweyn.

Father Vilfred was astonished one morning to find himself summoned to the presence of Baron Jerrik. His wife gave him a worried look as he left their quarters.

"Yes Sire, you called for me?"

"I did Father Vilfred. I need your assistance."

The priest suddenly became wary. Jerrik was speaking in a conciliatory tone and had even addressed him properly. *Something is afoot,* the clergyman thought. He rephrased his question, "Yes Sire, what will you have me do?

"Father Vilfred, I am going to hold a feast in the honor of Sweyn who is seeking the crown of all of Denmark. I need my mother, who knows of these things, to make all the arrangements for this event. She has the experience necessary to make my occasion successful. I expect that she will refuse to accept my call for help. She and I have some differences."

"True enough Sire."

"Hear me out!" Jerrik's calm tone had disappeared.

I've said too much, the priest thought. *What does this wild man want me to do?*

"I want you to go to my mother and ask her to arrange the affair for me" Jerrik said.

"But Baron…"

"Father Vilfred, you are to tell her ***this***! There is a benefit for her. If she does as I request, I will allow her to leave her rooms and return to the full freedom of Castle Egeskov. There is also a penalty. If she refuses me, she will never be allowed to leave her quarters until the day she dies…but also in turn, you Father Vilfred and your family will be banished from this manor."

Father Vilfred gasped at the thought of being deprived of his comfortable home. He knew too, that Baroness Ingeborg relied heavily on him for moral support. She might refuse the request just to spite her son. Yet the banishment of her priest might compel her to take up the task. *I don't wish to leave here and start a new parish somewhere else. I am too old,* the priest thought. *Castle Egeskov has been our home for many years. It is not easy to start over…even if anyone would have me. The Bishop will not help me…he thinks I am weak and useless. I must decide what to do.*

"I will talk to Lady Ingeborg as soon as I can, Baron"

"Do it right now!" Jerrik demanded. Then after a pause, he said, "Oh, and Priest, one more thing."

"Of course, Sire."

"Tell that meddling woman, I mean my mother, tell her that I expect that she and my sister will attend the banquet. Do you understand? I will not honor my part of the bargain unless the both of them attend. *They must be there.* I want this to be a family affair."

Strange, very strange, Father Vilfred thought. *He is plotting something.*

"He wants me to do…what!" Ingeborg protested. She fumed but rapidly regained her traditional poise. "Father Vilfred, what else is going on here? Why would that wretched son of mine choose to have the Danish nobility fêted here in Castle Egeskov? He is, if anything, a devious person. He knows that you are valuable to me, so I will honor his request. But you must learn what you can about this affair."

Adalena was equally disturbed…especially by the demand that she attend the banquet. "Mother I hate him. I won't go!"

"We both must attend dear. Now that I consider it, here is a wonderful opportunity for us…or rather for you."

"What are you talking about mother?"

"Our our castle will be filled with nobility, you will be able to see eligible young men. They in turn will see you. Since you are almost eighteen, it is well past time that you find a spouse."

"No mother, no, no, no! I choose not to give myself to a man. I think I might become a nun. Father Vilfred can guide me in my desire for God."

The gathering became a huge success for Baron Jerrik. His mother had planned well. The guests were sated with food, drink and delightfully entertained. Best of all, Jerrik had cemented relations with Sweyn, the foremost pretender to the Danish throne. His plan had worked. He summoned his mother and sister to the castle's great hall in order to congratulate them.

"You have done well. I am pleased."

Adalena and her mother simply nodded without smiling. The event had been an exciting time especially for the young Adalena. It was a party where she mixed freely with equally ranked nobility whom they seldom saw. It was also her first banquet as an adult. Ingeborg, however, was still cautious. Her son was being un-naturally generous with compliments. *Was there something else happening?*

"I have exceptionally good news," Jerrik crowed. At the end of our banquet I met privately with Sweyn and his second son Ulf. You will be delighted to know, my dear sister," Jerrik's voice was now dripping with sarcastic pleasure, "that Ulf has agreed to take you as his wife."

"No," Adalena screamed in surprise. "I will not marry that ugly animal. I will kill myself befo…"

Adalena did not finish her complaint. Her brother had stepped forward and slapped her so hard that the young girl sank to her knees. "You will do as I command. You are but a woman! I am the master of this noble house and you will do as I say." Jerrik was livid.

Ingeborg stepped between them. "You cannot do this to your sister, Jerrik. Did you not notice Ulf? Did you not see the rash on Ulf's hands and face? His hair is falling out in patches. Ulf has all the signs of the French disease!" Ingeborg was shaking and equally upset as she helped the sobbing Adalena to her feet.

"You cannot do this! His disease will kill her," she screamed at her son.

"She will be his bride, and I will be part of the royal Sweyn family.

"Mother you cannot stop this marriage. I have already agreed to it. Now end your wailing. I have worked hard to achieve this tie between our families. It will be done! This wedlock that I have arranged will unite my Barony to the house of the next king of Denmark." Jerrik's high pitched voice echoed throughout the great hall. "Be joyous with me. I have finally found a worthwhile use for my simpleton sister!"

Father Vilfred was as distraught as he had ever been in his entire life. He had been immediately set upon by Ingeborg and Adalena as they returned to their rooms. Each begged him to intervene. Both women were bawling their pleas through a flood of tears. It was beyond his powers to help. He knew that. Feudal custom allowed the Lord of the Manor to make marriage decisions. There was no appeal, except to the Pope. That occurred only when situations involved morals or Papal politics. Adalena's impending marriage, especially since it would unite two noble houses, would not be questioned.

Two days later Father Vilfred received a new and much heavier personal burden. He received word from his Bishop of the results of the Second Lateran Council. This formal church meeting had been recently completed in Rome.

Canons 6, 7 and 11 had repeated the First Lateran Council's condemnation of marriage and concubinage among priests, deacons, sub-deacons, monks, and nuns. Unexpectedly the marriage to his wife of many years had been declared invalid. He was directed to abandon his family. She and his son Ramius and their two daughters would now have to make their way in the world without him. Father Vilfred in turn, was ordered to live a celibate life. He was torn asunder by love for the Church and love for his family. How could he abandon either of them?

For weeks he kept secret the decrees of the Council. He barely slept and would eat little. His wife noticed. "What is wrong husband?" she asked. "You can't let Adalena's forthcoming marriage bother you so much. I have heard that she and her mother are pleading daily with Baron Jerrik to cancel the union. It is a civil matter and not at all religious. It can't concern you. The servants tell me Baron Jerrik has often taken to hiding to avoid those pampered yowling women."

Father Vilfred lowered his head to his chest. He finally informed his wife of the sad directives from the canons of the Second Lateran Council. Her response was to send their three children to bed. Then, in whispered tones she offered a plan to her husband.

"Where is Father Vilfred? I want him here now!" Baron Jerrik was in a rage.

Out of breath, the priest ran into the Great Room. ""You called for me Sire?"

"Don't play that stupid mousey priest game with me. You know I called for you!"

"Yes Sire. Of course I do."

"Of course I do, of course I do! You are a babbling nincompoop. Is that all you can say? I don't understand as to why I tolerate you in Castle Egeskov. You do me no good...no good at all." Jerrik continued his tirade for several minutes as the chastened priest assumed a humble posture.

This is dangerous, he thought. *I must remain tranquil and watch my words carefully.*

Jerrik gradually calmed. Now his voice was barely a whispered growl. "Are you acquainted with what my stupid sister is now threatening to do? Did she tell you she will kill herself before marrying Ulf? Did she?"

"No sire."

"Well she informed me….me…the rightful Baron of this manor…that…that she would defy me and take her own life. That is a sin, as you taught us Father Vilfred. Is that not so? Tell me!" Jerrik's voice was a sharp rasp.

"You are correct Baron. It is a mortal sin to die by your own hand."

"And my mother stood beside Adalena as she threatened this horrible act. She told me that she agreed with all of this.

"You Father, *you* Father Vilfred, must put a stop to this deathly talk. I have made a pact with our soon to be King Sweyn. I will not be made the fool. This marriage between my sister and Ulf will give me great power in the kingdom. You must force Adalena to do the decent thing and go through with it. Help me Father."

The Priest followed the Baron as the younger man paced the Great Hall. Jerrik was frustrated that his plans were being mired by an uncooperative sister. He worried that he would not be in good graces of soon to be King Sweyn. Ulf and Sweyn had both been quite taken by Adalena's unblemished fresh beauty. Ulf eagerly wanted her.

Again Jerrik pleaded, "Help me Father. I am in pain."

"Yes Baron. I have a thought…no more of an idea."

"Out with it man. Tell me, what can you suggest? Adalena cannot kill herself. I won't allow it!"

"Baron we must wipe this idea of death out of your sister's mind. I am at fault. My religious teachings obviously failed with your sister and your mother. You are correct. They are on the verge of damning their immortal souls to Hell forever. They need a stronger guidance in our faith than I can provide."

"What are you proposing, Priest?"

"I suggest that I take them...no better yet, you order them...to make a retreat to the Cistercian Abbey at Om. The Abbot Jens is the most persuasive religious man I have ever met. I think he is a saint. He will convince your sister to live by her religion and obey your lawful order to marry Ulf. Your troubles will be over."

Ingeborg and Adalena both fought bitterly to avoid taking the long journey to Om Abbey. Jerrik was unwavering. They would go and Father Vilfred would lead them. They demanded that their servants accompany them to comfort them for the difficult trip. Jerrik was agreeable to almost any concession in order to achieve his political goals. He desperately sought peace and quiet in his castle. A week later the Baroness, Adalena and all of the party they requested, entered the vast grounds of Om Abbey.

"Father Vilfred, you did it," Ingeborg said laughing.

"My brother is such an idiot," Adalena added. "He is so stupid that he never realized that Om Abbey is outside the realm of Sweyn's control. He cannot make us return."

"True enough, daughter. He is so dense I dislike admitting I bore him. He would never imagine that we took with us a great deal of gold from my husband's treasury. It will make us welcome here for life. But you Father, what of you and your wife and children?"

Father Vilfred displayed a broader smile than either lady had ever seen. "I have gained as much as you Baroness. This Abbey is under the jurisdiction of the Diocese of Aarhus. The bishop there is an old friend and will allow me to stay as a married man with my wife and daughters and little son Ramius. Like you, we will never return to Castle Egeskov unless…unless..."

"Unless what Father Vilfred?" Adalena said in a trembling falsetto voice.

"Unless Sweyn overcomes the other pretenders to the crown and rules all of Denmark. Then we all might have to return and face Jerrik's wrath."

The ship carrying the ambassador and the supposed Baron Haakon was in sight of the Danish shore. Rogaard did not know what to do. If Prince Valdemar found that he had paid a great price to ransom a common huscarl it would not go well. Then again, the possibility of his maintaining the identity of the Baron was impossible. He would be exposed as soon as they visited the Prince's court…maybe even before that. He thought, *I will be punished…even killed…or the worst of fates…placed in a dungeon to die slowly.*

Rogaard decided to confess. With halting speech he explained everything to the ambassador.

"How could you do that? The ambassador demanded.

"They would have killed me if you had not ransomed me and Pehr." Rogaard replied.

"True, but have you no regard for me?" The ambassador crassly demanded. "Now I must tell Prince Valdemar that I gave his gold for the wrong man. I cannot do that. I could be stripped of my position by the Prince. We must delay your presentation to the Prince until I can decide how to explain all of this. It will take time."

The ambassador found lodging for Rogaard and Pehr at a port inn. Weeks later he returned to the two men. "I have not yet seen the

Prince. There is great turmoil in the land. There is a civil war brewing between Prince Sweyn, Prince Canute and Prince Valdemar. Each of these three claims the throne of Denmark. Various nobles are taking sides. The son of Baron Haakon is…"

"I know him, his name is Jerrik," Rogaard interrupted.

"Yes, well he is aligning himself with Sweyn. In fact he has promised his sister to Sweyn's second son, Ulf."

"What…what that cannot be. She is an innocent virgin and Ulf is…is,,,"

"Rogaard calm yourself. She is just another female. The world is filled with them."

"Yes, but I have special feelings…" His voice drifted off to silence. There was no reason to expose his desires for the Lady Adalena.

"You will remain here Rogaard and not reveal your true identity to anyone. I will take your servant Pehr and return to Prince Valdemar's Court. It seems that because of all the turmoil with three pretenders seeking the crown of Denmark…it seems that Valdemar has forgotten about my mission to ransom you…no…I mean the real Baron Haakon." Anger was building in the ambassador's voice. "We will talk again but only through your man Pehr. I hope in fact I never see or hear from you again. You could cause my life at court to end."

With those words, the ambassador took Pehr and left in a huff.

Rogaard spent his days wandering the small port town. As time passed he learned more of the raging civil war. He came to know that Canute and Valdemar had been raised together along with Valdemar's brother Absalon. They, like Sweyn, had blood-line claims to the throne. Each of the antagonists was powerful enough to stop the other two.

After months of no contact from Pehr, Rogaard decided to set off to Valdemar's court. He had never met the Prince and would offer his services as a huscarl. If his life-long good luck held, he would not be recognized and could get away with the scheme. Upon entering the Prince's estate he was surprised to immediately meet Pehr.

"Where have you been you faithless dog? I rescued you from the Rus and now you abandon me?"

"Master, I could not leave here. The Ambassador made me a servant to one of the lesser nobles and I could offer no valid reason to return to you. My departure might expose you to Prince Valdemar. I am sorry." Pehr thought, *I hope he accepts my excuse. This is the best life I have ever had...food...a good bed...warmth. Why would I chance my well being with a simple huscarl? I was never coming back.*

"I think I understand Pehr. Yet it seems to me…"

"Wait master Rogaard. I have news that will be of great interest to you. It is about Lady Adalena."

"What is it Pehr? Tell me now!"

"The servants of this court hear a great deal while tending their masters. We often share the information…"

Rogaard grabbed Pehr's shirt with an iron fist. "Tell me now. Out with it. What is the news of Lady Adalena?"

Pehr could see the young man was frantic. It suited his purpose. No longer must he provide reasons why he failed to return to Rogaard. "Master I am told that the Baroness Ingeborg, Lady Adalena, their handmaidens and their priest Father Vilfred and his family all fled to Abbey Om. They deceived Baron Jerrik by telling him that Adalena would kill herself if she was forced to marry Ulf. The Baron only wanted the union to advance his position with Sweyn. He can't get them back because Abbey Om is in lands controlled by Absalon."

Rogaard hugged the frail Pehr. His joy was so great the servant thought he might be injured. He finally freed himself and directed Rogaard to the commander of the Prince's guard. Here Rogaard portrayed himself as an experienced Crusader who wanted to join the impending conflict. He was immediately accepted by the under-manned contingent.

As time went by Rogaard was able to put names with faces. Valdemar was always accompanied by his half brother Absalon. He learned of Absalon's desire to support his half-brother as king, while he himself favored a position in the church.

Absalon, like Rogaard, had spent a great deal of time in Paris and was tutored directly by a Bishop there. Canute and Valdemar were friendly rivals while Sweyn was willing to use any means to get the Danish crown. The Ambassador, the man who had ransomed Rogaard from the Rus had disappeared.

Pehr often visited Rogaard daily and offered bits of gossip. Then without warning he disappeared for a period of time. Days later the little man came running to Rogaard. "Master, I have just learned of a great danger to you."

"What is it Pehr."

"I had been sent with others to help with the arrangements for an important banquet. It will be hosted by Sweyn at his stronghold. He has invited the Valdemar, Canute and Absalon to attend. The banquet is to make peace between all warring parties in Denmark."

"So again tell me Pehr why are you out of breath? What is the great danger to me?"

Pehr breathed loudly several times. His lungs had been damaged by the cold Rus winters and he had difficulty catching his breath.

Finally, "Remember the days when you were a prisoner in Prince Alexander Nevsky's castle and we talked and talked?"

"Of course you foolish old man. Actually you saved my sanity. I was alone for…for I don't want to think about how long. That was torture. Now what is the news? What are you trying to tell me?"

Pehr stuttered trying to find the words. "You told me about your life in Paris. You said that you and Jerrik had to leave because of the French king's whore named Abrial."

"I did tell you that. What has that got to do with me now?"

"Master, Abrial is here now in the court of Sweyn. She was bought here by one of the nobles loyal to the Sweyn and now services him. If she sees you, your identity may unravel and you will be recognized as one of Baron Haakon's men. They will think you a spy since Baron Jerrik had pledged himself to Sweyn. You might be killed if she identifies you."

"Thank you Pehr. I will stay away from that banquet, that woman enjoys watching men die."

"There is more master."

"What?" Rogaard was now disturbed and perhaps just annoyed by all of this.

"Master, I stayed with the other servants for the days of organizing the banquet. We are not just stupid blocks of stone. We stand by quietly to serve but we also listen and learn. Servants will tell each other what their masters say and do. By luck, I got to know Abrial's maid quite well, if you understand what I mean. She told me everything."

"Get on with it man."

"Abrial was practicing her profession with her new paramour while her maid waited behind a drape. Men talk at times like this while women such as Abrial appreciate the value of knowledge. It gives them power over men. Her lover was laughing wildly about the banquet. He confided in her that the party is a sham. Sweyn intends not to make peace, but rather to kill all three of those who oppose him…Valdemar, Absalon and Canute just after they are seated."

"My good god," Rogaard muttered. "I must stop this."

Rogaard, a huscarl, was not in a position to directly approach nobility. He spent days agonizing as to how to speak directly to Valdemar. Finally on the day they were to travel to the banquet Rogaard violated custom and directly approached Absalon. His personal bodyguard tried to block him, but Rogaard shouted, "You are in danger sire!"

Both Absalon and the bodyguard grasped the hilts of their swords. The bodyguard positioned himself in front of Absalon. "What is it huscarl?" the Prince demanded.

Rogaard put one knee on the floor and bowed his head. "Sire, my servant was part of the group you sent to Sweyn's great hall to prepare for the banquet. There he found a whore I knew in Paris and…"

"You have been to Paris huscarl?"

"Yes Sire."

"Why?"

It was too late now for caution. Rogaard had to tell the truth. "I was sent there by Baron Haakon. I was ordered to protect his son, now the Baron Jerrik, from harm."

Hmmm, Absalon murmured. "I was in Paris myself. What is the name of this whore?"

"Abrial."

"I have heard of her. She was the concubine for the King of France. It is true she is here with Sweyn's nobles. Get on your feet huscarl. Look me in the eye. What is your name? How did you get here?"

"Rogaard sire. I was the bodyguard to Baron Haakon after my father, the captain, was killed by the Livs. I was captured by the Rus. They thought I was the Baron and they held me for ransom. Your man came to Novgorod and paid them gold for me thinking that I was Baron Haakon.

"Please Sire do not punish your ambassador. It was not his fault. He had never met me. He could not know that I was not Baron Haakon. I know I wasted your gold."

"Rogaard, you are a remarkable man. You tell me all this knowing the danger to yourself. Do not concern yourself about the ambassador. He kept part of the ransom for himself and has fled to England. Now, tell me where is Baron Haakon?"

"He is dead Sire. He perished on the ice when the Rus surprised us."

"And you are loyal to the House of Haakon and now Baron Jerrik."

"No Sire. I hate Baron Jerrik. He is stupid and has caused many problems. We grew up together at Castle Egeskov. He often caused me grief. Jerrik was sent to Paris for education, but I had to attend the lectures while he gambled and whored."

Absalon smiled at the younger man's truthfulness. "So you are not a spy or loyal to Jerrik who we know is siding with Sweyn?"

Rogaard shook his head in agreement. Then he delivered the concern that King Sweyn intended to kill them all at the banquet. Absalon left Rogaard and retreated back into the stronghold without another word.

Rogaard was mystified. No seeming concern from Absalon. No punishment for having accepted the ransom. Nobility was certainly strange. Later in the morning a guard came and ordered him to report to Prince Absalon. He recognized the same fear that he had experienced so long ago when Baron Haakon called him for getting young Lady Adalena muddy and wet. Again his special luck held. He was simply directed to accompany the group to Sweyn's banquet. He was to stay outside the great hall in the town of Roskilde.

Waiting at the door of the banquet hall, he smelled the food being served and found he was quite hungry. A serving girl came out the door of the great hall with bowls holding uneaten meat. Rogaard took one of the bowls for himself.

At that moment the sound of fighting with screams of anguish suddenly filled the air. Rogaard threw down his food and rushed into the dimly lit room. Light came from only the few candles not destroyed by the fighting. There was one huge fireplace providing additional dim light. Sweyn's men were attacking the guests. Valdemar was wounded in the thigh but used his cloak to ward off the attackers. He fled past Rogaard out the front door. In the dim light he found Absalon who was cradling a man in his lap. This man's head was cleaved nearly in two. Absalon was covered with blood and seeping brain material. He was crooning, "Valdemar, Valdemar."

Rogaard grabbed Absalon and pulled the prince to his feet. "Sire, I recognize the cloak. That is Canute who has been killed. Valdemar has escaped. You must go now before they kill you. I will stay to delay them and fight for you."

Absalon quickly ran out of the great hall seeking refuge from the men chasing him. The town of Roskilde was one of the largest in

Denmark and contained several royal estates. Absalon lost his pursuers and managed to make his way to his mother's fortified house. Valdemar arrived at the house later that night. Then both safely made their way back to their protected estate. In the morning a slightly wounded Rogaard also returned.

Canute was dead. Sweyn had clandestinely perforated his own robe with a knife and displayed it to the townspeople. He claimed it was he who had been viciously attacked. It caused the start of full scale open warfare.

Sweyn immediately launched an invasion of the lands loyal to Valdemar. In the battle that followed, his army was roundly defeated. As Sweyn retreated he was caught alone in a swampy bog weighed down by his heavy armor. Peasants trailing Sweyn easily killed him. Now Valdemar was the sole surviving pretender. He would now be crowned the King of all Denmark.

Rogaard was substantially rewarded for his part in first warning and then saving Absalon. King Valdemar made Rogaard a Knight, the lowest rank in the aristocratic system. Finally Rogaard was a member of the nobility. Absalon gave him gold and title to some parcels of land. Rogaard set out as quickly as possible for Abbey Om to find Adalena. Their meeting would not be joyous.

"Rogaard, you are alive. I…I can't believe it." Adalena clutched him tightly for just a moment. As he returned her embrace she unexpectedly backed away.

"Adalena, is something wrong. I came here to ask you to marry me. I have thought of no one but you for all the time I was away in Paris or on the crusade or in prison or fighting for Valdemar. I love you. Do you not love me too?"

Adalena began to weep. She held up her hand to stop Rogaard as he tried to hold her and comfort her. "Rogaard, I cannot see you again…you are the only man…" She could not finish. Sobbing she ran back to her cell in the Abbey.

Rogaard sought out Father Vilfred in hopes of gaining some understanding. What could be wrong? He had a title, albeit a minor title, some land and money. Now all he needed to make his life complete was Adalena.

"Rogaard, you have been away a long time." Father Vilfred spoke in hushed tones. You know Lady Adalena was threatened with marriage to that sickly Ulf. She needed refuge and Abbey Om offered that to her. Her demented brother could not reach her here. Further, she thought you dead with her father. She expressed to me that she really had feelings for you, but you were gone. Adalena then decided that her only path was to give herself to God. She and her mother Ingeborg both took their final vows as nuns here in the Abbey almost six months ago."

The new Knight turned beet red with anger. "I will get the vows reversed. I will ask Absalon to revoke them. King Valdemar had Absalon appointed the Bishop of all Denmark. He can release her. I will petition him to do so. Tell Adalena what I am going to do."

"I will do that young Knight. I am not sure she will agree to what you are doing, but I will tell her."

Father Vilfred met with Ingeborg and Adalena. He felt it better to explain once, to both of them, what Rogaard was doing.

"Oh Father, can Rogaard do that. Can he relieve me of my vows?"

"Certainly not by himself Adalena. I believe he might be able to persuade our new Bishop, Absalon, to grant his request. He saved the

Bishop's life and fought for King Valdemar. He might be successful in this quest. We must await his return"

Ingeborg spoke up. "Adalena listen to me. Even if he managed to get you relieved of your vows, Rogaard is still a commoner...a peasant. You cannot marry such a man; it is below your station."

"I don't care about that mother. I think I love him."

Ingeborg huffed. "Are you ever going to outgrow your silly girlish thoughts daughter? You are nobility. A marriage like this is just not proper. He is little better than a serf. I never approved when your father allowed him to be in the castle...to be your playmate. It was scandalous."

Father Vilfred watched the scowling Ingeborg and the tearful Adalena as they argued. Finally he said "I think you need to know that Rogaard is now a member of the nobility. King Valdemar knighted him and he has lands and money of his own."

"See mother..."

"Hummph," Ingeborg growled in a low voice. "I will not let you marry that churl."

"It is my decision mother! I will do as I please."

"You are a nun daughter. You have promised yourself to God."

"Let me alone mother. If Rogaard manages to get me relieved from my vows, I will decide. And if I choose him...so be it. You or Father Vilfred will not make this decision for me."

The priest shook his head; He needed to add something, something for the Church. Finally, "Adalena you must seriously weigh the fact that you promised yourself to God. You made a vow. Perhaps it can be cancelled but you still made that pledge to the Almighty."

"Ha, Father! Pledges! What about you? You are still married and living here with your wife and three children. You were ordered to live a celibate's life. Are you doing that…tell me, are you celibate?" Adalena was furious.

Father Vilfred shuffled his feet and blushed deeply.

There was nothing more he could say. He wandered back to his quarters in hopes of some consolation from his wife. As he entered the room his son Ramius greeted him. For some unknown reason the young boy was smiling brightly.

Then, looking directly at his father, Ramius pulled his left thumb and forefinger over his nose closing both nostrils for just a moment.

A BIT OF HISTORY

In 1139, the Second Lateran Council officially imposed mandatory celibacy on all priests. Every priest's marriage was declared invalid and all married priests had to separate from their wives — leaving the women to whatever fate God had in store for them, even if it meant making them destitute.

What is known as "The Blood Feast of Roskilde", where Canute was killed is described by the Danish historian Saxo Grammiticus, in a series of books titled 'The History of the Danes'. It was the most ambitious literary undertaking of medieval Denmark and is an essential source for the nation's early history. It was written in the 12th century.

After Valdemar became king, the bishopric in Sjælland was vacant. The church had to elect a new bishop. Although Valdemar wanted to give his friend Absalon the office, the king had to follow rules. Valdemar needed to invent a manner, not too obvious, to influence the canons of Roskilde. They had to do the electing.

The canons said they had a choice of three candidates as a successor for Bishop Asser, who had died. They added Absalon's name, obviously to please the king. Valdemar said that he would observe the election and he would not interfere. The canons were to elect the new bishop themselves. The King sat down leaning on his sword while keeping a strict eye on every canon. Each official had to pass Valdemar in order to write his choice in a book. Every one of them wrote the name 'Absalon'.

Epilogue

Have you ever closed your nostrils by pinching them using your left thumb and forefinger?

Special thanks for getting this book into print to:
Joann Barclay, Dr. Julie Aspenleiter,
Mary Ellen Clarke, Marilynn Lane, James Rowe,
David St Amour, David Smithson, and
Ed Younis

And a very special thanks for in-depth editing to
Margaret Arton and Sister Frances Ann Thom OSF

Made in the USA
Charleston, SC
14 January 2014